David E. Bjork's book weaves the th[...] judgment, showing how the eccles[...] of discipleship. It is an affirmation o[...] [...]to be life-long learners, and their "playing coaches" to faithfully equip them for the daily journey of faith and witness. Read it with an open mind!

William R. O'Brien
Missionary in Indonesia for 10 years and Founding Director of the Global Center at Samford University's Beeson Divinity School, Alabama, USA

Dr David E. Bjork's *Every Believer a Disciple!* is an essential addition to the library of all Christians who desire a clearer understanding of Jesus' call to "make disciples of all nations" as a natural part of their everyday life in the twenty-first century. He has not written another "how-to" book with formulaic strategies but rather a plea for Christians to take discipleship seriously by going deeper into their own relationship with God (Father, Son, and Holy Spirit) and being available and intentional in accompanying fellow disciples on a journey that leads to a fuller, richer, more purposeful relationship with God and with one another. Readers from all Christian faith communities will be renewed in mind and in soul and they will be equipped to share Jesus' love and truth with a world that desperately needs both.

Dr Thomas Jones
Chair of History, International Studies & Social Studies
Taylor University, Indiana, USA

In this book Dr Bjork speaks from careful research and Biblical study to point out how today's organized church has allowed institutional concerns to overshadow its primary mission of discipleship multiplication as outlined in the Great Commission (Matthew 28:18-20). The principles he shares are more than theory, Dr Bjork has been putting them into practice for over forty years.

David Mann
World Partners Director

Out of the wealth of his years of experience ministering in Europe, Africa and North America, David E. Bjork has written an honest book with a courageous look at the most fundamental assignment Christ gave the church – discipling. I love this book because Bjork is willing to calmly and lovingly, but strongly, challenge many commonly accepted practices and assumptions in the evangelical movement. For instance, one of the most insidious and pervasive lies the modern evangelical church believes is the old lay/clergy dichotomy. But Bjork makes a compelling and persuasive case based on Scripture that ministry is not a task reserved for the "elite, full-time Christian workers" in the church. Rather, all vocations are holy and every believer should be engaged in ministry. You will enjoy the powerful personal examples Bjork shares out of his own years of rich experience. Following the biblical pattern Bjork so ably sets forth in this book will change the church. Converts will be truly discipled and trained to disciple others. Pastors and laity alike will be energized and active. The church will grow by focusing on its core task of making disciples. Believers will experience a more vital and fruitful life in Christ. Read this book and be changed.

Daryl McCarthy
Vice President of Academic Programs and Strategy
European Leadership Forum

Every Believer a Disciple!

Langham
GLOBAL LIBRARY

Every Believer a Disciple!

Joining in God's Mission

David E. Bjork

Published 2015 by Langham Global Library
an imprint of Langham Creative Projects

Langham Partnership
PO Box 296, Carlisle, Cumbria CA3 9WZ, UK
www.langham.org

ISBNs:
978-1-78368-872-2 Print
978-1-78368-870-8 Mobi
978-1-78368-871-5 ePub
978-1-78368-869-2 PDF

British Library Cataloguing in Publication Data

Bjork, David E. author.
  Every believer a disciple! : joining in God's mission.
  1. Spiritual direction--Christianity. 2. Witness bearing
  (Christianity) 3. Missions--Theory. 4. Christianity and
  culture.
  I. Title
  253.5'3-dc23

  ISBN-13: 9781783688722

Cover & Book Design: projectluz.com

To all who have accompanied me, each in his or her
own way, as I have followed Jesus:

Diane, my wife and best friend;

David and Lois, my parents;

Dean & Dorothy Truog, Aral & Irene Dyksman, Paul & Beth Ronka,
Len & Diana Sunukjian, Bill St Cyr, Ben & Mary-Jean Jennings,
Dave Imbach, Gordon Mollett

CONTENTS

Acknowledgments xi

1   Introduction 1

2   Does Our Strategy of Church Planting Produce Disciples? 11

3   Does Jesus Really Want Us to Make Disciples? 37

4   What Does a Disciple of Jesus Look Like? 53

5   The Way of Transformation 71

6   Two Major Objections. 89

7   The Disciple of Jesus and the Glory of God 111

8   How to Begin and Sustain a Disciple-Making Accompaniment 129

9   The Disciple of Jesus, the Demon, and Deliverance 151

10 The Disciple of Jesus and *Ecclesia* 169

11 How to Help the Members of an Ecclesia-Institution
    Make Disciples of Jesus 189

12 The Disciple of Jesus and Unity 207

Bibliography. 225

Scripture Index 237

Acknowledgments

I am deeply grateful to my "son in the faith," Alain Germain, for the precious assistance that he gave in the writing of the French version of this book. He helped me to sharpen my thoughts and express them appropriately in his mother tongue.

Vivian Doub and Claire Moore of Langham Partnership worked toward the production of this book. They represent, for me, the best example of a publisher who is truly serving the work of God in the Majority World.

1

Introduction

Several weeks ago a seminary student showed me his research project that begins with these words: "The primary mission of the church in general, and our church in particular, is evangelization." Among those who identify themselves with Jesus Christ today, many would be in agreement with this student. For these people the word 'evangelization' sums up the entire mission of the church (Congregation for the Doctrine of the Faith, 2014). Because Jesus Christ is the unique mediator, the one in whom salvation is found for all of humanity,

> It is always of utmost urgency to collect souls through evangelization. The eternal destiny of men and of nations hangs in the balance. Each generation plays a strategic role. We are not responsible for previous generations, and we cannot carry the full responsibility for those to come; but we are confronted by the present generation. God will hold us responsible for the way in which we respond to the challenge of our day. (Graham 1977, 102)

While recognizing that the evangelization of those who do not know Christ must be our major preoccupation, can we reduce the mission of the people of God to the scheme: *Evangelization – Church – Evangelization*? Certainly one begins with evangelization by which men and women are led to accept Jesus Christ as their Lord and Savior. Then, those converts are made members of a local church body. And finally, they are included in the process of the evangelization of others through their testimony and their participation in evangelistic crusades organized by the church. When Jesus gave the Great Commission, was this what he had in mind?

> All authority in heaven and on earth has been given to me. Therefore go and make disciples of all nations, baptizing them in the name of the Father and of the Son and of the Holy Spirit, and teaching them to obey everything I have commanded you. And surely I am with you always, to the very end of the age. (Matt 28:18–20)

This scheme: *Evangelization – Church – Evangelization*, tends to place the implantation of churches at the center of its mission. "The implanting of the church is a means by which converts may be kept, edified and trained to become witnesses. For this reason, the implantation of the church is, in its very essence, the execution of the divine Commission" (Kapitao).

According to this view, each Christian is supposed to become a 'soul winner' and evangelization is considered to be the very reason for which the church exists. For this reason the church must "continue to grow numerically or cease to exits" (Phalippou 2005, 87).[1] The goal of evangelism becomes therefore the salvation of souls and the growth of the church.

In this book I am going to question many of our understandings and missionary practices that are based upon this scheme. I will suggest that this missionary model lacks a biblical foundation, devaluates the role of the laity in the church, institutionalizes spiritual reproduction, and legitimizes Christian superficiality and mediocrity.

Is Discipleship Reserved for 'Super Christians'?

The word 'disciple' is used 269 times in the New Testament. The word 'Christian' shows up only three times. It was introduced precisely in reference to disciples who, in their context, could no longer be considered a Jewish sect. Michael Wilkins, professor of New Testament at Talbot School of Theology describes the notion of a disciple in these words:

> In the Gospels, the word 'disciple' is the term the most often used to designate those who follow Jesus, and who are called by the early church 'believers', 'brothers/sisters', 'followers of the Way', or 'saints'. (Wilkins 1992, 40)

---

1. Translations of quotations from French to English are the author's own throughout the book.

In other words, the New Testament is a book that talks about disciples, was written by disciples and for disciples of Jesus Christ. What is the most important is not the choice of terminology. What counts is the tie to Jesus and the life-long experience of imperfect people being transformed into his likeness. It is a sort of pilgrimage which begins with the new birth, passes through the phases of spiritual infancy and adolescence to attain maturity and spiritual reproduction. This is not a lifestyle that is reserved for a handful of elites or outstanding spiritual athletes. In the New Testament, the disciple is the ordinary (normal, basic) believer. He is the regular believer who follows Jesus and lets him reshape his life.

Disciples Who Aren't Disciples

For several decades Western churches have not made discipleship a condition for belonging to their communities of faith. One needn't be a disciple, or even desire to become a disciple. This doesn't exclude the individual from the faith community. A person can be born again, baptized, and become a member of the community without demonstrating any of the signs of growth in Christian discipleship. North American evangelicals and Pentecostals, for instance, do not require that people demonstrate Christ-likeness in their way of thinking, their temperament, or their teaching before being admitted among the faithful of the local gathering. Bill Hull writes that the vast majority of American evangelicals do not feel that it is really necessary to live according to the teaching of Jesus. In their opinion, if Jesus is necessary for everyone's salvation, only a few are called to really follow his example (Hull 2010, 11). Clearly then from an institutional perspective, discipleship is largely optional.

This is not secret. The best literature on the subject of Christian discipleship either says outright, or implies, that believers needn't be disciples – even after they have spent their entire lifetimes within a faith community. A well-known book in the English-speaking world, *The Lost Art of Disciple Making*, presents the Christian life in three stages: the convert, the disciple, and the worker (Eims, 1980). One must follow a process to aid the individual to move from one stage to the next. Evangelization produces converts, instruction in the fundamentals of the faith produces disciples, and a deeper level of training produces workers. Disciples and workers, it is said, can renew this process through evangelism, but only workers are truly capable of producing disciples through instruction.

This portrait of life within the faith community is globally realistic in its representation of the practice of North American Christianity. Our experience in France and in Cameroon leads us to believe that its influence goes even farther. But doesn't this model make discipleship optional? This seems clearly to be the case. It makes any progress optional, for it is not patently obvious that the disciple would choose to become a worker. So a large number of converts choose what kind of believer they wish to become from among the models that are proposed. And many of them choose to not become – or at least they don't chose to become – disciples of Jesus Christ. This explains why churches are full of disciples who are not 'real' disciples, or disciples who are 'undisciplined' (Willard 1988, 258). Most of the problems that are encountered in our faith communities are rooted in the fact that many of the faithful have never decided really to follow Jesus Christ.

When I was young, the message that was preached far and wide within American evangelicalism was: "Come to Jesus just as you are. Receive from him, by faith, the gift of forgiveness for your sins. This will cost you nothing. It is a gift of his grace. You have nothing to lose, and everything to gain. He will save your soul and will prepare a place for you in paradise." The only problem with this message is that it focalizes on Jesus as Savior and leaves in the shadows the fact that he is also Lord. The idea behind this message was that one could present Jesus in this way to bring the most souls to salvation. Later the notion of Christ's lordship could be introduced. Unfortunately, this deformed gospel message produced a large number of believers who are convinced that they are 'born again', but who have no desire to really become like Jesus.

A Defective Model of Missions

A different model was inaugurated by the Great Commission that Jesus gave to those who had begun to follow him. The first objective that he established for the members of that early faith community was that they use his power and authority to make disciples of all nations (Matt 28:18–19). And in the process of making those disciples, they should be baptized in the name of the Father and of the Son and of the Holy Spirit. They should also be taught to obey everything that Jesus taught. The first faith community followed that mandate, and the result was remarkable.

However, under the influence of historic events, that model was replaced by: "Make converts (to Christ and to a particular church) and baptize them so that they become members of that church." In the next chapter we will examine carefully how the model that Jesus left was replaced by the present model, and why this exchange is tragic both for the Christian community in the West and in emerging nations. But I want already to underline the fact that our current understanding of what it is that Christ expects from us is producing only a small number of people who truly live like his disciples. But making disciples of Jesus should be the heart of all we do. And it is obvious that if we haven't made disciples of our converts, they will find it nearly impossible to teach others how to live according to the life and teaching of Jesus.

Of course, we are doing many good things in Christ's name. For example, in his name we evangelize souls. And it is in his name that we care for the sick, cast out evil spirits, and teach the illiterate. In the name of Jesus we plant churches and spend billions of dollars on buildings and technology. To accomplish what we perceive to be the task that our Lord has given to us we train pastors, evangelists and missionaries in our Bible schools and seminaries. In fact, we are quite active, doing all kinds of things to accomplish what we believe to be our mission. However, I will argue in chapter 3 that the most important thing that we have to do is our mission *as it has been defined by Jesus*. I will also maintain that Jesus was very specific when he stated what it is that he expects from us. I will close the chapter by suggesting that the mission given by Jesus is both ingenious and strategic.

The vast majority of the pastors that I know would say that discipleship, or spiritual formation, is the primary work of the church. However, since we don't all have the same definition of what a disciple looks like, we aren't in agreement about the goals of our activities. For example, certain believers see spiritual maturity as the fruit of biblical knowledge. For those with this understanding, it becomes important that the believers know the Bible from cover to cover. In other faith communities, the disciple is first and foremost a soul-winner. In those circles, disciples are recognizable by the fact that they regularly invite friends, neighbors, and unsaved family members to the church where they can hear the gospel message and be converted. In their opinion the most important thing they do is to invite people to church where they can hear the good news. Another Christian spirituality understands the disciple in much more communitarian terms. The faithful who are influenced by that vision define disciples as those who share their lives with others in deep and meaningful relationships. For these people discipleship is a question of goodness and justice, the fight in Jesus' name against all forms of evil in society. For others, disciples are known by their compassion and charity toward all. Others yet define disciples by their sanctification and upright lifestyle. In this view, disciples of Jesus avoid sin and separate themselves from the world. And many Christians today believe a disciple of Jesus is above all a person of worship. Worship and praise are the center of his life.

In reality, what we see is that each faith community makes disciples according to its understanding of what is most important. In chapter 4 I will argue that we have not been assigned the task of making disciples that look like us, or who reflect the values of our church tradition or spirituality. When Jesus Christ gave the Great Commission, it was not so that Catholics would make Catholics, that Baptists would make Baptists, that evangelicals would make evangelicals, that Pentecostals would make Pentecostals, etc. For this reason we will examine what a disciple of Jesus looks like apart from our particular interpretations.

In fact, one could argue that within our particular communities of faith – whatever the church tradition – spiritual depth and maturity are remarkably absent. The challenge facing Christians, whatever their race, sex, education, social or economic status, is to live according to the gospel message. However, there is evidence that in spite of all of our activities – the multiplication of our meetings, and the refinement of our strategies – the lives of many of our faithful are not being deeply transformed. In chapter 5 I will draw from a several year- long study of thousands of Christian communities to describe the conditions that promote deep spiritual transformation.

Some people are convinced that we have good reason to believe that we are not really called to make disciples of Jesus. These people recognize that Jesus made disciples, but fail to see that model in the Acts of the Apostles or in the Epistles. In their eyes the coming of the Holy Spirit and the birth of the church have replaced the model of disciple with that of 'believer', 'faithful', 'member', 'baptized', 'saint', 'brother/sister', etc. This is the first major objection to the argument that we are called to make disciples of Jesus: Paul (and the other apostles) didn't work to make disciples of Jesus. They labored instead to establish faith communities. Other people suggest that we cannot make disciples of Jesus and that attempts to do so often result in spiritual abuse. These people point to examples of individuals who overemphasize certain biblical principles, demanding that their 'disciples' be submitted (like sheep are submitted to a shepherd), and demanding that they obtain the approval of their leader before making any major life decision. In chapter 6 I will respond to these objections. I will begin by answering the question: Was the apostle Paul a disciple of Jesus? Did he make disciples of Jesus? Next, I will affirm that we can make disciples of Jesus without falling into the trap of spiritual abuse, and I will suggest several warning signs that a relationship of spiritual accompaniment is beginning to move in a wrong direction.

If one were to take a survey asking Christians what is the ultimate goal of a believer, many would respond: "To live for the glory of God." And I would agree with them. Because the highest aim of the believer is to live for the glory of God, and Jesus sends us to make disciples of the nations, I assume that there is a solid link between the glory of God and the action of making disciples of Jesus Christ. Jesus himself underlined this tie when he stated: "This is to my Father's glory, that you bear much fruit, showing yourselves to be my disciples" (John 15:8, NIV). In chapter 7 I will examine what bringing glory to God actually means, and I will show why making disciples of Jesus is the best way to bring glory to our heavenly Father.

Sometimes we think that to make disciples of Jesus everyone must follow the same path or go through the same process. Unfortunately, we look for a method or a strategy that seems to have worked in one church situation and we try to apply it in our own context. But that approach does not work when it comes to making disciples of Jesus! Perhaps that is why the Bible does not give us a lot of specific instructions about how to go about making disciples of Jesus. There is no sort of "Four Spiritual Laws" for the making of a disciple of Jesus. Instead, the biblical text offers organic metaphors that describe the spiritual growth that is at the heart of that process; like sowing and reaping (John 4:37; 2 Cor 9:10), planting and watering (1 Cor 3:6), growth (1 Pet 2:2; 2 Pet 3:18) and bearing much fruit (Matt 7:17–20; John 15:1–16; Gal 5:22). In chapter 8 I will not attempt to give a process to follow. On the other hand, I will suggest several ideas about how you might initiate and sustain, in synergy with the Holy Spirit, a personal and individual accompaniment of someone who is in a position of vulnerability and openness to the teaching of Jesus.

In the personal accompaniment of an individual who is following Jesus, we wish to help that person to make Jesus the Lord of each aspect of his or her life. But in that process we sometimes run up against roadblocks, moments when the person whom we are accompanying can no longer move forward for reasons that even she does not understand. Those obstacles to growth are sometimes the work of demonic forces. Recognizing and overcoming those handicaps to spiritual transformation is the subject of chapter 9.

Some faith communities work harder at the evangelization of non-believers than they do at personal accompaniment in discipleship. We encounter this all over Africa, but it was already a reality in much of the

Evangelical movement in North America. During the First International
Consultation on Discipleship, John R. W. Stott highlighted the "strange and
disturbing paradox" of contemporary Christianity. He made that observation
in the form of a warning: "We have experienced tremendous growth in the
number of our faithful without having a corresponding growth in discipleship.
A superficial discipleship does not please God" (Stott 1999, 28). However, the
rapid expansion of faith communities is not the only force that is working
against the accompaniment in discipleship.

One of the greatest obstacles to discipleship is the institutionalization
of faith communities. The movements that foster the forming of disciples
of Jesus must constantly be wary of institutionalizing tendencies that would
stop their progress. C. S. Lewis said: "There is within every church something
which sooner or later militates against the very reason for its existence. We
must work with all our force, by the grace of God, to keep the church on the
path of the original mission which it received from Christ" (Vaus 2004, 167).
Lewis warns against institutionalization.

Many spiritual revivals have begun as movements wherein people have
sought to be more like Jesus and have attempted to accompany others in that
process. In chapter 10 I will examine the legitimacy of those movements and
the tensions that their members have encountered as they fought the forces
of institutionalization.

In one sense we can say that each faith community makes disciples,
because the word 'disciple' means an 'apprentice' or a 'student'. Like I said
earlier, each faith community shapes its members according to what it
values. Each faith community makes disciples according to its definition of
discipleship. One problem is that this takes place more often than not within
a context that devalues the role of laypeople[2] and overestimates the place of
the clergy, the 'religious professionals', in the process of multiplying disciples
of Jesus Christ. For this reason in chapter 11 I look at the question of the
relationship between the clergy and the laity within the institutionalized
community of faith. And I propose a few ways that the vision and practice
of personal accompaniment in discipleship might be reintroduced into an
ecclesial context that has somehow lost that perspective.

---

2. In the French language the word *Laïc* (layperson) is often used to designate that which is
independent of, or even opposed to, all religious belief. In this book I use the word much
more in the Anglo-Saxon way to distinguish simply between believing men and women and
people who have been formed for various Christian ministries in church institutions. I will
develop more fully that distinction in chapter 11.

Jesus said that we should be recognizable as his disciples by the love that we have for each other (John 13:34–35). Later, the apostle Paul would present the unity of believers with Christ as the basis for their unity with each other: "Is Christ divided?" asks the apostle, "Was Paul crucified for you? Were you baptized into the name of Paul?" (1 Cor 1:13). The answer to these questions is clearly No! Jesus Christ is not divided! And our spiritual predecessors, our ecclesial tradition, and our particular experiences are not the source of our salvation. In spite of what we might think, we have not been baptized into the name of a particular Christian heritage. In the last chapter I will ask whether or not we can legitimately recognize the presence of disciples of Jesus in religious circles that do not share our spirituality or even all of our beliefs. And, if such is the case, what relationship should we seek to have with those disciples of Jesus who do not look like us?

Note:

At the end of each chapter you will find a few reflection questions to help you think a bit more deeply about what you have read. You will profit the most from this book by taking the time to answer these questions.

Questions to Think About:

1. How do you define a disciple of Jesus? What are some major characteristics of a disciple?

2. Based on the definition that you just formulated, for what reasons would you say that the Christian assembly that you are part of is successful or unsuccessful in making more disciples of Jesus?

2

Does Our Strategy of Church Planting Produce Disciples?

Discipleship and the idea of making disciples is very fashionable in Christian circles these days.[1] But in spite of its recent popularity, it seems that we have somehow forgotten to ask ourselves if we are truly making disciples of Jesus. There seem to be some very convincing reasons to doubt that we are! In all honesty, a rapid examination of the church in the world reveals that, in one way or another, *we have emptied the Great Commission of its essence.* I will quickly examine three places where I have lived and worked for Christ: the United States of America, France, and Cameroon, to illustrate what I mean.

According to a study done by the *Barna Group* in 2009, in spite of the fact that the majority of Americans call themselves Christians and say that they know the contents of the Bible, less than one out of ten of them demonstrates that knowledge in his daily lifestyle (Barna). This being the case, it is not surprising to learn that in spite of mega-churches like Willow Creek,[2] evangelistic crusades, church-growth experts, diplomas, radio and television broadcasts, material resources, etc., American evangelicals display

---

1. A Google internet search on the word "discipling" produces 137,000 results, "disciplemakers" produced 78,800 hits, and the word "discipleship" produced 10,400,000 results on 16 December 2011.

2. Willow Creek is both a church and an organization. The Willow Creek Community Church near Chicago, was founded in 1975 by Bill Hybels with the help of Gilbert Bilezikian. This large church is characterized by two values: fostering authentic long-term relationships through a network of small groups, and making the gospel available to those who have no ties to the church. The Willow Creek Association gathers more than 10,000 churches (from 35 different countries and representing 90 denominations) who are seeking to innovate in the communication of the gospel message within their specific cultural environment.

one of the smallest growth rates in the world (Mandryk 2010, 916)! In reality North-American Christians are leaving the church at such a rapid pace that non-church-going has become the religious experience of the majority of the American people (Dempsey, 1997). That mass exodus of North Americans out of the church led Josh McDowell and Dave Bellis to publish in 2006 a book with a shocking title: *The Last Christian Generation*.[3] In this book McDowell explains that the title of the book was not chosen for sensationalism, but only because he felt that if something is not done immediately to change the spiritual state of the children of Christians in the USA, their parents will be the last Christian generation in that land (McDowell, 2006, 11). He sounds this warning bell after learning that between 69 and 94 percent of Christian adolescents abandon the church in their late teens, and few of those young people ever return.

In France where I served for thirty years as a missionary, the religious scene illustrates the evolution that has been taking place across Europe for several decades. In 1986, 91 percent of the French, 15 years of age or more, identified themselves as Catholics. That number fell to 69 percent in 2001 (Mermet 2001, 280). In 2002 only 7 percent of French adults (18 years of age and older) regularly practiced their faith and 44 percent of French adults who identified themselves as Catholics stated that they never attend church services.[4] In a study done in 2003, which asked the same questions of the French that had been asked ten years earlier, all of the indicators of Christian belief had dropped.[5] That survey revealed that fewer of the French believe in the existence of God and in the primary Christian beliefs than was formerly the case. They attend church services less, pray less, and fewer of them claim that Christian faith plays an important role in their lives than was true ten years earlier.

Today, 20 percent of the French say that they are agnostic, and it is in France, among all of the Western European nations, that we find the largest

3. See also Ron D. Dempsey, 1997. *Faith Outside the Walls: Why People Don't Come and Why the Church Must Listen* (Macon: Smyth & Helwys Publishing); and Alan Jamieson, 2002. *A Churchless Faith: Faith Journeys Beyond the Churches* (London: SPCK).

4. It is true that the total number of Evangelical Protestants has grown from 0.4 percent of the total French population in 2004 to 0.8 percent in 2012, but the overall tendencies that I have described here remain the same. http://www.crosswalk.com/news/religion-today/what-nobody-is-saying-about-france.html?utm_source=Crosswalk_Daily_Update&utm_medium=email&utm_campaign=04/10/2012.

5. According to a telephone interview of 1,000 French adults, done on 21 March 2003 by the CSA, the results of which were published in an article that appeared in "*Le Monde*", 17 April 2003, signed by Xavier Ternisien.

percentage of convinced atheists (14%). While it is true that a slowly growing number of French young people affirm their belief in God, their image of him is far removed from the personal God of the Bible (Brechon 2004, 39). Even those French men and women who continue to attend church services on Sundays admit that they are more attached to the humanistic values that they find in their faith than they are to the doctrines and dogmas of their religion (Muller & Bertrand 2002, 24–25).

Today I am situated in Cameroon where, in spite of the fact that the church has been growing rapidly for several decades, observers say that Christian nominalism[6] is a greater problem here than in most other African countries (Mandryk 2010, 191). It is clear that all of sub-Saharan Africa is one of the most religious areas of the world. In Cameroon, in particular, nearly nine people out of ten affirm that religion occupies a very important place in their life (Pew Foundation, 2011). At the same time a significant number of those people who claim to be deeply committed to Christianity include practices from African traditional religion in their daily lives. In Cameroon almost half of the people who were questioned about their beliefs and practices stated that sacrifices to ancestors and spirits can protect them from harm.[7] And an important percentage of Cameroonian Christians say that they believe in the protective power of talismans or amulets. Many people confess that they consult traditional healers when a member of the family gets sick, and a large number of them keep sacred objects such as skulls or animal skins in their homes and participate in ceremonies honoring their traditional ancestors. The fact that the churches are more turned toward the conversion of non-believers than toward the formation of disciples has produced believers who are often superficial, ignorant of the Holy Scriptures, syncretistic, tribal, and ignorant of the importance of their mission (Grebe 1997, 67–75). In short, the Cameroonian churches reflect many of the same imperfections that we find in the Western churches that birthed them.[8]

---

6. The expression 'nominal Christians' is used when a large number of individuals, for one reason or another, want to be known as Christians even though they have lost contact with the church, no longer believe in the basic Christian doctrines, live lifestyles that are not in accord with the values of the kingdom of God, or maintain no living relationship with the Lord because they ignore the means of grace that he has placed at their disposal for their spiritual support (Gibbs 1994, 15).

7. These general observations are based on more than 25,000 one-on-one interviews, done for the Forum on Religion and Public Life by the Pew Center of Research in more than 60 languages or dialects, in 19 different countries in Sub-Saharan Africa, from December 2008 to April 2009.

8. I recognize that African Christianity is largely the fruit of African rather than

These rapidly drawn portraits of the church in the USA, in France and in Cameroon, reveal the symptoms of a sickness that has reached pandemic proportions. We have obeyed the injunction of Christ to go into all the world, but we have been very ineffective in the forming of disciples. We have evangelized and made converts. We have baptized and made members of the church. We have established schools and Bible or theological institutions and produced pastors and priests. We have founded hospitals and orphanages and cared for the needy. We have trained missionaries and workers and sent them out to plant new churches. But when we look at all of that activity, the question that remains is: *Where are the disciples*? If we were truly in the process of forming people who are committed to following the example and teaching of Jesus with complete faithfulness, would the church look like it does in the USA, in France and in Cameroon?

For more than a century it has been widely admitted that the most definitive missionary mandate the church has received is found in the words of the risen Christ to his disciples: "Go and make disciples of all nations" (Matt 28:19). Unfortunately we have understood that we should go into all the world and plant churches (Bjork 1997, 56–69), with the conviction that those churches would make disciples. But that is not what Christ said! he gave us the specific mandate to make disciples, and he promised specifically to build his church (Matt 16:18). Our work is to facilitate the encounter with Christ and to accompany those who turn from their sin in attaching themselves to his person and teaching. The goal is that those individuals be filled with the knowledge of his will through all wisdom and understanding, in order that they might live a life worthy of the Lord and please him in every way, bearing fruit in every good work and growing in the knowledge of God (Col 1:9–10). That is the objective of the mission that Christ gave to his disciples (and that he has given to us), and it is his responsibility to build his church.

The fact that we have reversed the roles (in seeking to plant churches in the hopes that they will produce disciples) is, in my opinion, one of the main reasons why we are not reaching our world for Christ. Many misunderstandings about our mission, associated with that wrong interpretation of our task, are in reality keeping us from doing that for which Christ has sent us into the world. More than forty years ago I read an exposition of Ephesians 4:11–13 that impacted me deeply. That study showed

---

Western initiatives (cf. Walls 1996, 85–89). I maintain, however, that the ecclesiastical and missiological models of the West continue to influence what is experienced on the African continent.

that this text of Scripture teaches that God has given Spirit-filled leaders to his church with the unique goal of making disciples of his people (by being models, mentors, coaches and trainers), so that 'ordinary' Christians would do his work in the world. If it is true that the communication of the Christian faith is primarily the work of Spirit-filled laymen and women, and that Christian leaders serve primarily to facilitate, strengthen and guide laymen and laywomen in that work, then we must examine again many of our practices. For, in reality, the laypeople are too often seen as simple "scouts who, returning from the 'outside world' with eyewitness accounts and perhaps some bunches of grapes, report to the 'operational basis'" (Bosch 1992, 472). Our ecclesiastic model overlooks the fact that they are the operational base from which the *missio Dei* proceeds. It is, in fact not *they* who have to 'accompany' those who hold 'special offices' in the latter's mission in the world. Rather, it is the *office bearers* who have to accompany the laity, the people of God (Hoekendijk 1967, 350).

Moreover, I am convinced that the fact that we implant churches that center all their activities around the Sunday worship service, with its professionalization of the witness of God's people, has largely silenced the communication of the laity.[9] For it seems undeniable that, in spite of the rediscovery of the notion of the priesthood of all believers, the dominant model is that of Christian ministry monopolized by men who have been consecrated to that end. In spite of the fact that Jesus of Nazareth broke with the Jewish tradition by choosing his disciples not from the priestly class, but among fishermen, tax collectors and the likes; and despite the fact that Pauline churches were not called 'synagogues', but simply 'gatherings' (cf. 1 Cor 11:17, 18, 20, 33, 34; 14:23, 26) and the fact that most of these took place primarily

---

9. Rick Wood, Editor of *Mission Frontiers: The News and Issues Journal from the US Center for World Mission* (July–August 2012) maintains that the popular models of church life are a global problem! He writes: "If I could say one thing to church planters around the world, it would be this, 'Please do not follow our popular Western example of how to do church.'" We have failed miserably to equip the people in our churches to be disciple-makers and church planters. We have failed miserably to instill in believers the biblical vision of the Great Commission. What we are currently doing in most churches is not effective in equipping believers for the work of ministry. All of us need to rethink all of our assumptions about what church is suppose to be and focus on discovering the principles and practices that God uses to make disciples, and create church-planting movements that build his kingdom. If most pastors continue to focus on growing their existing church attendance rather than on building God's kingdom by equipping their people to be disciple-makers, then we will continue to get the stagnant results we currently see in the Western church. The goal of the church must be that every believer is involved in ministry and that every believer is trained and equipped to be a disciple-maker or church planter."

in private homes – for nearly nineteen centuries, and within all ecclesiastic traditions – the ministry has been almost exclusively understood in terms of consecrated ministers (Bosch 1992, 468).

In addition, the notion of a minister placed at the center of the church and endowed with considerable authority[10] has led the church to be understood as a strictly sacred society guided by 'internal leaders' with the priest or pastor installed in a privileged and central position (Burrows 1981 [1980], 61, 74). The results of such a view of the church are evident everywhere. Recently, for example, my wife and I attended a worship service in a new protestant church that was celebrating their thirteenth week of existence. That community of about sixty members (including the children) was renting a building for three hundred dollars a month. And the pastor had committed himself to produce a daily radio program (at a cost of an additional one hundred dollars a month), even if the faithful of the congregation were giving only around twenty dollars a month. All of the activities of this Cameroonian church (with two pastors, a youth group, a prayer coordinator, a choir, etc.) are organized before there is a congregation large enough to need those structures. The 'visionary' pastor, who 'implanted' that congregation seems to be reasoning more out of a logic centered around himself and his role in the community of faith, than out of a sensitivity to the real needs of his faithful. Here in Cameroon it is not unusual to find pastors who claim to have received a vision from God and who insist that their faithful enter into that vision by submitting to their authority. These pastors sometimes call themselves prophets, and by so doing affirm that those who enter into their projects will receive a 'prophet's reward' (cf. Matt 10:41).[11] We have heard pastors publicly scold parishioners who did not regularly attend their meetings saying: "You disappoint your pastor"; or affirming that those who disobey their pastor are sinning.

According to Mark's gospel, Jesus established twelve people among his followers "that they might *be with him* and that he might send them out . . ." (Mark 3:13–15). An honest appraisal of the condition of the church convinces us that we are not forming enough disciples through the activities of our communities. One cannot make a disciple of Jesus in a classroom, or

---

10. In the Protestant perspective, this notion can be widely found in the three ministries of Pastor, Elder and Deacon.

11. In a recent tract calling for funds to support the young church that we visited, one is promised that if she gives ten dollars a month to support that project, God will: (1) transform the person's defeats into victories, (2) help the person to overcome natural limitations, and (3) manifest in new and surprising ways his power in the person's life.

in a Bible school, or during a seminar. Because a disciple of Jesus cannot be made without spending lots of time together, one-on-one, in a real sharing of life. Where can those who follow Christ enter into that kind of deep and intimate relationship where they can learn together how to follow Christ in all of the areas of their life? I suspect that in reality we (missionaries, pastors and other leaders of the church) seek more to recruit laypeople as members of our ecclesial communities so that they support the structures, programs and activities of the church, than we do to form them as disciples of Christ who are equipped and sent out to evangelize and accompany others in Christian discipleship. Somewhere along the line we have replaced the church that said, "I go to you," with a church that says "come to me."

Several decades ago the veteran missionary, Bob Evans, had this to say about the importance of making disciples:

> We must train the nationals. Discipleship both inside and especially outside the institution should be taking place on all levels. The question to be asked of the missionary is, "Where are your disciples?" To the extent that they are saved, motivated and trained, to that extent we are successful. (Smeeton 1980, 216)

I have been a missionary for more than forty years. But I must admit that I find it difficult to promote the missionary enterprise as it has been pursued for the past century. Do we really believe that people will be ready to pray for, financially support, and give their lives to Christian missions that have been largely emptied of their essence? Who wishes to spend the rest of his life planting churches and promoting programs that do not produce the deep life transformation that is the goal of Christian discipleship? Honestly, I am surprised that we are so committed to our religious activities that we refuse to ask ourselves the question, "Where are our disciples?"

In December 2010, Rick Wood, the editor of *Missions Frontiers* wrote:

> The dirty little secret of missions is that we are sending missionaries all over the world who have not demonstrated the ability to make disciples who can make disciples. Most have not seen or participated in effective models of church planting or discipleship at home, but we send them out in the hope that going cross-culturally will turn them into effective church planters and disciplers. This is wishful thinking at best, and it has to change. (Wood, 2010)

Are we ready to critically examine the missional paradigm that has dominated our understanding and fashioned our approach for more than a century? Are we going to continue to give ourselves to the planting of churches in the hope that, contrary to the experience of others, our churches will be successful in making disciples of Jesus Christ? If we continue to do what we have always done, we will continue to obtain what we have always obtained. It is not through doing what we have always done, but with more zeal, or in using better methods, that we will obtain different results. And if we Western missionaries are not ready to do what is necessary to put discipleship back at the heart of our missional preoccupations, how can we hope that our sister churches from the Southern hemisphere enter into that process?

Financing the Mission of the Church

We have seen how, in accomplishing their plans, Western missionaries passed their ecclesiastic model largely unchanged to the growing church in the rest of the world. One of the major problems with that spread of their model is that it is not based on the formation of laymen and women, disciples of Jesus, who produce other laypeople who are disciples of Jesus and who reproduce their life with Jesus in the lives of others. Quite the contrary, the model based on the priest or pastor who functions as the center of the church with the worship service perceived as the climax of Christian experience has been imposed on others as the only valid and acceptable pattern. I want now to examine a second difficulty that arises from the fact that the 'mission churches' have been modeled on the example of the West in spite of the fact that economic and social structures are totally different. The results of that disparity are often catastrophic.

In the West for the past two centuries, there has been an unprecedented multiplication of 'full-time' missionaries, completely financed by the gifts of others. That was made possible by two unique phenomenon: the colonization and industrialization of the West. Colonization added three important elements to the missionary expansion of the church: (1) access to mission fields, (2) a means for monetary exchange, and (3) social stability allowing the proclamation of the gospel. Industrialization added a level of production that gave people more financial means than what was needed for their own survival. That meant that they could consecrate a part of those goods for the financing of the mission of the church if they so wished. That had not been the case before the beginning of the twentieth century. Up to that point, the large majority of Christian missionaries had to work in one form or another to finance their own mission (Burthwick 2012, 172).

In the *Evangelical Missions Quarterly*, Donald K. Smith, professor at Western Seminary, writes:

> Historically, missions from the West began when those nations were not wealthy. The Moravians worked to support themselves wherever they went, even selling themselves into slavery to reach the slaves in the Caribbean. For years William Carey received no financial support in India but worked in various jobs to support his Bible translation efforts. His lifestyle in India was little different than it was when he was a cobbler in England. In fact, only in the last century have missionaries felt it necessary to be fully supported from the homeland. (Smith, 1999)

Between the time of William Carey (1761–1834) who is considered the "father of contemporary missions" and the emergence of 'faith missions'[12] with J. Hudson Taylor (1832–1905), the typical missionary was a person from a humble and modest background: an artisan, worker or farmer (Walls 1996, 171–172). They were people accustomed to working with their hands to meet their own needs. But during the past 100 years 'full-time missionaries', supported by the gifts of others, have become so much the normal model that this means of financing the apostolic work of the church has become the very definition of the word 'missionary' (Smith, 1999).[13]

However, we must realize that the impact of colonization and industrialization is over. With the fall of the Berlin wall in 1989, the last colonial empire, the Soviet Union, collapsed. That being the case, new countries emerged. The empires that had offered missionaries access to unreached peoples were gone forever. In their place it is nationalism that defines the new era. And it is not surprising that these nations do not want a foreign society to impose on them its culture, economic system or religion.

---

12. The beginning of 'faith missions', which consists in sending missionaries without a fixed salary, depending on God to respond to the prayers of the faithful to meet their physical needs through the gifts of supporters, has had a significant impact on evangelical missions to the present.

13. "Tent-making is another biblical model. Unfortunately, it is relatively unsupported by churches, or rather, the churches don't bother to organize their human resources according to that model. Many pastors would be able to largely support their own ministry were they to work, for example, part-time in a business setting. They could, in that way, support an additional pastor . . ." Henri Bacher, 2008. "Sur la vie de l'Église : le chantier des finances". http://www.lafree.ch/details.php/fr/reflexion_vie_d_eglise.html?idelement=663

Moreover, often these nations cannot perceive Christianity any other way than as a foreign religion that threatens their indigenous culture. For these reasons there are an increasing number of countries that refuse visas or residence papers to Christian missionaries.

Today more that 80 percent of the world's population lives in lands that do not give visas to 'full-time' missionaries. But they do welcome missionaries who work in fields where their skills are needed and sought (Siemens, 1999). Why is this the case? Because those nations want to develop, and they know that in order for that to happen, they need help. And what is the greatest physical need of those nations? The development of businesses – no other durable economic development is possible without that. Without an economic development based on the creation of businesses and micro-businesses, those nations will not escape from the interminable cycle of dependency upon other nations.

Two notable traits characterize the new world situation. First, there is a growing consensus that free economies do better than controlled ones, and an agreement that a government by and for the people is better than a totalitarian regime. Second, those forces are tied to new means of communication and transportation that foster the international exchange of goods and services.

And what about the mission of the people of God in all this? The door remains open to missionaries, but it is not the same door that was open earlier. It is a door that is open to those who are ready to work to meet their own physical needs and those of the mission (as the vast majority of Christian missionaries have always done). The door that has been open to vocational ('full-time') missionaries is now largely closed, and every day that passes it closes a bit further.[14] But the emerging countries welcome, and even seek after, qualified people who can assist them in their development.

In reality, as we have already noted, the model used by Western missionaries, and largely adopted by the churches of the Southern hemisphere, aims at evangelization and the multiplication of churches, but largely overlooks the role of the laity. In the same way, that model stresses the training, sending and financing of full-time pastors and missionaries, and devaluates the role of 'lay missionaries' who do the work of the Christian ministry while at the same time working with their hands to meet their physical needs.

---

14. Twenty or so years ago, Kennon Callahan dared to affirm that the days of the professional Christian have passed (1990. *Effective Church Leadership* [San Francisco: Harper-Collins]).

The Biblical Foundation of a Lay Mission[15]

There are many scriptural examples of God calling men and women to serve him in foreign lands without renouncing their secular work. Abraham, for instance, raised livestock all his life.[16] Joseph and Daniel served faithfully as government officials. Nehemiah was a governor. Queen Esther, the servant of Naaman, and many others were used by God outside of their land and in the exercise of their normal employment (Nunn 2007, 8).

In the same way, in the early church, the spread of the Christian message was primarily the fruit of lay missions, when 'anonymous Christians' communicated their faith during their trips and chance encounters sparked by persecution (Daniel-Rops 1965, 100–101). "Those who had been scattered preached the word wherever they went" (Acts 8:4). This text underlines the fact that Christianity was originally a lay movement. It was laymen and women who followed the coastal plain as far as Phoenicia, crossed the sea to Cyprus, or traveled north to Antioch (Acts 11:19–21). Those anonymous laypeople evangelized as much as did the apostles. And they were the ones who took the revolutionary initiative of communicating the gospel message to Greeks who had no ties to Judaism, and then of launching the Gentile mission from Antioch (Green 2001, 208). That missionary action of laypeople took place 'naturally':

> They were scattered from their base in Jerusalem and they went everywhere spreading the good news which had brought joy, release and a new life to themselves. This must often have been not formal preaching, but the informal chattering to friends and chance acquaintances, in homes and wine shops, on walks, and around market stalls. They went everywhere gossiping the gospel;

---

15. The word 'laity' is not in the New Testament, even though it has solid biblical backing. The New Testament expressions all designate a community that defines itself in reference to God (or to Christ): church (*ecclesia*) of God or of Christ, people (*laos*) of God, body (*soma*) of Christ. The members of that community are 'called' (*kletoi*), 'saints' (*hagioi*), 'disciples' (*mathetai*), but more than anything else 'brethren', and 'fellowship' (*adelphoi, adelphotes*). The word 'laity' (*laikos*) is very rare among Christians before the third century. But after that period there arose the idea that the laity play an earthly, temporal role, in opposition to the *ministers* (1 Cor 4:1; 6:4), *rulers* (Rom 12:8; 1 Thess 5:12), *pastors* (Eph 4:11), *leaders* (Heb 13:7, 17, 24), *elders* (Tit 1:5), *doctors* (Acts 13:1; 1 Cor 12:28), *shepherds* (Acts 20:28) (Congar, 1962).

16. Cf. Genesis 12:5: "Abraham took his wife Sarai, his nephew Lot, all the possessions they had accumulated and the people they had acquired in Haran, and they set out for the land of Canaan . . ."; Gen 13:2, "Abraham had become very wealthy in livestock and in silver and gold."

they did it naturally, enthusiastically, and with the conviction of those who are not paid to say that sort of thing. Consequently, they were taken seriously, and the movement spread, notably among the lower classes. (Green 2001, 208–209)

The Scriptures offer us many examples of godly men and women who were used by the Lord in the course of their secular work. Lydia (Acts 16:14) was a seller of purple, Zenas was a lawyer (Tit 3:13), Erastus was the city's director of public works (Rom 16:23), Priscilla and Aquila were tentmakers (Acts 18; Rom 16:3; 1 Cor 16:19; 2 Tim 4:19). Luke, a physician by profession, was at various times a companion of Paul (Col 4:14).

There are a growing number of Western missionaries who are adopting the 'tentmaking' model in an attempt to gain access to people who live in lands that are closed to 'traditional' Christian missionaries. That situation sometimes creates tensions and raises significant ethical questions. For in some cases those missionaries see their secular work as a simple means to gain access to those with whom they desire to share their faith, while their 'real work' (hidden from the sight of government officials) is the evangelization of souls and the implantation of churches. In other words, they see their secular work as a means by which they can accomplish something else. I am suggesting that embracing a missional paradigm centered on the formation of disciples who are reproducing their life with Christ in the lives of others (in place of the missional paradigm centered on the implantation of churches and the professional clergy) might diminish that tension.

The scheme of using secular roles to obtain access to those whom we wish to influence for Christ is understandable in the light of the influence colonization, industrialization and specialization had on the historical development of the dominant paradigm of vocational missions, supported by the financial gifts of Christians. When countries began closing their borders to that kind of missionary, in their desire to make disciples of the nations, they simply added secular roles to their 'full-time missionary' profile in order to obtain the necessary visas. Often, this was done without seriously considering the biblical model of the apostle Paul who was a tentmaker.[17]

---

17. Daniel-Rops offers the following information: "The work that he did throughout his missionary career to supply for his needs by working with his hands, was it the same work his father had done? A *skenopoio*, a *tabernacularis*, that could be a tentmaker, a humble employment working with leather and scissors. This seems too modest an employment for his family, and one might wonder if Saul didn't adopt this work precisely after breaking with his relatives following his conversion. But we must not lose sight of the fact that in Israel manual

Consequently, Western missionaries have largely overlooked the power and genius of Paul's examples. The apostle did not make tents with the goal of gaining an access to unreached peoples. In fact, he probably never even entertained that kind of reasoning, for as a Roman citizen, he could go wherever he wanted. But the apostle had other very convincing reasons to deliberately choose to work to support himself rather than to receive gifts from others to finance his mission.

Did the Apostle Paul Work to Finance His Mission by Choice or out of Necessity?

At this point in our reflection, we must ask if the apostle Paul deliberately choose to work to earn his living rather than receive financial support from others in support of his mission. This is a very important question. You might think that Paul received financial gifts when he could, and that he worked with his own hands only when that kind of support was lacking. But the testimony of the New Testament suggests otherwise. The New Testament affirms specifically that the apostle Paul worked in Galatia, in Corinth, in Thessalonica, and in Ephesus (1 Thess 2:9; 2 Thess 3:7–8; Acts 20:31–35; 1 Cor 4:12; 9:6 [this last text refers to the ministry of Paul and Barnabas which took place in Galatia]).

But the text that most helps us to understand Paul's position on this point is found in the ninth chapter of the first epistle to the Corinthians that was written from the city of Ephesus during the apostle's third missionary journey. In that text Paul defends his apostleship in front of opponents who had been criticizing his mission. Those enemies had criticized his apostleship on the ground that he had not exercised all the rights one might expect an apostle to use.[18] In defending the authenticity of his mission, Paul develops the most

---

labor accompanied the life of the intellect, and the most celebrated doctors of the Law had earned their livelihood by making clothes or preparing food" (Daniel-Rops 1965, II, 60).

18. It is interesting to note that even Jewish priests, living in Jesus' day, had to work with their own hands to provide for their needs: "They numbered seven thousand two hundred, grouped into 24 sections. All the service of each of these sections took place during one week, two times a year. And all of the priests were united for the three annual pilgrimages. The rest of the time they lived in their homes, working to meet their own needs and those of their families. Some among them learned to read and became scribes; but the majority of them were artisans, or in commerce, or worked the land. Their income was small. During their weeks of service, they could partake of the part of the sacrifices that was reserved for the priests. They also received the tythe. The rest of their revenue came from the work of their hands once they returned home" (Beaude 1983, 53–55).

convincing arguments found in the Bible to establish the rights of apostles and other Christian leaders to be supported financially in the ministry. Then he proceeds to say three times that he did not and will not exercise these rights (vv. 12, 15, 18).

It is important to remember that it was while he was staying in Ephesus, during his third missionary journey, that the apostle wrote this letter. The claim that he had not used his privilege to 'not work' covers therefore the bulk of his years of ministry. This leads me to believe that his 'normal' practice was to work with his hands to provide for his own needs. Moreover, Barnabas is associated with Paul in this text (v. 6). This is the case in spite of the fact that Barnabas had not collaborated with Paul since their separation during his first missionary journey (cf. Acts 15:32–41). Evidently Barnabas had continued to work to support his own ministry after their disagreement.

Paul develops his thinking further yet when he is forced, once again, to defend his apostleship in 2 Corinthians. He argues there that rather than weakening his apostleship, the fact that he refused to receive support from the Corinthians meant that he could serve them gratuitously and more effectively. This policy, which enabled Paul to boast that he was preaching the gospel free of charge, differentiated him from less scrupulous charlatans whose motives were corrupted. Paul was determined to demonstrate that his affections were set on the Corinthians themselves (cf. 6:11, 12; 7:2, 3), not on what they owned and could share with him. He argues that it is not part of children's obligation to save up and provide for their parents, but only parents for children (11:7–11; 12:14–16). The apostle announces that his policy toward support will not be altered (11:12).

The only text that seems to contradict the observation that it was Paul's policy to use his own resources rather than depend on the gifts of others is found in the middle of his defense in 2 Corinthians. He says: "I robbed other churches by receiving support from them so as to serve you . . . for the brothers who came from Macedonia supplied what I needed" (11:8–9). However, for a number of reasons, this text does not weaken my conclusions. First, our understanding of these couple of verses must be placed within the context of Paul's larger argument developed in 1 Corinthians 9 and 2 Corinthians 11. Second, in these verses Paul uses a powerful irony and exaggerates in order to shame the Corinthians. Third, the epistle to the Philippians clarifies this text when Paul affirms that "not one church shared with me in the matter of giving and receiving, except you only" (Phil 4:15). This they seem to have done on one or two occasions when the apostle had been in Thessalonica, and perhaps once when he was in Corinth. We can conclude that the Church of Philippi was the only one that sent money to aid the apostle Paul, and that this happened only a few times. Finally, the apostle wouldn't have had to defend his policy of not receiving gifts from others had this not been his habitual way of acting.

The New Testament presents us with some other relevant information concerning the practice of the apostle Paul. First, how much did he work with his hands? In 2 Thessalonians 3:8 we read: "Nor did we eat anyone's food without paying for it. On the contrary, we worked night and day, laboring and toiling so that we would not be a burden to any of you." Here the apostle explains that he worked in the morning and the afternoon, in other words 'full-time'.[19]

Second, that practice was so important to the apostle that he paid for his own meals rather than profiting from the hospitality of others. Third, the co-workers of Paul seem to have followed his model. According to 2 Thessalonians 3:7–9, Silas and Timothy worked as well to cover their needs. Eight times in these verses Paul uses the first person plural 'we': "For you yourselves know how you ought to follow our example. We were not idle when we were with you, nor did we eat anyone's food without paying for it. On the contrary, we worked night and day, laboring and toiling so that we would not be a burden to any of you. We did this, not because we do not have the right to such help, but in order to make ourselves a model for you to follow" (2 Thess 3:7–9; 1:1; 1 Thess 2:9).

A careful reading of the New Testament reveals that the apostle Paul chose deliberately to work to support his ministry rather than to depend on the gifts of others. Moreover, his explanations teach us that he did so for specific reasons.

---

19. But the description of Acts 18:2–4 also shows the difficulty of that option: Paul, could only give a small amount of his time to preaching the gospel, only on the Sabbath, because the rest of the week he was busy making tents to earn his livelihood. The arrival of support enabling him to announce the gospel full-time is one of the accents that Luke gives in verse 5: "When Silas and Timothy came from Macedonia, Paul devoted himself exclusively to preaching . . ." It was not only the arrival of his companions, but even more importantly the financial gift they carried from the believers in Philippi, that enabled Paul to quit working in order to devote himself exclusively to sharing the message of Christ (See Phil 4:15–19; 2 Cor 11:8–9).

Reason 1: To Lend Credibility to the Gospel He Communicated

The first reason why Paul chose to work to sustain his ministry rather than to depend on the support of others is spelled out in 1 Corinthians 9:12 "... to not hinder the gospel of Christ." To what hindrance might the apostle be referring here? I believe that he is alluding to the obstacle of suspicion. Had Paul been supported materially by those who benefitted from the gospel, some people might have doubted the truth of his message because they could question his motives. But no one could claim that Paul preached the gospel in order to better his financial situation! No one could say, "Paul you make converts and plant churches because that increases your monthly salary," nor could they say, "Paul you evangelize and plant churches because that is what you are paid to do. It's your job." When in a touching scene the apostle says goodbye to the leaders of the community of faith in Ephesus, Paul closes his admonitions by underlining his personal example:

> I have not coveted anyone's silver or gold or clothing. You yourselves know that these hands of mine have supplied my own needs and the needs of my companions. In everything I did, I showed you that by this kind of hard work we must help the weak, remembering the words the Lord Jesus himself said; "It is more blessed to give than to receive." (Acts 20:33–35)

Suspicion of our motives remains an obstacle to the furtherance of the gospel today. People know that money is important, and they are often wary of the reasons why we share the message of Christ. When we were missionaries in France people often asked us how we managed to finance our ministry without a 'normal' job. And here in Africa that question is not less important. Time and time again we have had Africans explain to us that becoming a pastor is a good way to earn one's livelihood. Several weeks ago, for instance, we were visited by a pastor's son who said that he hoped one day to either become a civil servant, or an ambassador, or a pastor. For this young man, to become a pastor had little to do with the gifting or call that comes from the Spirit of God, and much to do with how to earn a living. I remember as well the words of the real estate agent who helped us find our apartment in Yaoundé. That man, who displayed no signs of a vital and personal relationship with Christ, explained how one day he hoped to become a pastor and start a church as a means to finance his retirement years. Everyone here seems to know that whoever can get a microphone, if they display enough enthusiasm, they can begin a church in their living room.

In fact, just a couple of months ago a new group was planted that way in the courtyard of a building two houses away from where we live. This is seen as a legitimate way, among others, to earn a living.

Reason 2: In Order to Identify with Others

In 1 Corinthians 9 the apostle Paul moves beyond his right to financial support to discuss other areas of life in which he forfeited his right to freedom in order to win more to Christ.[20] Paul applied this principle to all of the situations in which he found himself – he would identify himself with others for their sake: with the God-fearing Jews (Acts 13:16–41), with the pagan Greek philosophers (Acts 17:16–34), and with political leaders (Acts 24–26). In this text where Paul states that he has chosen to minister to the Corinthians without charge and not making use of his rights as a gospel minister, he says that he did so "to become all things to all men . . . for the sake of the gospel" (1 Cor 9:22-23).

Because work is such a central component of human life,[21] working to earn one's livelihood is one of the deepest means of identifying one's self with others.[22] By working with his hands, Paul placed himself on the same level as those around him. He shared their joys and their difficulties. He relied as much on what he could earn as they did. He shared their fatigue at the end of the day. He had to put up with difficult clients and handle the various situations of the workplace ethically. No one could say: "Paul, you don't understand my fatigue or the pressures that I face at work."

The gospel calls us to a conversion of all of the areas of our being, to a transformation of each aspect of our existence. That deep change takes time. Few are those who are converted after having heard the gospel message for

---

20. The word 'job' (*métier* in French) comes from the Latin word "*ministerium*" (ministry). Every 'job' is a ministry, a service. And as a ministry to God and to men, work has value, even when accomplished in painful or boring conditions. The ministry develops the person. We are all 'full-time' for the Lord. In his epistle to the Colossians, Paul writes: "And whatever you do, whether in word or deed, do it all in the name of the Lord Jesus, giving thanks to God the Father through him" (Col 3:17).

21. It offers, among other things, the possibility to realize by the exercise of the capacities of the individual, the means of social integration beyond the circle of family and friends, and an activity that is useful for society.

22. We should mention here the example in the 1970s of 'working pastors' in French Protestantism, motivated as much by the desire to share the life of working laypeople as by the desire to save the meager financial resources that had been designated for missions. We can also mention the *Mission de France* with its 'working priests' in the Catholic world.

the first time (Singlehurst 1995, 36). Most people must go through a long process that enables them to see the credibility of the gospel, recognize the lordship of Jesus Christ and his authority over their life, acknowledge their sinfulness before God and receive his gracious gift of forgiveness (Hunter 1992, 76–77; Flinn 1999, 54; Engel and Norton 1982, 44–45). Finally, people must submit to the rule of Christ and learn how to allow his Spirit to change their way of thinking and acting. That is the path of discipleship which is at the heart of the Great Commission.

We will see as we progress in our study of Christian discipleship that life transformation takes place in a context of personal relationships. The communication of the gospel begins with its authentication in our lifestyle (Park 2005, 156–157; Posterski 1989, 32; Aldrich, 1981). Non-believers must encounter the reality of the gospel in the lives of followers of Christ who demonstrate its validity through their integrity, their sacrificial service, their charity, their joy, their attachment to the person and teaching of Jesus (Stone 2007, 259; Pippert, 1979). The followers of Jesus are constantly being watched by others at their place of employment. The missionary who works to support himself has the opportunity to live the gospel in front of others day after day (Hunsberger 2008, 71). In spite of our fascination with mass evangelism and our attempts to communicate the gospel through the formal activities of the church like Sunday School, door-to-door visitation, literature distribution, small Bible study groups, radio or television programs, or the Sunday worship service, the fact is that the gospel message advances through direct and intimate interpersonal attachments that lead to discussion of things that matter (Webber 2001, 75; 2003, 58). Only rarely does a person experience life-transforming conversion in an evangelistic crusade, or having received a Bible or piece of Christian literature, or by following a radio broadcast or a television program, outside of the presence and influence of friends. Practically all of those who are converted during an evangelistic campaign found themselves in that context through the invitation and influence of a friend.

The missionary who, like the apostle Paul, works at a secular job to earn his own livelihood, will 'naturally' enter into lasting relationships with others. It is within the context of those relationships that the validity and relevancy of the message of Christ will become evident to non-believers. Even in a context of non-belief, or hostility toward the church, people can move toward Christ if we enter into deep and lasting relationships with them. Moreover, the disciples of Christ, 'lay missionaries', can penetrate all of the legitimate domains of human society and thereby reach those that the institutional church finds outside its sphere of influence.

Reason 3: To Establish a Model of Witness and Discipleship

The third reason why Paul chose to work to support his own ministry rather than rely on the gifts of others was undoubtedly to establish a pattern of Christian witness and discipleship that others could follow. This pattern entailed at least three aspects: it covers the totality of life, it demonstrates the value of human labor, and it is for laypeople.

a. Paul made this choice to establish a discipleship pattern that covers the totality of life.

Even if the word 'disciple' is nowhere to be found in the writings of the apostle Paul, it is undeniable that he modeled a discipleship that touched all aspects of life for his converts. In fact, he explains that he sought deliberately to be a model for others, and he exhorted them to follow his example: "Join with others in following my example, brothers, and take note of those who live according to the pattern we gave you" (Phil 3:17). "Follow my example, as I follow the example of Christ" (1 Cor 11:1). Notice that the apostle desired that others imitate in his lifestyle a conduct that was "worthy of Christ" (Phil 1:27–30). This meant for the apostle to try to seek the good of others rather than his own good in everything, so that many might be saved (cf. 1 Cor 10:31–11:1).

b. Paul made this choice to establish a discipleship pattern that demonstrates the value of human labor.

The apostle writes to the Thessalonians that it was in "laboring and toiling" that he and his companions had "worked night and day" so that they would not be a burden to any of them. They did not do this because they did not "have the right to such help," he explains, "but in order to make ourselves a model for you to follow" (2 Thess 3:8–9). The apostle Paul modeled a good work ethic in a lazy society. The Roman Empire was suffering from a bad work ethic. And the apostle wrote that many of the converts had been greedy swindlers, etc. (1 Cor 6:9–10). That aspect of discipleship is so important that the apostle mentions it seven times (Acts 20:35; Eph 4:28; 6:5–9; 1 Thess 2:9–12; 4:11: 2 Thess 3:7–10; Col 3:23; Tit 3:1). Working to get rich is not a good work ethic. To work with diligence and application in order to serve one's boss (as if one worked for Christ), to serve one's clients, colleagues and those in need as if they were family members, these are the elements that make a morally irreproachable work ethic. For that reason a biblical work ethic includes diligence, the pursuit of excellence, honesty and service.

c. Paul made this choice to establish a discipleship pattern for laypeople.

But let's look more closely at the appeal that the apostle made to laypeople to imitate his example and join him in the ministry. This is one of the themes that flows through each of the chapters of the epistle to the Philippians:

> I thank God every time I remember you . . . because of your partnership in the gospel . . . And this is my prayer: that your love may abound . . . so that you may be able to discern what is best and may be pure and blameless until the day of Christ, filled with the fruit of righteousness . . . to the glory and praise of God. . . . Whatever happens, conduct yourselves in a manner worthy of the gospel of Christ. Then, . . . I will know that you stand firm in one spirit, contending as one man for the faith of the gospel . . . Do everything without complaining or arguing, so that you may become . . . children of God without fault in a crooked and depraved generation, in which you shine like stars in the universe. . . . But whatever was to my profit I now consider loss for the sake of Christ . . . I press on toward the goal . . . I press on to take hold of that for which Christ Jesus took hold of me. . . . All of us who are mature should take such a view of things. . . . Join with others in following my example. . . . Whatever you have learned or received or heard from me, or seen in me – put it into practice (Phil 1:3–11, 27–30; 2:14–16; 3:7–21; 4:9).

Paul deliberately called laymen and women to imitate his example in living out the gospel. That is the missionary nature of the laypeople of God.

But when the faithful lay believers of his day looked at the life of Paul, what did they see? Did they observe only the way in which he preached to crowds or the miracles that God did through him? Or did they watch him witness day after day as he plied his trade? Both answers are undoubtedly true. I can hardly imagine the apostle who constantly sought opportunities to lead others to Christ not sharing his faith as he made tents. Acts 18 seems to justify this conviction. In that text we read how Paul found Aquila with his wife Priscilla, and because he was a tentmaker as they were, he stayed and worked with them (v. 3). Luke describes Aquila as a Jew who had been chased out of Rome by Claudius, the Roman Emperor. The book of Acts uses the title 'Jew' to designate Jews who did not believe in Jesus as Messiah. Apparently, Paul led Aquila and Priscilla to faith in Jesus as they labored side by side in their workshop.

In Acts 19 we find other fascinating details about the practice of the apostle. Luke informs us that Paul "had discussions daily in the lecture hall of Tyrannus," and that this went on for two years (Acts 19:9). A bit further he explains how the sick brought "handkerchiefs and aprons" that had been touched by the apostle and they were healed (19:12). This is the only place where the Acts of the Apostles mentions this kind of practice. But what were those 'handkerchiefs and aprons'? The Greek word *soudarion* means a facecloth used for wiping perspiration, and the word *simikinthion* means a workman's apron. So Luke is telling his readers that Paul's sweat-cloths and work-aprons used in his trade of tentmaking and leather working, were taken out to the sick and demonized, and through their application there were cures. It seems that Paul was using the hall between the hours of 11 a.m. and 4 p.m. – the time of the usual midday rest and after Tyrannus had dismissed his students and Paul had completed his morning's work. The text indicates that he went to the hall in his work clothes, taught awhile, and then returned to his work. According to verse 31 of chapter 20, Paul encouraged the Ephesian elders by claiming that he "had not ceased day and night" to warn each of them with tears. It is evident that this incessant activity of the apostle included the hours when he had been busy making tents. Apparently interested individuals even came to his workplace to meet with him.

By working with his hands, Paul established the norm for the apostolic mission of laymen and laywomen. He could authoritatively address the question of evangelism and disciple-making in the workplace because he practiced it himself. No one could respond to him with: "But Paul, you don't understand the tensions, injustices, poor treatment, lack of respect, fatigue, boredom, ingratitude or the mockery that I must put up with." The apostle lived in the secular world of everyone else. He set the norm for witness and spiritual reproduction in the realm of ordinary everyday activities through his own example.

During the first years of his ministry the communities of disciples founded by Paul did not have a pastor who depended on the financial contributions of the faithful for their personal needs. They had no professional clergy. The believers acted with the conviction that every disciple of Jesus reproduces his spiritual life and his faith with others (Neil 1990, 22). It is only later, after the communities had grown and the model of lay ministry had been established as the norm, and that leaders had emerged, that the apostle gave instructions in his pastoral letters about the financial support of those who teach the Word.[23] Paul's approach produced communities of disciples that were immediately autonomous and reproducing. This is one of the factors that explains the tremendous advance of the gospel during those early years.[24]

---

23. A careful reading of the Bible reveals that in the first-century church, money was largely used to help the poor and desperate. Paul even exhorted the pastors to care for the poor. In fact, it is to them that he said: "In everything I did, I showed you that by this kind of hard work we must help the weak, remembering the words the Lord Jesus himself said: 'It is more blessed to give than to receive'" (Acts 20:17, 28, 34–35). (cf. Earle E. Cairns, 1996. *Christianity Through The Centuries* [Grand Rapids: Zondervan Publishing House, 84]).

24. The Anglican evangelist David Watson has underscored the fact that "During the first two centuries, the church met in small groups in the homes of its members . . . Those two centuries witnessed the greatest advance that the church has ever experienced. The absence of church buildings was not an obstacle to the rapid expansion of the church; in comparison with the situation 2000 years after Jesus Christ, it seem rather to have had a positive effect." David Watson, 1978, *I Believe in the Church* (Great Britain: Hodder & Stoughton, 121).

In working with his hands to provide for his material needs, the apostle Paul offered a missional model based on the Incarnation and on spiritual multiplication. He wrote to his co-worker Timothy: "The things you have heard me say in the presence of many witnesses entrust to reliable men who will also be qualified to teach others" (2 Tim 2:2). Paul's disciples could see with their eyes how to apply what they heard from his mouth. And what he modeled was contrary to the example of many others:

> The church had the benefit of the model of Paul, who sought no financial aid for himself but took his place as any ordinary person, finding ways to support himself. This was one thing that set Paul apart from the professional public preachers who were such a nuisance in his day. Lecturers and spell-binding orators, expecting support from their listeners, wandered from town to town. There was also a large class of people that wandered about as mystery-mongers, exhibiting their own shows and collecting money from those who attended. Paul refused to be classed with such people. . . . In setting an example at Thessalonica, Paul says that he adopted the role of a 'nurse'. To have asked for support from these infant Christians would have been a denial of his nurturing spirit. (Gilliland 1983, 249)[25]

Reason 4: In Order to Rapidly Multiply the Communities of Faith

The fourth reason why Paul chose to work with his hands to provide for his physical needs rather than rely on the gifts of others is because it allowed the rapid multiplication of autonomous faith communities. In making disciples of Jesus who knew (through his example) how to accompany others on the path of obedience to Christ at the same time that they earned their livelihood, Paul didn't need to stay long in any single location. He often left the disciples after only a few months' presence, and only approved leaders for them during a later visit (cf. Acts 14:21–23). It was in Ephesus, the most important city in the Roman province of Asia with a fine harbor that served as a great export

---

25. See also Roland Allen, 1993, *Missionary Methods: St. Paul's or Ours?* (Grand Rapids: Wm. B. Eerdmans, 49–50).

center, that Paul stayed the longest (two years). From that location he and his companions strengthened the faith of the believers in the surrounding cities. In the space of a dozen years time Paul had founded ten communities of disciples that we are aware of. Others such as Laodicea, Colossae, and Hierapolis were begun by his team or by members of other communities. In short, the apostle expected the disciples to do the work of the ministry, and he expected leaders to emerge from among the members of that body to equip, guide and encourage them in that role.[26]

Reason 5: In Order to Multiply the Number of His Co-workers

The fifth reason for which Paul chose to work to support himself in ministry rather than depend on the gifts of others is that this policy enabled him to rapidly add members to his missionary team. During his dozen years of missionary journeys he recruited twenty-four people whose identities we know of into his team (plus those whose names are not mentioned in the New Testament text). The indications are that he added two or three new people to his team each year from among the members of the communities of disciples. Only Silas came from Jerusalem. The others were the Turks, Kazakhs, and Spaniards of his day.

But how could he add members to his team at such a rapid pace? Because the members of his team followed his example and each person worked to meet his own physical needs while giving himself totally to the ministry. The apostle confirms this observation in 2 Thessalonians 3:7–10 when he uses the word 'us' to explain how he, Silas, and Timothy worked in order to give the believers in Thessalonica an example to follow. In other words, Paul led an entirely mobile and self-supporting team. They could rapidly reproduce their life as a disciple of Jesus in the lives of a handful of others, and then rapidly leave for a different location taking with them one or two promising disciples for further training. They were functioning out of a ministerial paradigm solidly based on lay missionaries. They did not need to wait for their members to complete their studies at the local seminary, or round up supporters who would pledge to underwrite their missionary endeavor.

---

26. It is evident in the New Testament that the first-century believers met generally in homes (Acts 2:46, Rom 16:3, 5; 1 Cor 16:19; Col 4:15; Phlm 12). There was a rapid expansion of the universal church when the faithful met regularly and locally in small communities. Each member seems to have been active in the Body of Christ when the meetings took place in their private homes.

Conclusions

Because people learn through examples that serve as models, the way in which Western missions have sent vocational workers ('full-time') has been repeated around the globe. That model has been embraced in spite of the fact that it marginalizes the role of lay believers and has proven itself to be largely ineffective in the multiplication of disciples of Jesus Christ. Moreover, it has developed an entire ecclesiology to justify its way of doing things. According to that ecclesiology, because vocational Christian workers serve Christ 'full-time', they have received a 'special call', a 'vocation', and are therefore more important in the kingdom of God than are simple lay believers. It follows that because laypeople have not received a special call, they only serve Christ 'part time', and one finds it difficult to imagine how they could contribute anything really significant to the community of faith. Instead, the laypeople are sometimes seen as a sort of second-class citizen.[27] One could conclude from that situation that laymen and laywomen don't have the same spiritual potential as do pastors or priests, and by extension, the same access to the life of the Spirit of God.

We began our reflection by observing that the missionary model that has been adopted in the West for more than a century, and that is now being followed in the Southern hemisphere, is largely defective. That model, based on the implantation of churches functioning around the Sunday worship service with its preaching, liturgy and professional clergy, only too rarely produces lay disciples of Jesus Christ who are actively reproducing their spiritual life in the lives of others. We have also shown how the means of financing 'full-time' missionaries is, in reality, a historical anomaly. According to the biblical model, which is also the model that has been the most practiced since the time of Christ, disciples of Jesus works with their hands to meet their physical needs. This was the case of the apostle Paul and the members of his missionary team. The fulfillment of the Great Commission, "make disciples of all nations", is inextricably tied to our way of financing that missional enterprise. I am suggesting that we must return to a more biblical understanding of the goal of our mission (with the valorization of lay disciples of Christ who reproduce their spiritual life in the lives of others), and of the financing of that mission

---

27. In certain traditions, the laypeople only serve to influence temporal society in a way that orients it toward the kingdom of God as we wait for the 'Day of the Lord'. This is in contrast with those who, responding to a call of God, leave the world and the affairs of this age and devote themselves to the service of God and the affairs of his kingdom.

(based on the revalorization of lay missionaries who serve Christ 'full-time' while they work with their own hands to meet their physical needs).

Questions to Think About:

1. How would you describe the 'average' believer in your faith community? What words would you use to depict his life with Christ and his commitment to the mission of the people of God?

2. The author in this chapter argues that the professionalization of the ministry in the person of the pastor, the evangelist, and the missionary has the effect of demobilizing the laity and centers the life of the faith community in the Sunday morning activities. What do you think of this evaluation?

3. The author of this chapter insists that the question of money, and the financial support of Christian ministry, has too great an impact in defining the role of the various actors in the mission of the church. What examples could you give to either confirm or refute that argument?

3

Does Jesus Really Want Us to Make Disciples?

The ancient Greeks seem to have made a distinction between three kinds of time: *chronos* time, *kairos* time, and *aion* time. *Chronos* time, is physical time. It allows us, through its units of measure such as seconds, minutes, hours, etc., to segment time into past, present, and future. *Kairos* time is an extraordinary moment, a point of decisive balance with the notion of a 'before' and an 'after'. It is a moment when a particular, vital event takes place. *Aion* time designates an indefinitely long period, without limits, that can signify destiny, an age, or eternity. These three words are all found in the New Testament text, and even though biblical scholars continue to discuss the major differences between them, they are in agreement that the biblical text mentions 'particular' moments when God has intervened decisively in time and space. We read for example that at the beginning of his public ministry Jesus proclaimed: "The time (*kairos*) has come, the kingdom of God is near. Repent and believe the good news!" (Mark 1:15). And the apostle Paul maintained that the life and work of Jesus marked the *kairos* – the decisive and critical moment in the execution of the divine project for humanity (Eph 1:10).

During the years of Christ's earthly existence, attention is especially given to the *kairos* of his death and resurrection (cf. Matt 26:18 and John 7:6). This explains why the four gospel writers consecrate one third of their text to describing that 'hour' in Jesus' life. That 'moment' was crucial for our justification (Rom 4:25), our liberation from the power of sin (Rom 6:4–10) and our liberation from the power of death (Rom 8:10–11).

Moreover, in 1 Corinthians 15 Paul explains six disastrous consequences if we eliminate the *kairos* of the resurrection: If Jesus of Nazareth has not been raised from the dead, (1) it is senseless to preach Christ (v. 14); (2) faith in Christ is useless (v. 14); (3) all the witnesses and preachers of the resurrection are liars (v. 15); (4) those who have placed their confidence in Christ remain in their sins (v. 17); (5) all the believers in the First Covenant (through Israel) are lost (v. 18); and, (6) those who follow Christ in this life are to be pitied more than anyone else (v. 19). Without the resurrection, it is quite certain there would have been no Christian church. With the ignominious death of their Master, his disciples were utterly confused and afraid for their own lives. There is no possibility that they could have continued as teachers of the Nazarene's doctrines, and even less that others could have been persuaded to follow them in those circumstances (Green 2001, 50).

A second *kairos* moment took place during the feast of Pentecost, when God the Father gave the gift of the Holy Spirit to the disciples. Before enduring his passion, Jesus had assured his followers that it was best for them that he leave. "But I tell you the truth," he said, "It is for your good that I am going away. Unless I go away, the Counselor will not come to you; but if I go, I will send him to you" (John 16:7). The departure of Jesus and the sending of the Spirit marked a major transformation in the relationship between the disciples and their Lord. Before that *kairos* moment Jesus was physically present; the disciples could count on him when things got difficult (see Mark 4:35–41 and Luke 9:37–45).

Now, in his absence, the disciples would need to learn how to live in relationship with him, counting solely on his spiritual presence and his promise: "I will not leave you as orphans; I will come to you" (John 14:18). Beginning with the Pentecost event the disciples who had accompanied Jesus in Galilee had to learn a new way of relating to their Master. And everyone who, for the past two thousand years, has begun following Jesus of Nazareth must live that same type of relationship with Christ. All of the disciples of Jesus, from the moment of his ascension and the giving of the Spirit, learn to know Christ and to be refashioned into the image of their Lord through the spiritual presence of the Counselor. It is the primary role of the Holy Spirit to make Jesus known (John 14:26; 15:26; 16:13–14). For this reason we can affirm that the Holy Spirit was given because Jesus is Lord (Congar, 1984).

This leads us to a third *kairos* moment, another event chosen by God that holds a foundational importance in the New Testament. It is an occurrence that took place between the resurrection of Jesus Christ and the sending of the Counselor on the day of Pentecost. The biblical text speaks of this incident in this way:

Then the eleven disciples went to Galilee, to the mountain where Jesus had told them to go. When they saw him, they worshiped him; but some doubted. Then Jesus came to them and said, "All authority in heaven and on earth has been given to me. Therefore go and make disciples of all nations, baptizing them in the name of the Father and of the Son and of the Holy Spirit, and teaching them to obey everything I have commanded you. And surely I am with you always, to the very end of the age." (Matt 28:16–20)

Here we have the text that will be at the heart of our reflection in this chapter where I will propose a response to the question: "Does Jesus really want us to make disciples?" In the previous chapter I attempted to demonstrate how our current ways of understanding the role of the pastor in the faith community, and the corresponding professionalization of Christian witness by 'full-time' ministers, has largely replaced the notion of lay disciples of Jesus by that of laypeople who financially support the ministry of their pastor. This substitution puts the Sunday worship service – its support, development and duplication – at the center of ecclesial preoccupations and relegates lay discipleship to the periphery. In spite of our observation that our Sunday programs are very ineffective in forming disciples of Jesus, we don't dare question the biblical legitimacy of the supremacy that we grant them. We therefore perpetuate a model based upon the conviction that evangelism gives birth to a community that exists to evangelize and produce other communities. We argue that this is the assignment that Jesus gave to those who follow him, and that the Holy Spirit helps us in this project.

I will organize my thoughts around four essential elements that spring from a study on this text from Matthew's gospel: (1) Our mission, as Jesus defines it, is the most important thing that we have to do; (2) The apostolic nature of this assignment contributes significantly to its importance; (3) Jesus was very specific in the assignment he has given; and, (4) This mission is both ingenious and strategic.[1]

---

1. In the rest of this chapter the author is relying on information drawn from the materials of the "Keystone Training DVD's and Manual" developed by Richard Greene, edited and published in 2007 by World Partners, Fort Wayne, Indiana.

1) This Mission is the Most Important Thing That We Can Accomplish

According to Matthew's account, when the resurrected Jesus came to meet the eleven disciples in Galilee, his first words were: "All authority in heaven and on earth has been given to me" (Matt 28:18). Certain biblical scholars suggest that these words were directed toward those disciples who doubted the reality of his resurrection, and who therefore wondered if they should prostrate themselves at his feet or not (v. 17). However, the majority of those scholars who have studied this text see in these words of Jesus a singular affirmation that gives an extraordinary importance to the words that will follow. When the risen Christ appeals to his absolute authority, this conditions what he will say, its application, and the means of its realization. Let's look at these elements in order.

To correctly understand the importance of these words of Jesus we must keep in mind that authority is defined as the power to command individuals and events. The word 'power' signifies the ability to realize what one desires. Throughout the days of his ministry, Jesus of Nazareth demonstrated his authority and his power. He established it when he proved himself stronger than the forces of nature or of evil spirits (Mark 4:35–41). His incomparable power and authority were evident when he brought back from the dead a young girl (Mark 5:21–43), a young man who lived in the village called Nain (Luke 7:11–17), and his friend Lazarus (John 11:38–44). Jesus also displayed real authority in his teaching which placed him ahead of the Scribes (Mark 1:22). On one occasion he claimed that his teaching would never pass away (Mark 13:31). His authority is such that he could cast out an evil spirit by a single word (Mark 1:21–28), heal through a simple touch (Mark 5:27–32), and even forgive sins (Mark 2:10). However, it is only after his resurrection, when "God (had) exalted him to the highest place and gave him the name that is above every name" (Phil 2:9), that Jesus gave this instruction to his friends.

Finally, notice that Jesus claims to have received "*all* authority". We have just seen that during the years of his public ministry Jesus demonstrated in extraordinary fashion his authority and outstanding power. Like the other gospel writers, Matthew underlines with insistence the authority of Jesus, the Messiah (see 7:29; 10:1, 7–8; 11:27; 22:43–44; 24:35). But what is it that has changed now that Jesus is resurrected from the dead? What changes is that the spheres in which he now exercises his authority are enlarged. They include the heavens *and* the earth, in other words, the entire cosmos (Carson 1984, 594). Before the events of his death on the cross and his resurrection, Jesus had received from the Father authority on earth. But now, God the Father has "put everything under his feet" (1 Cor 15:25–28). He is now the one through whom *all* the authority of Almighty God is manifested.

By tying what he is about to say to his power and absolute authority, Jesus is making it clear that no other authority can annul this commission. Be it on earth or in heaven, no one has the power to alter or modify it. This is perhaps the reason why for the past two thousand years the words he gives in this text have been considered the most complete and definitive description of the mission that Jesus left for his followers. In other words, this is the most important work that anyone who follows Jesus can do. It is the number one missional priority of the people of God. It is the supreme commandment that those who follow Jesus exist and work to obey. It is the assignment given to each and every person who identifies him or herself with Christ.

Second, when Jesus affirms his absolute power and authority, he is signifying that at his name every knee should bow, in heaven and on earth and under the earth (cf. Phil 2:10). Jesus knows that he is about to send his followers to make disciples of all the peoples and ethnic groups on earth, without distinction or exception. His words are reassuring: "All authority has been given to me . . ." he has already obtained the authority over all these peoples and their gods (1 Cor 8:5–6), and over every power and authority (Col 2:10, 15). When men and women become disciples of Jesus they learn day by day how to submit their lives to his lordship. For the disciple this results in a continual transformation that is almost endless. The disciple of Jesus is always discovering elements in her way of thinking, of speaking, and of acting that must be remade into the image of her Master. This is true whatever the person's ethnic origin. Because Jesus Christ is already Lord and the measure of every human being, his disciples can go to encounter others with full confidence!

Finally, by tying this commission to his power and unequaled authority, Jesus insists that his followers must do what he is about to command. He has received all power and authority over their lives. This realization explains perhaps why the term *kurios*, (Lord), became the central confession of the disciples concerning Jesus (cf. Rom 10:9; 1 Cor 12:3; Phil 2:11). This word designates the one to whom a person or thing belongs, the one who can decide that person or thing's purpose and fate. Jesus has received all authority. He is therefore the Master, the Lord. This truth shines brightly in Matthew's gospel. In that gospel this title appears uniquely in the mouth of disciples and of those people who are suffering and pleading for Jesus to intervene in their situation. It is noteworthy that those who oppose Jesus call him either 'Master' or 'Rabbi'. Matthew systematically distinguishes between these groups of individuals (Bosch 1992, 75). Where Mark or Luke have the disciples calling Jesus 'Master' or 'Rabbi', Matthew uses 'Lord'. As a result, the opponents of Jesus never call him 'Lord' in Matthew's gospel, and the disciples never address him any other way. In other words, Jesus, for Matthew, is not only a leader of men, like Moses, but truly the Lord of the disciples, the one who has received all authority in heaven and on earth.

This means that the commandment that Jesus is about to give is not a simple program, or method, or strategy, or formula among others that you or I can add or subtract from our ministry according to our preferences! And at this point in our reflection I will go so far as to state that because Jesus is the Lord of lords, and since he has commanded us to make disciples that will make disciples, if you are intentionally working to make disciples of Jesus who make disciples of Jesus in obedience to what he expects of us, you are in the process of obeying him. This signifies also that if you are not intentionally working to multiply disciples of Jesus who make disciples of Jesus, you are doing something other than what he expects from you.

Let's look again at the biblical text to determine if I am correct in making this kind of assertion.

2) The Apostolic Nature of the Great Commission is an Element Which Contributes to its Importance

In the introduction of his letter to Theophilus, Luke writes:

> In my former book, Theophilus, I wrote about all that Jesus began to do and to teach until the day he was taken up to heaven, after giving instructions through the Holy Spirit to the apostles he had chosen. (Acts 1:1–2)

Notice that Luke speaks of *instructions* that Jesus gave *through the Holy Spirit* to the *apostles* he had chosen. These words are meaningful. First, Luke speaks of 'instructions' that Jesus gave before he was taken up to heaven. He is certainly referring to the command that the men and women who accompanied the Lord Jesus during his ministry on earth received to continue his work. This is why the words of Jesus to his disciples, recorded in the text of Matthew 28 that we are in the process of examining, are called the Great Commission. The word commission refers to the giving of authority to someone to perform a particular task of duty. It also refers to the task itself. It is not the person who receives the commission who determines the nature of his mission. He has been mandated to execute the task that has been received. And in the case that interests us, the commission that Jesus gave to his followers is neither a missionary option, nor a missionary suggestion, but an absolute command: "Go and make disciples of all nations!" (Matt 28:19).

Two elements of this commission raise it above the level of a simple plan, strategy, idea or project. These two elements are its authority and its precision. Note that the word 'therefore' figures at the beginning of verse 19 in most English translations. This word is absent in some of the ancient manuscripts; however, it finds its logical place in this text. For as we have already noted, the *kairos* moment had arrived when Jesus received all authority in heaven and on earth. He can now command his followers to go to and make disciples of the nations. When Jesus gave this commission he sent his followers to do a specific and distinct job. He sent them out to accomplish the precise assignment of making disciples of all nations. This is an apostolic work. And even if *all* of Christ's followers aren't 'sent' to the nations in the sense of crossing cultural and linguistic frontiers, *every one of them* is called to participate in the apostolic work of making disciples of Jesus Christ. We will examine the specificity of that commission a bit further on in this chapter.

The apostolic nature of the commission that Jesus gave to his followers is reinforced by the fact that it is linked to the work of the Holy Spirit (Acts 1:1–3). This echoes the testimony of John who affirms that the sending of the followers of Jesus is inextricably tied to the sending of Christ himself by the Father in the Holy Spirit (John 20:21–23). The Gospels state that at the beginning of his public ministry, the Spirit of God descended like a dove on Jesus (Matt 3:13–17; Mark 1:9–10; Luke 3:21–23; John 1:32–34). Christ came into the world to do the will of the Father in the power of the Holy Spirit. Having accomplished that task he now sends his disciples to continue that work in his physical absence. For this reason, John's gospel says, "He breathed on them (like the Creator 'breathed' into the nostrils of the man he had formed from the dust of the ground [Gen 2:7]) and said, 'As the Father has sent me, I am sending you . . . Receive the Holy Spirit'" (John 20:21–22).

Finally, the importance of that commission is reinforced by the information that Luke furnishes when he writes that the Great Commission was given to the 'apostles' that Jesus had chosen. The title 'apostle', as it is used by Luke, designates the Twelve that Jesus had chosen to be with him and to participate in his work (Mark 3:13–19). But even more widely, the word designates someone who has been sent – a delegate or a messenger. We have just seen that Jesus saw himself as the one who had been sent by the Father.[2] And through this commission, he sends his followers in the same way to accomplish the specific assignment of making disciples.

3) Jesus Gave an Assignment Which is Very Specific

What does the Great Commission actually say? Make disciples! This command is really only one word in the Greek text, the verb *matheteuein*, which is used in the imperative mode *matheteusate*. Moreover, it is the primary verb of the text, the very heart of the mission. The two participles, 'baptizing' and 'teaching' are clearly secondary to the verb 'make disciples'. The primary verb in this sentence tells us what we are to do, and the participles describe how we are to do it. In a word, the mission aims at allowing all human beings the privilege of becoming true disciples of Jesus Christ. We should remember that for Matthew, the word 'disciple' does not refer solely to the Twelve. It is for him the only word to designate those who follow Jesus, and he uses it far more often than the other writers (Bosch 1992, 73). And even if in his gospel, Matthew uses words like send, go, proclaim, heal, exorcise, make peace, witness, and teach, it is the verb 'make disciples' that designates the objective of the mission.

"Make disciples!"

According to Matthew 4:19 a disciple is someone who is transformed by Jesus because he has been called to follow him. The verb the most often associated with a disciple is *akoluthein*, "to follow in the footprints of someone". To make disciples is simply to personally and individually accompany people in their apprenticeship to Jesus. It is not only a matter of leading people to confess their sins and place their confidence in Jesus for salvation. It is not only a question of teaching others what Jesus taught. Nor is it limited to putting others in a place where they can testify, explain the gospel message, lead a Bible study, preach, pray for the sick or cast out evil spirits. It is much deeper

---

2. There are a number of words of Jesus in the synoptic Gospels that reveal the extent to which he was conscious of the fact that he had been sent from the Father (Matt 15:24; Luke 4:18; Matt 10:40; Mark 9:37; Luke 9:48; 10:16). The gospel of John records thirty-nine phrases spoken by Jesus that reveal that understanding (i.e. John 5:30, 36, 38; 6:29, 57; 7:16, 29; 8:16, 42; 10:36).

than all that. The words of Jesus are clear: "A student (disciple) is not above his teacher, nor a servant above his master. It is enough for the student (disciple) to be like his teacher, and the servant like his master" (Matt 10:24). Here is a foundational text, central to the biblical portrait of a disciple. The disciple is modeled after the image of Jesus.

"Go and make disciples!"

Tied to the commission to personally and intentionally accompany others on the path that leads to Christ-likeness, the Great Commission of Matthew 28:19 is the explicit command to go. "Go and make disciples!" It is surprising to see the ease with which we have transformed that command to "Go and make" into "Come and watch!" The apostolic models that dominate our circles today are centered on evangelistic campaigns, Sunday meetings, Bible studies, meetings of different Christian associations or movements, etc., where people are invited to *come* (sometimes accompanied by their non-believing friends or family members) and *watch* like spectators. Instead of stimulating a centrifugal movement that pushes the faithful to those who are 'outside', our incorrect interpretation of the work that Jesus has assigned to us reinforces a contrary centripetal movement.

"Baptizing them in the name of the Father and of the Son and of the Holy Spirit"

Biblical scholars tell us that the rite of baptism was well known in the Jewish world and was certainly not introduced by John the Baptist (Matt 3:1–17; 4:18–22; Mark 1:16–20; Luke 3:15–18; 5:1–11; John 1:19–34), or by the baptism mentioned here (Dockery 1992, 56–57). They also inform us that the rite of baptism at the time of Jesus was, for the Jew, a public expression of repentance and faith, the decisive act of commitment (Dunn 1962, 122). In other words, the rite of baptism did not necessarily mean a change of religious identity (Bjork 1997, 84). When Jesus associated the rite of baptism with the making of disciples, he was not saying that the person must become a Christian! In receiving baptism, the person publically expressed his decision to begin walking in the footsteps of Jesus. Baptism is a 'visible word' of the Christ-follower addressed to his family and people (Spindler, 2001).

I will say it again, from a socio-religious perspective, the rite of baptism in water signified for the first-century Jews that the person being baptized was identifying solemnly and definitively with the person in whose name he or she was receiving baptism. In a fascinating article entitled "Proselytism, Mission, and the Bible", Eugene P. Heideman indicates that in both the Old and the New Testaments, conversion was not a call to a change of community so much as it was a call to new obedience to God. To illustrate this point from the New Testament Heideman points to the Day of Pentecost when Peter called upon the crowd of Jews and proselytes 'from every nation' to repent and be baptized, without expecting them to change their community identity. Even the rite of baptism did not, according to Heideman, entail a change from one human community to another:

Conversion and baptism did not mean a change in human community or citizenship in the New Testament. As we have already noted, throughout the New Testament, Jews who are baptized remain Jews and continue to identify with the temple and the synagogue. The Samaritans, the Ethiopian eunuch, and Cornelius the Roman do not change citizenship when they become followers of Jesus. Rather than a change of affiliation in the human community of converts, the undergirding idea of being 'in Christ' is to experience a new birth 'from above' (John 3:3) and to gain citizenship in heaven (Phil 3:20).

Baptism today is often viewed both within the church and by those outside as the rite that symbolized the breach in relationships whereby a person leaves one community to become a member of another. Baptism in the New Testament, however, did not have that character (1996, 11).

The rite of baptism is, therefore, the public sign of the relationship of voluntary submission to Christ that is at the heart of discipleship (Beasley-Murray 1954, 90–92).

"Teaching them to obey everything I have commanded you"

For Matthew, discipleship is learning to live according to the model and teachings of Jesus. It highlights orthopraxy, an irreversible transformation in the relationship with God and with others. It is not an attempt to earn salvation through good works. Matthew tells how, during the institution of the Last Supper, Jesus proclaimed: "This is my blood of the covenant, which is poured out for many for the forgiveness of sins" (Matt 26:28). The other synoptic writers don't allude to the forgiveness of sins in their narration of the Last Supper of Jesus. For Matthew, the disciple of Jesus does not seek to conform his life to the example and teaching of Jesus in order to save his soul. On the contrary, for Matthew, what God did in Jesus Christ – the forgiveness of sins – is the point of departure for a new life for the disciple.

But the Great Commission given by the resurrected Christ reminds us that salvation involves much more than the forgiveness of our sins. Because Jesus Christ has received all authority, he is Lord of all humankind and of all of the aspects of human life. Abraham Kuyper, Dutch academician from the Reformed Church, was undoubtedly correct when he said: "There is not one square inch of all of creation over which Jesus Christ does not cry out: 'This is mine! This belongs to me!'" (Kuyper, 1931). For this reason the teaching of Jesus addresses all of the areas of human existence. Jesus explains, for instance, the ways in which we should handle conflict (Matt 5:24–25), how to live our sexuality (Matt 5:29–30), how to communicate (Matt 5:34–37), how to respond to appeals for assistance (Matt 5:38–42), how to respond to those who oppose you (Matt 5:44), how to practice the different spiritual disciplines (Matt 6:1–18), the kind of goods we should seek after (Matt 6:33), how to respond to those who disappoint us (Matt 7:1), what to do when the person with whom we are sharing doesn't appreciate our message (Matt 7:6), how to pray (Matt 7:7–8), how to determine the ethical thing to do (Matt 7:12), how to react to false prophets (Matt 7:15), whom we should fear (Matt 10:26–28), how we should treat our parents (Matt 15:4), how to respond to a legalistic mindset (Matt 16:6), how we should treat the helpless (Matt 18:10), how to respond to those who treat you wrongly (Matt 18:15, 21–22), how to respond to consumerism (Luke 22:15), how to regard marriage (Matt 19:6), whom we should invite to our receptions (Luke 14:12–14), the attitude that we should have toward civil authorities (Matt 22:19–21), how we should receive his teaching (John 14:15), how we should treat the other disciples of Jesus (John 21:15–16), the goal of our mission (Matt 28:19), and, what we should teach those whom we accompany on the path of discipleship (Matt 28:20).

The disciple is the person who, desirous to be like Christ, applies systematically and intentionally Jesus' teaching in each of the areas of his or her life. In this way, even today, whatever our ethnic origin, our social status, our education, our sex, our religious identity, or our age, we enter into his school as apprentices or students.

4) The Mission Which We Have Received is Both Ingenious and Strategic

Jesus established some criteria so that we can evaluate our life as his disciples. Among these we find that of bearing fruit – "This is to my Father's glory, that you bear much fruit, showing yourselves to be my disciples" (John 15:8).

These words come from the teaching in which Jesus compares his disciples to branches that are attached to the true vine (in other words, himself). In this discourse, he underlines with force the idea that the disciple must 'remain' or 'abide' in him (v. 4–7), and in his love (v. 9–10). He insists that to 'remain' in his love, the disciple must obey his commands, live according to his teaching, put his instructions into practice (v. 10). And he adds: "You are my friends if you do what I command" (v. 14). At the close of this discourse Jesus comes back to the notion of fruit-bearing: "You did not choose me, but I chose you and appointed you to go and bear fruit – fruit that will last" (v. 16).

We can see from this teaching that through a person's attachment to Jesus, and the adjustment of one's behavior to his teaching, that person enriches his own life. Notice also that when an individual learns not only to believe in Jesus, but also how to do what the Master said, to live according to his teaching, that person profits fully from his friendship (see also John 14:21). And in words that resemble those of the Great Commission of the gospel of Matthew, Jesus says that his project is that the people who live in that fashion 'go' (". . . appointed you to go" [John 15:16] and "Go" [Matt 28:19]) and that they ". . . bear fruit – fruit that will last" (John 15:16) and ". . . make disciples" (Matt 28:19).

All those who live by the life of Jesus have been chosen and appointed to bear fruit that will last. Sometimes we think that only pastors, elders, deacons, evangelists, missionaries, monks and nuns, and other 'consecrated' people have been called to that task. But just as all are called equally to 'remain' in Christ, drawing life and strength from him, putting into practice his instructions, all are appointed to bear fruit. And Jesus declares that two significant things are accomplished when we bear fruit: (1) his Father is glorified, and (2) we show ourselves to be his disciples.

When Jesus says, "showing yourselves to be my disciples", the verb of that phrase is the Greek word *ginomai* which signifies; become, begin to exist, come to be, be made. We literally become the disciples of Jesus when we bear fruit. And Jesus himself will evaluate the quality of the fruit that we bear (Matt 3:7–10; 7:15–23; 13:23; 21:43; Mark 4:20; Luke 3:9; 6:43–49; 8:14–15; 13:6–9; John 4:34–38; 12:24; 15:1–8; Col 1:10; Jude 1:12). This means that we are all called to bear fruit. If it is true that we are not all called to preach, or lead a Bible study, we are all called to fruitfulness. If we have not received the gift of an evangelist, and are not all called to cross cultural and linguistic barriers for Christ, we are nevertheless all called to be fruitful. Fruit bearing is not a luxury reserved for pastors, priests, missionaries and others who serve

Christ 'full-time'. Why is this the case? Because Jesus said that when we bear fruit his Father is glorified.

When the disciples of Jesus accompany others on the path of discipleship, and those individuals repeat the process with others (and this is the meaning of bearing fruit), the redemptive projects of God the Father are realized, and he is glorified. Paul says that in this way we serve to celebrate God's glory (Eph 1:10–12). And he specifies that it is for that reason that we have been adopted into God's family (1 Cor 10:31). We will come back to the tie between the disciple of Jesus and the glory of God in chapter 7.

Christ says that all those who remain in him, drawing strength and vitality from his life, glorify the Father as they reproduce in the lives of others that same attachment to him (John 15:8). And he warns that every branch that does not produce fruit is 'cut off' from him by the Father, and that every branch that does bear fruit is pruned so that it will be even more fruitful (John 15:2). We are all called to accompany others in the footsteps of Jesus. No one is exempt. Every person who has responded to Jesus' call to 'follow' him is a part of the process that God the Father has inaugurated to extend his Reign. We know this to be true because Jesus made disciples, and he commanded his followers to do the same thing.

Jesus Christ could have chosen any variety of methods to spread the good news and advance his kingdom. He could have ordered an angel to circle the earth, like a satellite, proclaiming his message in the appropriate language as he passed over each people group of the planet. He could have orchestrated things so that the printing press, the radio and the television were invented before his coming. Jesus could have been a famous author, a radio Bible teacher, or the first televangelist. God could have done all of these things.

But instead, Jesus decided to base his work on the people who would become his disciples, and who would then accompany others in the same process. This is, in fact, a quite ingenious method for several reasons. First, anybody can do it. One needn't be a seminary student or a pastor to accompany someone else on the path of discipleship. Second, this is something that one can do with the means that one has already. It isn't necessary to rent a building, own an automobile, have access to a sound system, or finance a publicity campaign to accompany someone in discipleship. Third, the process of making disciples who accompany others in discipleship produces more 'workers' who are really engaged in the harvest. Tied to that multiplication of 'workers' in the harvest, one can observe that evangelistic campaigns (without the personal and deliberate accompaniment that is at the heart of discipleship) *adds* people to the faith community, while the process of making disciples *multiplies* the people of God.

The Value of Fruitfulness

The divine projects are accomplished through God's benediction: "Be fruitful and increase in number, fill the earth . . ." (Gen 1:28). This blessing was given to every noteworthy person or group in the Bible. It constitutes the base of each of the covenants that God has made with humankind. Fruitfulness was the first benediction and the first commandment given by God. He has chosen to establish his reign or authority through the propagation of divine offspring (cf. Rom 9:8; 1 John 3:9; 1 Pet 1:3). Jesus Christ affirmed that natural and spiritual value when he declared; "I chose you and appointed you to go and bear fruit" (John 15:16). The value of fruitfulness is each person who follows Jesus who bears fruit!

When each person who remains in Jesus and draws life from him bears fruit in accompanying others on that same path, the principle of multiplication begins. This process can seem long and not very productive at first. Imagine, for instance, that as an evangelist a person can lead one person a day to convert and embrace Christ. In the period of one year, that evangelist would see the salvation of 365 souls. It is not possible to lead one person a day to conversion *and* to spiritual maturity. It takes more time than that to reach maturity and the ability to reproduce that relationship to Christ in the life of someone else. Imagine that I can do that in the period of one year. In other words, in the one year that I accompany a person toward spiritual maturity as a disciple of Jesus, the evangelist sees the conversion of 365 souls. Suppose that at the end of that first year, I suggest to the person that I have been accompanying that we begin praying that we can see the conversion of two other people the second year, and that we will reproduce the process that we have gone through together in the lives of those new converts during that second year. At the end of the second year, if we have reproduced the process of spiritual reproduction and personal accompaniment in following Jesus, there are now four of us who are following Christ. During this same period the evangelist has continued evangelizing one person a day so he has seen the salvation of 730 souls during that same period of time.

The process of spiritual multiplication seems much less fruitful than the addition of the evangelist if we consider only the first years. But at the rate of multiplication used in this illustration, each disciple producing a new disciple each year, the result would largely overtake the fruit of the evangelist who is converting one person a day, for after about ten years, see what will happen as indicated by the following table.

Evangelism and Multiplication

Year	Evangelist (1 soul a day)	Disciple (1 disciple a year)
1	365	2
2	730	4
3	1,095	8
4	1,460	16
5	1,825	32
10	3,650	1,024
20	7,300	1,048,576
30	10,950	1,073,741,824
33	12,045	8,589,924,592

Jesus knew that even though there is a place for preaching and mass evangelism, the success or failure of his movement would depend on the small number of people who truly followed him. His strategic investment into the lives of those individuals, through a process of personal accompaniment, was the key that assured the future of his movement and the growth of the kingdom of God he proclaimed.

Conclusions

When we look closely at the Great Commission that Jesus gave to those who followed him (Matt 28:16–20), we observe that he mandated them to do one thing – make disciples. That is the specific assignment of the Great Commission. When Jesus said to make disciples, he didn't mean something else. His language is clear and specific. It is amazing how, in reading this commandment of Christ, we have understood: "Go into all the world and plant churches, and the churches will make disciples." The assignment of the Great Commission is the making of disciples. It is neither the planting of churches, nor the creation of evangelistic cell groups, nor the training of leaders, nor the planning of meetings, nor charitable activities in his name (even if all of these things are good and play a role in the life of a disciple). Jesus said, "Make disciples" because he wants disciples.

Questions to Think About:

1. According to the author, for what reasons must we take seriously the Great Commission as it appears in Matthew 28:18–20?

2. Summarize in your own words the Great Commission. In your opinion what are the notions that are the most important in that commission? Why?

4

What Does a Disciple of Jesus Look Like?

We have just seen that Jesus Christ wants us to make disciples of all nations. Every person who enters into God's family by the new birth (cf. John 3) is called to be a disciple of Jesus who reproduces that vital relationship with Christ that he possesses by accompanying others on the path of discipleship. Every disciple is called to make disciples. Jesus clearly said to the men who had followed him during three years on the roads of Galilee that they were to make disciples everywhere. And he promised to accompany them in that task up to the very end of the age (Matt 28:20).

Naturally, almost every church does all that it can to make disciples. When there is an evangelistic crusade, or a pastor preaches, or a layperson leads a Bible study, when the faith community celebrates the Lord's Supper, or spends time in prayer, the faithful experience things that can help them to grow spiritually in Christ-likeness. However, we must go further. It is true that this model of the church is now to be found everywhere, and is thriving in Asia and in Africa. Nevertheless, I have underlined in chapter 2 the observation that in reality few of the faithful are becoming spiritually mature and reproducing what they have received because of these ecclesiastic activities. I also indicated that this way of understanding our call focuses the attention, energy and physical means of the communities on the 'religious professionals' and their Sunday morning activities. A growing number of Christians are asking if this is sufficient or if we aren't missing something. In our way of doing things, something seems to not be quite as it ought to be. Are all of our activities, all of our reunions, all of our programs, really accomplishing the mission that we have received from the resurrected Christ to "Go make disciples of all nations"?

In this chapter I will examine the attributes of a disciple of Jesus. For the call that we have received is not to make disciples who look like us. They are his disciples, and not our own. In the same way, we are not sent out to make disciples of our church tradition. When Jesus Christ gave us the missionary mandate it was not so that Catholics would make Catholics, Baptists other Baptists, evangelicals more evangelicals, Pentecostals new Pentecostals, and so forth. Jesus sends Catholics to make disciples of Jesus, and this is true for all the others as well.

Let's think a minute about why Christ has come into this world. Why was Jesus born?

Why Has Christ Come into this World? Why Was Jesus Born?

The responses to these questions do not vary much. "Jesus was born to bring salvation to the world," say some. "Christ has come into the world to show us the way to the Father," affirm others. Some suggest that Jesus was born to take away our sin and to procure forgiveness for our transgressions. "Christ has come to reconcile us to our Creator and to give us access to heaven," attest others. Many Africans are convinced that Jesus was born to conquer occult powers, the forces of evil and death, and that he brings us healing and true life.

There is truth in each of these responses. But didn't Jesus Christ also come to do something that very often is hidden from our sight, and yet largely defines what his disciples look like? I am thinking of what Jesus said when he was interrogated by Pilate shortly before his death (John 18:33–38):

> [33] Pilate then went back inside the palace, summoned Jesus and asked him, "Are you the king of the Jews?"
>
> [34] "Is that your own idea," Jesus asked, "or did others talk to you about me?"
>
> [35] "Am I a Jew?" Pilate replied. "It was your people and your chief priests who handed you over to me. What is it you have done?"
>
> [36] Jesus said, "My kingdom is not of this world. If it were, my servants would fight to prevent my arrest by the Jews. But now my kingdom is from another place."

[37] "You are a king, then!" said Pilate. Jesus answered, "You are right in saying I am a king. In fact, for this reason I was born, and for this I came into the world, to testify to the truth. Everyone on the side of truth listens to me"

[38] "What is truth?" Pilate asked.

The question Pilate asks – "What is truth?" – is difficult to interpret. What is he actually expressing? His skepticism, his misunderstanding, his impatience, his hopelessness, or his sincerity? No one knows how to answer that question. But when Jesus says that he came into the world to testify to the truth, his message is clear. By that word he is affirming that his person, his actions and his teaching bring to light all that we can confidently know about ourselves and the world we live in.

Jesus maintained that he was born, that he came into our world in response to the fundamental desire of humankind to orient existence according to trustworthy guidelines. In this, he presents himself as the response to the most basic question of human life.

We evangelicals sometimes are so desirous to see in Jesus the Savior of our souls, that we lose from sight the fact that he is much more than that. Jesus was not only born to die on a cross. He did not come into our world only to enable us to enter into paradise. His life, his death on the cross, and his resurrection serve that goal. They allow us to be reconciled to God the Father (2 Cor 5:18–19), deliver us from condemnation (Rom 8:1; 1 Thess 1:10), from death (1 Cor 15:54–55; 2 Tim 1:10; Heb 2:14–15), from the power of our sinful nature and of this world (Rom 7:23–25; Gal 1:4; 5:24), from all powers that are opposed to God (Col 2:14–15; 2 Tim 4:18), and it is true that they guarantee us an inheritance that can never perish, spoil or fade (1 Pet 1:4). However, when he explains his coming to Pilate, Jesus mentions none of these things. Instead he says: "For this reason I was born, and for this I came into the world, to testify to the truth."

It seems to me that many of the people in our churches have placed their faith in Jesus for their salvation. They have received from him the forgiveness of their sin, they hope in eternal life, but they have not grown as his disciples because they have not understood his link to the truth.

In order to expose the tie between Jesus as the truth and the life of the disciple, I will lean primarily on the writings of John. My thoughts will be organized around three key elements: (1) Jesus communicates the truth, (2) Jesus acts in truth, and (3) Jesus is the truth.

But first, let's come to an agreement about the meaning that we will give to the word 'truth'.

Toward a Definition of the Truth

Great thinkers of the past have believed that one of the central tasks of human existence is discovering the truth about human beings, the world they live in, and ultimate reality that gives meaning to everything else. Buddhism, which denies the existence of God, affirms nevertheless the need to discern what is real, and to adjust our thoughts, our emotions, our commitments, and our actions according to that understanding. Fundamentally, the question of the truth refers to what we can know confidently about ourselves and our world.

This observation allows us to define the truth as that which corresponds to reality. Are certain things or experiences real? Or are they only appearances, illusions, or phantasms like the Hindus believe? How might we comprehend and account for the reality of our being and our existence in the world? Are our beliefs only dreams, projections of our imagination, which have no correspondence with what really exists? If that were the case, we would be no more than religious fools or passionate madmen. Folly does not allow one to discern between what is real and what is only a delirious hallucination.

The problem is that in the end reality will catch up with us whatever our belief might be. The man who falls from the tenth floor of a building can yell during his fall as he passes by each window – "So far so good!" But there will come a moment when he will encounter the hard reality. The truth, in its biblical sense, is not only that which corresponds to reality in some abstract way. Biblical truth is trustworthy, worthy of personal commitment; it gives meaning to our actions.

It is noteworthy that the Old Testament does not have a Hebrew word for 'truth' (Meyer, 1988). For the Jews, the truth is not so much something that a person believes, as it is to adjust one's way of living so as to correspond with the reality in which one believes. The arguments with the 'false prophets' are a good example of the way in which the Bible speaks of the truth. The false prophets are morally corrupt. They are "greedy for gain" (Jer 6:13; cf. Mic 3:5, 11), given over to adultery, liars and accomplices of evildoers, and tellers of reckless lies (Jer 23:30). For these reasons their message is disqualified. It is no more than "visions from their own minds" (Jer 23:16, 26). Biblical truth cannot be separated from a way of life that corresponds to a certain vision of reality. "Don't tell me what you believe," say the Jews. "Show me how you live."

Standing before Pilate, Jesus says that he is come into the world to display by his acts and words what is really real, full and complete reality. All that conforms to the life and teaching of Jesus corresponds truly to what really is; and whatever does not conform to the life and teaching of Jesus does not correspond to ultimate reality.

Jesus Communicates What is Real

In the Gospels, the word 'amen' is used one hundred times. Thirty-one times by Mark, six times by Luke, and twenty-five times, always in its double form, "amen, amen" by John. This word comes from a Hebrew verb signifying 'confirm, hold, establish, verify, be sure of' (Harris, Archer & Waltke 1980, 51). In English, some Bibles translate this word "I am telling you the truth", or "truly, truly I say to you", or "truly, I assure you", or "I declare to you the truth". Biblical scholars tell us that this double usage of 'amen' does not correspond to any Hebrew expression, and that it is consequently an invention of Jesus. When Jesus uses this expression he seems to be saying something like: "Listen to what I am about to say, because the words that I am pronouncing do not come from me (John 3:34). They reveal what is real."

Jesus talks about things as they really are. When he affirms the importance of reconciliation, for example (Matt 5:26), of giving liberally (Matt 10:42), of faith (Matt 17:20; John 5:24), of joy when he who was lost is found (Matt 18:13), of humility and trust in God rather than pride and self-sufficiency (Matt 21:31), of the need to understand the origin of what is good (Mark 3:28), what he says corresponds to reality.

Because the Father is both ultimate reality and the One who sent Jesus into the world (John 7:28), and because Jesus came into the world to reveal the Father, his teaching corresponds to ultimate reality (John 8:16).

In John chapter 8, Jesus distinguishes clearly between those who place their faith in him, and those who, following that act of faith, attach themselves to his teaching. The text tells us that after hearing Jesus speak of the manner in which he would die on the cross (v. 28), many people believed in him (v. 30). If it is by faith that one is saved, then we could say that many of those people were 'born again', that they became 'believers', were 'converted', or became 'Christians'. Addressing himself to these people Jesus said something like this: If you live in my teaching, if you allow my words to define your way of making sense of life, and if you live in conformity to what I say, you will truly be my disciples. You will understand what is real, and that understanding will free you from all illusion (vv. 31–32).

The Jews who had believed in Jesus were not bad Jews. They followed the Law of God, the Torah. However, Jesus told them that to be his disciples, they must 'dwell' in, 'hold' to, 'remain permanently' in, 'live' within, 'continue to exist' in his teaching. It seems that we sometimes find it difficult to remain permanently in Jesus' teaching.

Take, for instance, our experience in evangelical churches in Cameroon. Since we arrived more than three years ago, Diane and I have visited several different churches. We have often observed that there are very few sermons preached from the words of Jesus. We have listened to many that examined an Old Testament passage, or one from an epistle, but I can count on the fingers of one hand the ones that we have heard from the Gospels. I think also of the church buildings where the Ten Commandments are posted on the wall of the sanctuary instead of the Beatitudes. It is as if one goes to the foot of the cross for salvation, but to the feet of Moses or Paul for instruction. Jesus invites us to live in his words.

Have you ever wondered why the gospel of Matthew is placed at the head of the New Testament? It is not because it was written first. That place goes to Mark. The well-known biblical scholar, Raymond Brown, informs us that right from the first centuries Matthew was considered to be the 'founding document' that grounded the church in the teaching of Jesus (Brown, 1997). It seems that Matthew even organized his gospel in such a way that it underscores the fact that the disciple is one who lives in the teaching of Jesus. All of Jesus' major discourses in that gospel are addressed to his disciples (Matt 5:1; 10:1, 36; 18:1; 23:1; 24:1–3). Matthew insists that the teaching of Jesus gives his disciples understanding (Wilkins 1992, 183). Jesus communicates things as they really are, and the disciple learns to change his way of life so as to reflect that reality. According to Matthew, that total obedience to the teaching of Jesus – sometimes called *justice* (Matt 5:17–20) and sometimes called *love* (Matt 22:37–40) – is the major characteristic of a disciple. The disciples are, therefore, those who regulate and conform their way of living in accordance with the teaching of Jesus.

Jesus Acts According to What is Real

pels tell us that Jesus was not satisfied with simply teaching about al through his words. In his person we can visualize the *verbalization* of reality. In Jesus, ultimate reality is visible to our eyes. "And the Word was made flesh, and dwelt among us, and we beheld his glory, the glory as of the only begotten of the Father" (John 1:14).

Jesus said to his disciples, "He who has seen me, has seen the Father" (John 14:9). He is the visible expression of the real nature of the Father. He not only spoke of love; he loved in all truth. Sinners considered him their friend. He not only preached about forgiveness; he forgave. He not only taught about the need for justice and righteousness; he attacked the unjust and corrupt institutions of his day. He did not establish a theological faculty or a Bible college; he invited men and women to live with him twenty-four hours a day. It was precisely for that reason that they could witness his way of living with others as a concrete expression of grace and reality.

When he says that Jesus was "full of grace and truth," John helps us to understand what people saw when they spent time with Jesus. He does not say that Jesus was full of doctrines and theories, or that he was full of the Torah and commandments. Neither does he say that he was full of strategies or methods. Naturally these things have their importance; but whatever their importance might be, John insists on the fact that Jesus, who reveals reality by his teaching, reveals it, above all, in his relationships with others.

What struck those who scrutinized Jesus' way of acting with others? Jesus was generous with his time, with his love and with his power. He was real and transparent in his compassion and in his commitment to do the will of his Father. He was incredibly open with others. He welcomed all who approached him; the well educated and the illiterate, the rich and the poor, the powerful and the helpless, the passionate and the indifferent, the seekers and the blasé, the healthy and the sick. His openness to others was such that he was not labeled the 'teacher of sinners', or the 'reformer of sinners', but the 'friend of sinners' (Matt 11:16–19).

I think of an incident that took place in the USA several years ago that has been told by Keith Miller (Moore, 2010). After an especially tiring day at work, a man who lived in the outskirts of Chicago was in a hurry to catch the last commuter train of the evening. In his haste, he accidentally collided with a ten-year-old boy on the crowded train platform of the station. In the collision the young lad dropped a box he had in his arms and its contents scattered under the feet of the crowd. The man hesitated a moment. At the same time the station chief called for the last passengers to board the train and announced the closing of the doors. The man knew that he didn't have enough time to help the child and catch his train. However, he stop down what he had in his hands, excused himself to the boy who was in tears, and took the time to collect the child's items. When he had finished, the boy who had been watching him asked, "Mister, are you Jesus?"

Of course that man was not Jesus, but he was acting like Jesus. This is the goal of discipleship – to become so like Jesus that people cannot distinguish us from him. That is our destiny, isn't it? To be a disciple of Jesus is much more than simply being born again, learning Scripture verses by heart, attending church Sunday morning, or doing evangelism a half hour a month. Jesus teaches us through his example that we are not only called to proclaim or preach reality, we must also become reality ourselves.

"But," you might be thinking, "how can ordinary people like me or you, living in commonplace circumstances, follow Jesus and become like him?" "How can we resemble him every day of the week, and not only Sunday morning when we are surrounded by other people who encourage and help us?" "Can we be like Jesus, not only when we are praying, fasting, or meditation on the Word of God – but also in our way of thinking, our manner of speaking, in the desires of our heart, and in our relationships with others?" If Jesus' way of being corresponds best to what is really real, then we are called to resemble him, and that is truly what is also best for us.

Jesus is Reality

Jesus is much more than a simple messenger who is communicating through his teaching and way of living a reflection of what is really real. In witnessing faithfully to his Father, he witnesses to himself (John 8:18), because he and his Father are one (John 10:30). To know Jesus, is to know the Father (John 14:9). For that reason Jesus can say that he is, himself, the truth, the expression of ultimate reality (John 14:6). This is what John presents at the beginning of his gospel when he claims that Jesus is the *Logos* of God (John 1:1, 18). John presents Jesus as the ultimate revelation of God, as God himself; he who is the measure of all that pretends to be real. For this reason we can say that Jesus is both the object and the example of our faith.

Do you want to know what it means to be a human being? Examine the life of Jesus. Do you want to be pleasing to God? Walk in the footsteps of Jesus. Do you want to successfully resist temptation? Follow the example of Jesus. Do you want to better love those around you? Let Jesus guide you. Do you want to be a better teacher of others? Learn from Jesus. Do you want to heal the sick, cast out evil spirits, comfort and bring hope to the hopeless? Let yourself be led by the Spirit of Jesus. Do you want to be a more influential and effective leader? Let Jesus direct you. That is what disciples of Jesus do. They do not only count on Jesus for the salvation of their souls. They learn to think as he thinks, to act as he acts, and to feel as he feels.

Jesus said to his disciples, "Apart from me, you can do nothing" (John 15:5). That was not only true in his day, it remains true today. Without him we can do nothing, including and above all, live a life that corresponds to ultimate reality.

Jesus said to Pilate: "To this end I was born, and for this cause I came into the world, that I should bear witness unto the truth" (John 18:37). During his stay on earth, Jesus judged the thoughts of people's hearts, taught the ignorant, confounded the wise, comforted the distraught, forgave sinners, brought healing to sick bodies and deliverance to souls, and he glorified the Father. The actions that he performed in the sight of all, the ways that he saw those around him, the hands he placed on the sick, the moments that he selflessly gave to others, the nights that he spent in solitude and prayer, all of these instances of his life correspond to ultimate reality.

You cannot go beyond or do better than Jesus Christ. The apostle Paul states that we are all called to be transformed into his image (2 Cor 3:18). And he adds that, simply put, the goal of his ministry was that "Christ be formed in each person," for he realized that in him is concentrated the hope of future glory (Col 1:27).

A Disciple is Attached to His Master

The historians of religion tell us that Jesus was not the first master to have disciples. In fact, already in the seventh century before Christ, the person of the master, surrounded by a handful of disciples, and who progressively gathered other disciples, can be found in all of the religious, spiritual and philosophical traditions of the time (Lenoir 2008, 120–122). It was between the seventh and the fifth centuries before Christ that Zoroaster appeared in Persia, the Upanishad and Brahmanism in India, the Buddha, Jainism, Confucius and Lao-tzu, the prophets of Israel and important Greek philosophers from Thales to Socrates, without forgetting Pythagoras or Heraclites. As Frédéric Lenoir explains (2008, 113–114) up to that time in human history the relationship between individuals and God, or the gods, was in the hands of priests (2008, 113–114):

During thousands of years, the individual was not nearly as important as the clan, the village and the city. Good health, prosperity, and the survival of the group was much more important than that of each individual. Even if the individual prayed to the spirits and the gods to obtain their favors, domestic worship was insignificant compared to the grandiose rituals that were destined to guarantee cosmic order, and that were conducted by priests for the good of the society.

The discipleship that Jesus inaugurated when he called fishermen, tax collectors and others to follow him, was part of a tradition that was already several centuries old. However, even if there were similarities between the disciple of Jesus and other disciples in their relationships to their masters, we will see how the notion of Jesus/Reality or Jesus/Truth that I have exposed at the beginning of this chapter redefines the notion of discipleship.

Discipleship in the Semitic World of the Hebrews

The Hebrew word for disciple is *talmidh*, which signifies literally "one who is taught" (Wilkins M. 1992, 45). The prophet Ezra used this word to describe a community of musicians in the temple (see 1 Chr 25:8). To speak of disciples, Isaiah uses another word closely associated with *talmidh*, the word *limmudh* (see Isa 8:16; 50:4; 54:13). The words of Isaiah, "Bind up the testimony and seal up the law among my disciples!" seem to indicate that Isaiah had disciples (Isa 8:16). In the book of Jeremiah the word *limmudh* is translated as 'accustomed' in the well-known phrase, "Can the Ethiopian change his skin or the leopard its spots? Neither can you do good who are accustomed to doing evil" (Jer 13:23). Here the word signifies that the individual has learned what he or she has been taught, to do evil.

The use of the words *talmidh* and *limmudh* also indicate a personal relationship between the master and his student or disciple. The disciple submits to the master, accompanies him, and assists him and in the process learns from him. This is seen in the example of Moses and his disciple Joshua (cf. Exod 24:13).

We find that idea of apprenticeship in the word that is used to designate a disciple in the Greek text of the New Testament. I am referring to the word *mathetes*, which has as a root the word *math* (the mental work required to think well), that designates the person who learns from or follows, normally a person who is linked to a master (Wilkins M. 1988, 52). Michael Wilkins, who teaches the New Testament at Talbot School of Theology, describes the notion of a disciple in this way (1992, 40):

> The word disciple is the term that is used the most often in the Gospels to designate those who follow Jesus, and who are called believers, brothers/sisters, followers of the Way, or saints by the early church. . . . This word was used in this specific sense at least 230 times in the Gospels and 28 times in the Acts of the Apostles.

A disciple is therefore a convert who follows Jesus. The converts are those people who are born again. That new birth is indispensable for becoming a disciple. Disciples live a relationship to Jesus that engages all of the aspects of their lives. They neither follow a program, nor a class, nor an official curriculum. And it is not a training that is reserved for the newly converted. Nor is it a call to live a rigorous lifestyle reserved exclusively for pastors, monks, missionaries, priests, evangelists or prophets. We can add that one does not measure discipleship by the tasks that are accomplished, the acquiring of certain skills, or the accumulation of knowledge.

The Characteristics of Discipleship within the Rabbinic Tradition

When they heard Jesus say, "Make disciples," the first thought of Peter, James and John was undoubtedly that they would find other individuals that they would form exactly like they had been formed by Jesus. That is clearly the understanding of the disciple-making process that we find in the apostle Paul many years later (see 2 Tim 2:2). Each of these men understood that the order that they had received to make disciples implied the serious commitment of an apprentice to attach himself to a master. Let's look briefly at five characteristics of discipleship during the first century (Hull 2006, 63–64).

The choice to follow a master. Young men could enter different kinds of 'schools', each one conducted by a rabbi or a teacher. In certain cases, the students chose their teacher, and it is obvious that the teachers could either accept or reject the request of a student. If a man had not yet reached an elevated academic or social status at the time of his *bar mitzvah*, at around thirteen years of age, he chose rather the life of a farmer, a fisherman a carpenter, etc.

The fact that Jesus and his disciples had been artisans explains why they were not well received by the religious groups of their day. In reality, as the philosopher Henri Bergson explains so well in his book entitled *Les Deux*

Sources de la Morale et de la Religion (2013), right from the emergence of discipleship there were often tensions, always lively, between the two branches of religious experience, whatever the tradition or wisdom. Facing the priest who taught dogma and the rituals of worship and who is the guardian of the institution, there was the master who chose discourse and a personal relationship that transformed the existence of the student. The ritual of the priest was opposed by the transformation of the master.

The first-century disciple learned everything from his master. He learned his stories, his habits, his way of respecting the Sabbath, and his interpretations of the Torah. And when the disciple had learned everything that his master knew, he began teaching his own disciples.

At the heart of this process of transformation, one finds the commitment of a disciple to follow his master. Each disciple must commit to submit to at least one other person. Without that dimension, all the rest is weakened. The relationship between the teacher and his disciple creates a tie that is at least as important as that which ties a father to his son.

First-century discipleship was in many ways like the relationship between a slave and his master (see Matt 10:24). Once accepted as a disciple, the young man began as a *talmidh* or debutant. As such, he had to stand behind the others and could not express himself. After awhile he became a distinguished student who could approach the master and ask him questions. After that phase, he became an associate disciple who could sit behind the rabbi during prayer. Finally, he reached the highest level, disciple of the wise, and was considered the intellectual equal of his rabbi (Wilkins M. 1988, 123).

The memorization of the words of the master. Oral tradition was the primary means of apprenticeship. The disciples learned by heart the words of their master and then transmitted those words to others. Often the disciples memorized as many as four different interpretations of the major texts of the Torah. It is interesting to note that the process of discipleship does not require the ability to read a text. We live in a world where two-thirds of the population is illiterate and are oral learners (Lausanne Committee for World Evangelization, 2005).

Apprenticeship in the ministry style of the master. A disciple learned how his master observed the commandments of God, including how he kept the Sabbath, fasted, prayed, and said blessings during religious ceremonies. He also learned how his master taught, and all of the traditions that he respected.

The imitation of the life and character of the master. Jesus said that when a disciple is fully trained, he would be like his master (Luke 6:40). The highest ambition of a disciple was to be like his master. Paul told Timothy to follow his example (see 2 Tim 3:10–14), and he did not hesitate to call other believers to do the same thing (see 1 Cor 4:14–16; 11:1; Phil 4,9).

The training of his own disciples. Once a disciple had completed his training, he was supposed to pass on what he had learned by finding his own apprentices and training them. He would begin his own 'school' that would take on his name, for example, the 'house of Hillel'.

These five characteristics describe discipleship as it was lived during the first century. Jesus employed these practices with his closest associates. When he told them to make disciples, he expected them to find others with whom they would reproduce what they had received in these ways. When he told them to teach others to do all that he had taught them (Matt 18:20), they knew that this would require the same devotion that we find embodied in these five commitments.

What is Unique about the Discipleship of Jesus?

It is true that the rabbis of Jesus' day also had disciples. At first glance, it might seem that there are few differences between their disciples and those who followed Jesus. In both cases, the disciple is linked to a particular master. But in looking a bit more closely, two fundamentally different kinds of discipleship become evident (Bosch 1992, 36–39).

The disciples of the rabbis	The disciples of Jesus
The disciples of the rabbis could chose their own teacher and attach themselves to that teacher.	None of Jesus' disciples attached themselves to him of their own volition. Those who follow him only do so after they have received his call: "Follow me!" The choice is Jesus' not the disciples.
It was the law, the Torah, that stood at the center of Judaism. The candidates for discipleship attached themselves to a rabbi in order to better know the Torah, and uniquely for that. It was the Torah that was the authority in the relationship, and not the rabbi.	Jesus calls on his disciples to forsake all, not for the sake of the Law, but for him alone: "He who loves father or mother more than me is not worthy of me; . . . and he who does not take his cross and follow me is not worthy of me . . . and he who loses his life for my sake will find it" (Matt 10:38f).

In Judaism discipleship was merely a means to an end. Being a disciple, a student of the Law, was no more than a transitional stage. The student's goal was to become a rabbi himself.

The disciples of the rabbis were only their students, nothing more.

For the disciple of Jesus, however, the stage of discipleship is not the first step forward toward a promising career. It is in itself the fulfillment of his destiny. The disciple of Jesus never graduates into a rabbi.

Jesus' disciples are also his servants, something quite alien to the Judaism of his day. They did not just bow to his greater knowledge – they obeyed him. He was not only their teacher, but also their Lord.

Because Jesus is the Truth/Reality, his disciples do not make their own disciples, they only train others as his disciples. The disciples of Jesus never take the place of the Master. Today as before, Jesus commands us to make disciples. Of course in that process we will have teachers, mentors, guides and models, but they should never be taken for our masters. Of course we submit to authority, but it is a voluntary submission characterized by humility and charity. We, who are the disciples of Jesus today, are called, like those of the first century, to make disciples of Jesus.

A definition of a *disciple of Jesus*: A disciple is a student or an apprentice who follows the example and teaching of Jesus. A disciple has chosen to submit to at least one other person, with the goal of learning from the example of that person how he or she follows Christ. Because our character is developed in relationships with others, the goal of the disciple is to allow that relationship to fashion him or her more into the image of Christ.

Summary:

1. A disciple submits to a role model who teaches him or her how to follow Jesus.

2. A disciple learns the words, the teachings, of Jesus.

3. A disciple learns how to minister as Jesus ministered.

4. A disciple imitates the life and the character of Jesus.

5. A disciple finds and teaches other people how they too can follow Jesus.

Bill Hull points out that many Christian ministries possess three of these five elements. A small minority possess four, and very few practice all five. The most common elements are those listed under numbers two through four:

2. A disciple learns the words, the teachings, of Jesus.

3. A disciple learns how to minister as Jesus ministered.

4. A disciple imitates the life and the character of Jesus.

These are the least difficult of the five elements. People gladly study the Bible, and familiarize themselves with the way that Jesus ministered to others and discover his character. We must admit, however, that one needn't really change one's lifestyle to do that. So we have found ways of being Christians without becoming like Jesus. If the elements two to four are vital, it is the elements one and five that are at the heart of discipleship.

In reality, the majority of those people who consider themselves to be Christians do not practice the qualities two to five. But what is even more unbelievable is the fact that a person can practice the elements two through five and be considered a mature Christian leader. The fact that as disciples of Jesus we avoid submitting to others, and only rarely reproduce in the life of someone else what we have received, constitutes a major problem for contemporary Christianity. All five of the elements that are mentioned above are absolutely necessary for Christian discipleship. What I mean is that discipleship that brings about the transformation of character and spiritual multiplication is dependent on all five of these elements. It is through that kind of discipleship that the reign or the kingdom of God progresses. A disciple submits to a model who helps him to learn how to follow Jesus.

Most people never arrive at this point. This is, in my opinion, the primary reason why they either do not grow, or do not continue to grow. There is nothing more foundational to spiritual growth. The character of a person is developed in community, and that takes place only through submission. Paul taught that submission must be the experience of all (see Eph 5:21). It is this character trait that makes Jesus so attractive (see Phil 2:5–8). God resists the proud, but he gives grace to the humble (Jas 5:4). The New Testament teaches that we manifest the virtue of humility in our submission to other believers.

Submission to others is the proof of humility, and it is for that reason that character is shaped within community.

The genius of submission in the disciple-making relationship is that all are submitted. No one is the master. Both people are servants of Jesus Christ, and both benefit from their mutual discipleship relationship. Often, one of the two has more experience and might be considered the primary teacher, as the one who is teaching the other what it means to follow Jesus.

This kind of relationship offers the strength that is necessary to stand up under the difficulties that test our faith (cf. Ecc 4:9). Without this kind of support an event or a crisis can trouble our confidence in Christ.

Disciples Find and Teach Others What They Have Learned of Christ

One of the reasons why discipleship fails is that we do not expect the disciples to reproduce. Next time you are in a church service, I can pretty much predict what you will experience. There is little chance that I fail in my prediction. You will see people sitting in the same seats, talking to the same people, before and after the service. The songs, the sermon, and the testimonies will be very much like those of previous weeks. You and those around you know a lot about Jesus. You have spent years in meetings together. You have learned his words and his way of ministering, and you have committed yourselves to imitating his character. But you are sitting there, like last year, beside the same person in the same spot in the church.

I can predict this because that is how the churches that I have experienced in the USA and in France function. We organize evangelistic campaigns, and we try to mobilize the faithful to witness to their faith so that they will invite others to our meetings, but we progress little. Why is this the case? It is because discipleship has become optional. When we only practice four of the five elements of discipleship that Jesus taught, we are only ministering to ourselves. We speak among ourselves, we act among ourselves, and we address questions that interest us. We find ourselves in a closed system.

We are not truly disciples of Jesus until we are sharing with someone else what we have learned about him. That is the heart of the Great Commission: "I have given you my instruction, now go teach others" (see Matt 28:18–20; John 15:15–16; Acts 1:8). However, most of us must admit that we have never followed Jesus in that way.

What will discipleship look like in the African context in the coming ~~? The response to that question must be spiritual reproduction – the multiplication of disciples of Jesus who make disciples of Jesus. But when we look at the present situation, we are tempted to wonder if we aren't more interested in filling our churches than we are in making true disciples of Jesus.

Conclusions

"If you hold to my teaching, you are really my disciples," said Jesus to the Jews who had believed in him. "You will know the truth/reality," he added, "and that truth/reality will set you free" (John 8:31–32). In the gospel of Matthew we read that Jesus called his first disciples saying: "Follow me, and I will make of you . . ." (Matt 4:19). In these two texts we have the same idea. Disciples of Jesus are people who follow Jesus, who hold to his teaching, and who allow themselves to be 'remade' by the Master. They follow Jesus intentionally and actively with that goal in mind. Of course they know that their sins are forgiven and that eternal life with the Lord is their inheritance. But that hope does not produce inactivity. On the contrary, disciples seek to be reshaped by the Master in order to reflect him today in all of the areas of their lives.

The apostle Paul wrote: "My dear children, for whom I am again in the pains of childbirth until Christ is formed in you" (Gal 4:19). The word translated 'formed' is the Greek word *morphe*, which means 'fashioned or shaped'. When it is joined to Greek prepositions, it is translated by 'conformed' in Romans 8:29 and 'transformed' in Romans 12:2. The words of the apostle indicate that this transformation is not automatic, once and for all, and without effort on our part. They also affirm the idea that we need a personal accompaniment in order to foster that ever-deepening conversion of our way of thinking, of wanting, of choosing, of feeling and of expressing ourselves. In the following chapter I will look more precisely at this question.

Questions to Think About:

1. Now that you have finished this chapter, write a description of a disciple of Jesus, then compare that description with the one you wrote after reading the first chapter. In what ways are those descriptions the same, and in what ways do they differ?

2. The author maintains that few Christians are intentionally submitted to a model who is teaching them how to follow in the footsteps of Jesus. Why might this be the case in your opinion?

5

The Way of Transformation

The Great Commission is given to us by the gospel of Matthew (28:19–20): "Go and make disciples of all nations." This theme appears differently in Luke's gospel where he paints a portrait of Jesus as the "Light for revelation to the Gentiles" (Luke 2:32) and insists that in him "the glory of the Lord will be revealed, and all mankind together will see it" (Isa 40:3–5). In order to underscore his point that Jesus came for all people, Luke does not begin his genealogy with Abraham, father of the Jewish people (as is the case with Matt 1:1–2). Rather he begins with Adam, father of the human race, and ultimately with God himself (Luke 3:23–38). The universality of Christ's message is also revealed when, in that gospel, Jesus recalls the fact that the prophet Elijah was sent to a widow in Zarephath, and not to an Israelite, and that Elisha cleansed Naaman the Syrian, rather than a Jew (Luke 4:25–27).

In fact, Luke goes even further in the portrait that he paints of Jesus. In his gospel Christ not only calls non-Jews to follow him, but also those who live on the outskirts of society, like the sinful woman who anointed his feet with perfume (Luke 7:36–50), Zacchaeus the tax collector (Luke 19:1–10), the criminal who was executed beside him (Luke 23:39–43), the lost son (Luke 15:11–32, of the parable), the tax collector (Luke 18:9–14, of the parable), the Samaritans (cf. Luke 9:51–56; 10:29–37; 17:11–19) and the poor (cf. Luke 4:16–22; 1:52–53; 14:12–13). In short, Luke describes Jesus like a universal Savior who relates to people of all kinds. He hangs out with both the very religious Pharisees, and the hated tax collectors (Luke 5:27–32; 7:36; 11:37; 14:1; 19:1–10). He is also described as someone who cares for the victims of personal tragedy (Luke 7:11–17; 8:40–56; 9:37–43). While Matthew underlines the ties between Jesus and his teaching, Luke places the accent on the ties between Jesus and people.

And what is the heart of those relationships? For Luke, all people are called to follow Jesus, regardless of their race, their nationality, their ethnic origin, their sex, their rank in society, or their religious background. All receive the same call. Luke makes no distinction between a 'believer', a 'saint', and a 'disciple' (cf. Luke 6:13; 8:9; 9:54; 10:23; 11:1; 14:26; 19:37–39). All receive the same call to follow the same spiritual pilgrimage – a pilgrimage that Jesus made himself – a pilgrimage that allows the Spirit of God to act in the life of the disciple.

To better understand the way in which Luke describes discipleship to Jesus, I propose that we look quickly at four motifs, or themes, that he develops in his gospel (and in the Acts of the Apostles): the motif of a plan, the motif of the way, the motif of pilgrimage, and the motif of self-abandon.

The Motif of a Plan

At the center of the gospel of Luke we find the idea that in Jesus and those who follow him, God is in the process of accomplishing in our world his plans and his designs. Luke, more that the three other gospel writers,[1] emphasizes and brings this theme to the forefront. In his gospel we learn that the plan of God, realized in Jesus and his disciples, takes place when good news is preached to the poor (Luke 4:18–19), when the sick are restored to health (Luke 5:30–32), when he is listened to with attention (Luke 10:16–20), and when what was lost is finally found (Luke 19:10).

"It must . . ."

This divine plan or project is being fulfilled according to the will and logic of God. Luke brings this reality to the forefront by underlining the idea that the events that mark the life of Jesus were not arbitrary, but necessary. Luke says very often in his gospel that certain things 'must' (Greek: *dei*) take place. Out of 101 uses of the expression *dei* in the New Testament, 40 are found in the gospel of Luke and the Acts of the Apostles. Jesus *must* be about his Father's business (Luke 2:49), he *must* announce the kingdom of God (Luke 4:43), he *must* free the woman tormented by Satan (Luke 13:16). Certain things *must* come to pass before the end of time (Luke 17:25; 21:9). Christ *must* suffer, be

---

1. A number of texts that are unique to Luke underline this theme: Luke 1:14–17, 31–35, 46–55, 68–79; 2:9–14, 30–32, 34–35; 4:16–30; 13:31–35; 24:44–49.

put to death, rise from the dead the third day, and repentance and remission of sins be preached in his name among the nations, beginning at Jerusalem (Luke 24:46–47). This theme will be repeated throughout the Acts of the Apostles (cf. Acts 1:11; 3:21; 9:6, 16; 13:46; 14:22; 19:21; 23:11; 25:10; 27:24).

Luke illustrates the accomplishment of this plan by a geographic progression. At the beginning of his account, Jesus is in Galilee where he teaches and performs miracles (Luke 4:14–9:50). Then Luke follows the Master along the road leading to Jerusalem, the holy city where the work of salvation must be accomplished (Luke 9:51–19:44). This section of the gospel of Luke is different from all the other Gospels. Almost half of the teachings of Jesus and incidents that Luke describes in this part of his gospel are unique. It is here that we find a rich concentration of teachings and of parables (seventeen in all, out of which fifteen are only found in the gospel of Luke). The trip from Galilee to Jerusalem is not a straight chronological line,[2] because in Luke 10:38–42 we find Jesus close to Jerusalem, while a bit further in the same section, he is once again in the North. Luke does not tell us how Jesus moved from one village to the next. What he is attempting to communicate is especially how Jesus is initiating a new way of following God. This explains why, throughout this section, the words of Jesus have a more important place that the miracles he performs. The theme that Jesus develops is the total abandonment of self so that the plan of God might be accomplished.

The Motif of the Way

'Following Jesus' is synonymous with 'being a disciple'; but Luke describes it in a particular fashion – the disciples of Jesus are those who follow the Way. We have just seen how the geographic perspective of Luke, with Jerusalem at its center, concentrates our attention on Jesus during his trip along the way which leads to the holy city where he will suffer his passion in the complete abandonment of his life (Luke 9:51). Jesus' disciples are his companions during this trip (Luke 9:57). Thus, for Luke, a path, or a 'way' (*he hodos*) is a lifestyle revealed by God and an image of salvation. This notion led the early Christian community to identify themselves as the 'followers of the Way' (Acts 9:2; 19:9, 23; 22:4; 24:14, 22). Luke sees disciples as those who enter

---

2. When Luke presents the words or actions of Jesus, he is interested above all in their meaning. He manifests at times what seems to be a profound indifference to their chronology (Luke 4:16–30; 5:1–11; 24:51; and Acts 1:2–3, 9) or their locality (10:13–15; 13:34–35; 24:36–49).

the Way, and then progress along that path by following in the footsteps of their Master.

The use of the 'Way' as a metaphor of the Christian life is rooted in its use in the Old Testament. There one recognizes the character, the ambitions and the values of an individual by the 'way' he or she chooses to follow (i.e. Exod 33:13). More importantly, there is a tie between the 'way', 'the path', or the 'road', of God and his will or projects; like we find in certain Psalms:

- Psalm 25:4 – "Show me your ways, O LORD, teach me your paths."
- Psalm 27:11 – "Teach me your way, O LORD; lead me in a straight path."
- Psalm 86:11 – "Teach me your way, O LORD, and I will walk in your truth."
- Psalm 119:35 – "Direct me in the path of your commands!"
- Psalm 143:8 – "Show me the way I should go."
- Psalm 67:1–2 – "May God be gracious to us and bless us and make his face to shine upon us, that your ways may be known on earth, your salvation among all nations!"

Conscious of the fact that the first disciples of Jesus didn't call themselves 'Christians', but 'followers of the Way', Luke grabs that image to describe what it means to follow Jesus. Like the Master traveled toward Jerusalem where he would give himself totally out of love for us, disciples travel also toward the complete giving of themselves out of love for the Master.

The Motif of Pilgrimage

Discipleship begins when one enters the Way of salvation by faith (cf. Luke 7:50; 8:48; 17:19; Acts 10:43). In his gospel, as in the Acts of the Apostles, Luke uses the verb 'believe' to describe the act of becoming a disciple. And right at the start of his gospel he opposes two examples in order to shed light on the importance of faith. First, he gives us the example of Zechariah who did not believe the announcement of the miraculous birth of John the Baptist (Luke 1:5–20). Then he offers the example of Mary who believed that what the Lord said to her would be accomplished (Luke 1:45), and who, in a total giving of herself said: "I am the Lord's servant . . . may it be to me as you have said" (Luke 1:38). And it is for this reason that she is called 'blessed' and remains a model of a disciple.

"May it be to me as you have said! May everything that you have said come to place in my life!" That is the kind of faith that Mary possessed, the kind of faith that, according to Luke, characterizes the disciple.

Total Abandonment of One's Self

Discipleship begins when one enters the Way of salvation. It continues as the individual progresses on that path. In other words, Luke specifies that the total abandonment of one's self, the daily taking up of one's cross and following Jesus, not only defines how one enters the Way, it also describes existence on that path. For Luke, disciples are learning to abandon themselves totally to Jesus. We can find an illustration of what total abandonment means in the incident that is spoken of in 1 Kings 20:

> Ben-Hadad king of Aram, mustered his entire army. Accompanied by thirty-two kings with their horses and chariots, he went up and besieged Samaria and attacked it. He sent messengers into the city to Ahab king of Israel, saying, "This is what Ben-Hadad says: 'Your silver and gold are mine, and the best of your wives and children are mine.'" The king of Israel answered, "Just as you say, my lord the king. I and all I have are yours." (1 Kgs 20:1–4)

What Ben-Hadad demanded was total abandonment. And what Ahab gave him was what had been demanded – total abandonment. The words, "Just as you say, my lord the king. I and all I have are yours," could be uttered by every disciple of Jesus Christ as a sign of self-giving to his or her Master. I am repeating myself because we need to be reminded, the condition for life as a disciple of Jesus is a total abandonment into his hands.

Jesus said that those who would follow him, learn from him, and live as his disciples, must learn to daily deny themselves – to abandon themselves to him. This is what he meant when he said that we must take up our cross daily in order to follow him (Luke 9:23).

Why is it so difficult for us to hear these words of Jesus? We must humbly admit that we find it difficult to understand the impact that they must have had on those who heard him speak them. We live in a different age than the first disciples. Today, do we see the corpses of individuals who have been crucified on the sides of our streets? Do we ever encounter condemned people who are carrying their crosses to the place of their execution? In

Jesus' day many people carried crosses.[3] We should realize that before being widely used in the Roman territories, crucifixion was already practiced by the Persians, the Phoenicians and the Carthaginians. The Roman historian, Flavius Josephus, says that Alexander "crucified 800 Jews before his eyes and disemboweled in their presence, while they were yet alive, their wives and their children" (Josephus, 2014, LXII, 5, 4). In the year AD 66, just a few years after the gospel of Luke was written, Florus, governor of Judea, "had crucified 3,630 men, women and children." Shortly thereafter, in the year AD 70, Titus entered Jerusalem and had crucified the survivors who sought to flee. Flavius Josephus counted as many as 500 who were put to death in that way in a single day: "One could barely make the crosses fast enough, or find a place to plant them in the ground," he writes (Josephus 2013, LV, 11, 1).

Jesus borrows that terrible image to underscore the fact that the disciple must daily renounce the direction of his life, or the possession of himself. Paul takes up that same illustration when he declares, "I have been crucified with Christ and I no longer live, but Christ lives in me" (Gal 2:20). The first Christians also saw themselves as crucified with Christ. Tertullian, for example, one of the fathers of the early church, who lived between AD 160 and AD 220, wrote:

> When we go out and when we move about, at the beginning and at the end of all of our activities, when we get dressed, put on our shoes, bathe, eat a meal, light candles, when we lie down and rest, during each of these activities, we mark our forehead with the sign of the cross.[4]

What is the meaning of that gesture?

It seems that within the first Judeo-Christian communities, the faithful traced on their foreheads a mark that evoked the cross of Christ, and perhaps

---

3. The victim, whom one began to weaken through a beating, was condemned, not to carry the cross itself (which was much too heavy and bulky) but to drag the transversal beam of that cross, which was called the *patibulum* in Latin.

4. From *De corona mil.*, c. III. The same ideas are found in Cyril of Jerusalem: Catechism, XIII, 36. Finally John Chrysostom: "This sign of the cross, which formerly everyone was horrified by, and which is now earnestly sought after by all, is found everywhere: amongst those who govern and their subjects, amongst men and women, the married and those who are single, the slaves and those who are free. All trace unceasingly the most noble part of the human face and carry it engraved like a pillar on their foreheads. It is found at the Holy table, at the ordination of priests, it glows with the body of Christ at the mystical communion table. Everywhere one can find it glorified . . . And in this way everyone seeks after this marvelous gift, this indestructible grace." *Quod Christus sit Deus*, P. G., t. XLVIII, col. 826.

other things as well. For the book of Ezekiel proclaims that the members of
the messianic community would be marked by the sign of *Tav* (Ezek 9:4–6)
The *Tav*, the last letter of the Hebrew alphabet, designates *Dieu*, in the same
way that the *Omega* does in Greek. That letter, *Tav*, could, in Christ's day,
be represented by either the sign + or the sign x. We can therefore conclude
that the sign of Ezekiel, in the form of a cross, represents the name of the
Father. Hence the first Christians, predominantly of Jewish origin, marked
the day of their baptism by a *Tav* on their forehead, designating the name of
YHWH . . . In the book of Revelation, the evangelist and theologian John,
saw 144,000 people who had written on their foreheads the name of the Lamb
and his Father's name (Rev 14:1).. Once again, the sign of the cross traced on
the forehead, the *Tav* of the first Christians, designated the verb/word of the
Father, and his death on the cross. This gesture signified that they were set
apart for his service. (Molinier 2007, 2–3)

One of my professors suggested once in class that when the first Christ-
followers made that gesture, they remembered the words of the apostle Paul
to the Romans: "If you confess with your mouth, 'Jesus is Lord,' and believe in
your heart that God has raised him from the dead, you will be saved" (Rom
10:9). According to this professor, the first followers of Jesus, in marking
themselves with the sign of the cross, asked God to fill their thoughts with
his thoughts, their mouths with his praises, and their hearts with absolute
faithfulness.[5] One of the early Christian bishops of the fourth century,
Gaudence of Brescia (327–411) said:

> May the word of God and the sign of Christ be on your heart,
> on your lips, on your forehead, always; whether you are sitting
> down to eat, taking a bath or resting, whether you are leaving or
> arriving, during times of joy as in times of sorrow.[6]

In Matthew and in Mark, Jesus calls all those who want to follow him
to renounce themselves, and pick up their cross. Only the gospel of Luke
adds 'each day'. Luke insists, therefore on the need of a daily renewing of that
experience in the life of the disciple: a self denying that is continually renewed
and deepened, so that the disciple can be filled with divine life.

---

5. This is not far from the interpretation of Ambrose: "We have the sign of the cross on our
forehead, on our heart and on our arms: on our forehead, because we must always confess
Jesus Christ; on our heart, because we must always love him; on our arms, because we must
always work for him." Ambrose, *Life of Isaac.*

6. Gaudence de Brescia, Gaudentius, *De lect. evang.*, P.L., t. XX, col. 890.

The Importance of Depth

Through the pilgrimage described by Luke, we can understand that the cross represents the transforming work of God, the Holy Spirit, in the life of the disciple. It is when we pick up our cross that we are disciples. We cannot be counted among his disciples if we do not pick up our cross! Without the cross, there is no possible discipleship (Phillips 1981, 16–20). Christianity without that daily dying to one's self is nothing more than a philosophy. It is Christianity without Christ. This is true because the life of Christ is transferred by means of the cross. In the principle of the cross, it is not simply a question of the level of devotion that is needed to follow Jesus. The cross is also the *means* by which we follow him (Nelson 1994, 31–34). We follow Jesus by daily applying the principle of the cross in our lives (Luke 9:23). We do this as we submit to Jesus, and live for him, not for ourselves. The cross allows us to live as he died (Phil 3:10–12).

Thomas Merton seems to have had this truth in mind when he wrote: "Spiritual life is above all else, a life. It is not a subject to study and understand, but a life to be lived" (Merton, 1999). Our faith communities often lack that spiritual depth. Richard Foster claims that, "Superficiality is the curse of our age . . . in reality, our greatest need is not to have more intelligent and gifted people. More than anything, we need people who are deep" (Foster, 1899). Gideon Para-Mallam, Regional Secretary of the International Fellowship of Evangelical Students in English- and Portuguese-Speaking Africa claims that, "If there is a single challenge facing Christians in Africa today, it is the omission of not living out the gospel message as we should" (Para-Mallam 2013, 1). A bit further in his article he adds, "Christianity is not just an alternative religion (. . .) Our message must transform our personal lives, families, communities, nation and the African Continent." In order for this kind of transformation to happen, people must actively and intentionally seek a spirituality that comes only in obedience to Christ. And many of our faithful are not doing that.

Do you ever wonder whether our activities and programs really foster spiritual growth and the transformation of the lives of our faithful? Are we putting our resources into ministries that really change the way they behave? Do our meetings truly help those who come to them to become more Christ-like, or do they only serve to keep them busy? In the USA, one of the largest congregations, Willow Creek, did a study of several different churches based on a few questions. Twenty-four churches participated in the study. The conclusions that were reached applied to all of them: The numerical growth of a congregation is not an indicator of spiritual growth and the transformation of lives (Hawkins & Parkinson, 2007).

What Transformation is Not

But grow in the grace and knowledge of our Lord and Savior Jesus Christ. To him be glory both now and forever! Amen (2 Pet 3:18).

Many pastors that I know would agree with Bill Hull when he states that, "Discipleship, or spiritual formation, is the first and exclusive work of the church. All the rest, in the words of Solomon, 'is meaningless, a chasing after the wind' (Ecc 2:26)" (2004, 29). But even if every church trains its members according to its vision of what is important, we must recognize that our faith communities are not always producing the kinds of life transformation that we are looking for.

Before we examine more closely the Way of transformation, let's look at what spiritual transformation is not.

A. *Spiritual transformation does not precede our relationship to Christ.* People do not enter into relationship with Christ because of their good lives (Eph 2:8–9). The instant they place their confidence in Jesus, they are 'a new creation' in Christ (2 Cor 5:17). This is not a process, but an instantaneous and marvelous miracle. A process is undoubtedly necessary to expose people to the gospel and lead them to faith; but as far as the forgiveness of sins, the deliverance from darkness, and transference into the kingdom of Christ is concerned (Col 1:13), that takes place in a 'miraculous moment'. It is precisely at that moment that the believer receives from Jesus Christ all that is necessary for life and godliness (2 Pet 1:3). Spiritual transformation does not precede our relationship to Christ – it follows it.

B. *Spiritual transformation is not the same as experiencing the love of God.* What I mean by this is simply that one does not seek to be transformed spiritually as a method of experiencing more of divine love. For we can do absolutely nothing to increase God's love for us. Likewise, we can do nothing to diminish his love. According to Romans 5:1–11, God loved us while we were yet sinners. Before reconciling us to himself in Christ, while we were hostile enemies, he loved us with all the love that he is. He does not love us any more now than when we were rebelliously rejecting him.

C. *Spiritual transformation is not the result of time.* Some biblical texts indicate that as we advance on the Way of transformation, we progress from one spiritual stage to another. The apostle Paul, for instance, distinguishes between mature believers and those who, like children, are "blown here and there by every wind of teaching" (Eph 4:13). In like fashion, the author of the epistle to the Hebrews argues with conviction that the believers are not to remain spiritual infants (Heb 5:13). But spiritual progress is not automatic with the simple passing of time. Spiritual transformation defies the calendar. To the believers at Corinth Paul writes, "I could not address you as spiritual but as worldly – mere infants in Christ" (1 Cor 3:1). These believers had not grown in spite of their years of Christian life.

D. *Spiritual transformation is not the result of accumulated knowledge.* We sometimes think that spiritual maturity and depth depend on our knowledge of the Bible. But knowledge alone does not produce transformation. What is more important is what we do with what we know. Paul even warns us that knowledge puffs up (1 Cor 8:1). And when believers become proud of what they know, spiritual growth immediately slows down. On three different occasions the Bible warns us that God himself resists the proud (Prov 3:34; Jas 4:6; 1 Pet 5:5).

E. *Spiritual transformation is not the fruit of many activities.* Some people believe that in attending all of the activities that are proposed by their faith community (Sunday morning worship service, prayer vigils, Bible studies, etc.), they will grow spiritually. However, if you are involved day and night in religious activities, nothing guarantees that you are spiritually deep. Jesus himself seems to have doubted this when he declared: "Many will say to me on that day, 'Lord, Lord, did we not prophesy in your name, and in your name drive out demons and perform many miracles?' Then I will tell them plainly, 'I never knew you'" (Matt 7:22–23). Religious activities do not give access to new birth, or to spiritual transformation. Many of our religious activities seem to only produce a minimum of spiritual transformation. Observers like Dallas Willard estimate that, "What the majority of the faithful in our churches receive each week does not help them to progress spiritually" (Willard, 1990).

F. *Spiritual transformation is not tied to prosperity.* There is a certain kind of preaching and teaching that is widespread in the world today based on the idea that spiritual depth is linked to the blessings of health and wealth. For those who hold this position, the spirituality of a person allows him to obtain blessings through the confession of 'positive faith' and the 'principle of sowing and reaping' in monetary or physical goods. These teachers also teach that along with salvation, Christ promises material wealth, health and success to all who exercise faith. However, contrary to these doctrines, the Bible warns us of the dangers tied to seeking after material goods. Those who follow Jesus must not "be a lover of money" (1 Tim 3:3), and they should be "content with what they have" (Heb 13:5). For the love of money is the root of all kinds of evil (1 Tim 6:10). Jesus warned us: "Watch out! Be on your guard against all kinds of greed; a man's life does not consist in the abundance of his possessions" (Luke 12:15) (MacArthur 1990, 15).

The Goal of Transformation

The goal of spiritual transformation is clearly stated in 2 Peter 3:18 – "Grow in the grace and knowledge of our Lord and Savior Jesus Christ! To him be glory both now and forever! Amen." In this short letter Peter had already underlined the need to continually progress on the Way of transformation (1:3–11). Following Christ in one sense is like riding a bike. If you don't keep moving forward, you fall (Green 1968, 150). The apostle Paul explains that those who follow the path of transformation never fully arrive at the destination of a full knowledge of Jesus Christ in this life; which is why their goal is to continually get to know him more fully (Phil 3:10–13; cf. Eph 1:17).

What is remarkable in this text from 2 Peter is the link that is made between our progress on the Way of transformation and the glory of Jesus Christ. Notice that for Peter, the Jew, who would have learned by heart the solemn words of Isaiah 42:8 – "I am the LORD; that is my name! I will not yield my glory to another" – to attribute glory to Jesus Christ is a powerful confession of his supremacy (Blum 1981, 289). Notice also that it is our progress on the Way of transformation that brings glory to Jesus Christ. We will come back to this more fully in chapter 7.

Another monumental text from the New Testament will allow us to more fully understand the link between the glory of Christ and spiritual transformation. However, to present this text, I suggest that we first visit a study that was done in 2010 of the spiritual vitality and maturity of evangelical believers in North America.

The Process of Transformation

In 2008 a group called Lifeway Research did a study of 7,000 churches in North America. Their goal was to discover the principles of spiritual and organizational health that are operating in those communities. Spurred on by their findings, Lifeway Research began a new study in 2010 that sought to measure the spiritual vitality and maturity of evangelical believers. That research took place in three phases. First, a survey was done of twenty-eight recognized experts in the field of Christian discipleship. Following those interviews, and based upon the results, a questionnaire was developed and used to survey the opinions of 1,000 protestant pastors in the USA. The questionnaire sought to discover the kinds of discipleship had been put in place in the respective churches of those pastors, and their level of satisfaction with their discipleship program. Finally 4,000 North American Protestants (among whom 1,100 Canadians) were interviewed about their spiritual health, in English, Spanish and French. Here, in a single phrase, are the conclusions of that extensive and complete study (Geiger, Kelley, & Nation 2012, 16): "As far as life-transforming discipleship is concerned, most churches are failing."

One would probably reach the same conclusions were a similar study done in Europe, Africa or Asia. George Barna, who for many years has studied those who call themselves Christians, suggests that only about half of them actively seek to grow spiritually (Barna, 2001). Remember what we have already seen, that the goal of spiritual transformation is the glory of God through the presence of Christ living in us. The Scriptures associate that transformation with the word 'metamorphosis'. That term indicates a lasting and irreversible change at the core, and not a simple external alteration or modification of appearance. The apostle Paul describes that transformation in this way:

Now the Lord is the Spirit, and where the Spirit of the Lord is, there is freedom. And we, who with unveiled faces all reflect the Lord's glory, are being transformed into his likeness with ever-increasing glory, which comes from the Lord, who is the Spirit (2 Cor 3:17–18).

In this text Paul is alluding to Moses and his meetings with God on Mount Sinai (Exod 34:29–35). Each time Moses met with God, he left that encounter transformed – "his face was radiant" (v. 29). For that reason Moses "put a veil over his face" (v. 33) so as to hide the temporary nature of that transformation (2 Cor 3:13). Each step that Moses took as he left those meetings on Mount Sinai, distanced him from the presence of God.

Paul affirms that those who place their confidence in Christ have their face unveiled. The glory does not diminish for them, as was the case for Moses. On the contrary, because they never leave the presence of Christ, that glory only increases (see Col 1:27 and 2 Cor 4:6). It is as if they never leave the Mount of the encounter because the Comforter, whom the Father has sent to reveal the Son to us, lives in them. They benefit from a face-to-face with God that Moses never knew.

The language of the apostle in this text is extremely logical, since it is God who transforms by the Spirit whom he has sent, the Spirit of Jesus. We do not transform ourselves: ". . . we are being transformed into his likeness . . ." That transformation comes entirely from "the Lord who is the Spirit". But if it is God who transforms, how are we to understand the fact that so few of the faithful ever really grow? How can we account for the lack of depth and the small number of true disciples of Jesus in our faith communities? If it is by his Spirit that God transforms us, do we have a role to play? If it is God who leads the faithful members of your community to maturity, do you have anything to do in the process? Based on the research done by Lifeway Research, Eric Geiger offers an interesting response to these questions (Geiger, Kelley, & Nation 2012, 9):

> Yes, it was God who transformed Moses, but Moses had an active and important role to play in that transformation. His role was simple, but necessary. What did he do? He climbed the Mount. Moses placed himself in the right conditions to be transformed. He had discovered the right place that allowed God to act in his live; that is why he went up the Mount Sinai.

And he adds:

The right perspective is neither passivity (because it is God who transforms), nor performance (as if we were to transform ourselves), but a partnership. Transformation is a human and divine synergy[7] that lasts a lifetime (Geiger, Kelley & Nation 2012, 57).

In the previous chapter I argued two things that I will now bring back into our reflection. First, I maintained that Jesus Christ is ultimate reality – the measure of what every believer must live. And then I ended the chapter with the suggestion that the major reason why so many of our faithful do not grow, or continue to grow, is because they have not learned to submit themselves to a model who can help them to learn how to follow Jesus. At the beginning of this chapter I showed how Luke's gospel presents the Way of discipleship as a path of self-abandon (the principle of the cross). The study conducted by Lifeway Research confirms these observations. According to the analysis of their findings, the people at Lifeway Research indicate that the life transforming synergetic partnership between God and ourselves happens when there is the intersection of three realities. Going back to the analogy of Moses on Mount Sinai, it is when believers experience at the same time three elements that they are in the position to be deeply and lastingly transformed by the Spirit of God. These three elements are: (1) the teaching of Jesus, (2) vulnerability, and (3) a personal accompaniment.

When these three elements happen simultaneously, the person is in a position where growth in Christ most often occurs. In many of our assemblies there is teaching from the example and words of Jesus Christ. The message of Christ is sometimes received by people who are especially open and receptive due to diverse difficulties and trials of all kinds that they are going through. Sometimes the feeling of vulnerability and openness is stimulated by a spiritual encounter with the Truth/Reality that Jesus is and the realization that one is not living up to his call. At other times it is the crisis caused by the trial itself that makes the individual especially receptive to the Word of God. What is important is that these two experiences happen at the same time. For it is then that a deep transformation becomes a real possibility. However, in most cases these two realities are not sufficient to bring about the desired change. The fact that there is so little personal accompaniment in our faith

---

7. The word 'synergy' which is used in the Bible (Rom 8:28) means a coordinated action that exceeds the sum of their individual effects.

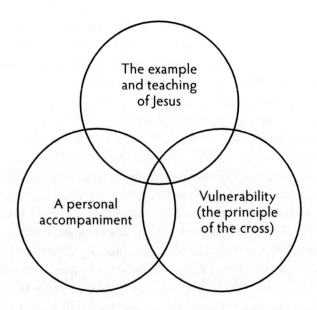

assemblies largely explains the lack of spiritual depth. I will draw from a personal experience to illustrate what I mean.

My Personal Testimony

After having completed a year of language study in France, right at the beginning of my missionary career, I was invited with my wife to join a missionary team that was getting settled in the city of Strasbourg. It was agreed that I would help these missionaries with their installation, and in exchange, they would train me in the ministry. So I served them with skills that I had acquired as a carpenter. In exchange, they let me accompany them on the university campus where they shared the gospel and led evangelistic Bible studies. After several months, one of these missionaries, Dean (he was called Daniel in French), said that he would like to talk.

Dean suggested on that occasion that we take a walk in the enormous park in the center of town because he had something important to share with me. During our stroll, and after he had shared some of the positive things that he had seen as I engaged with others on the campus, Dean said, "David, I have now been observing you for several months, and I have seen something in your life that does not conform to the example of Christ. If this does not change, you will not become the man that God wants you to be, and you will be handicapped in your witness to Christ." Then he asked, "Do you want me to continue? Do you want to know what it is that I see in your life?"

I felt a knot forming in my throat. Never before had a man whom I esteemed spoken to me in this way. Never had a friend said so directly that I had a serious problem in my life that needed to resolve, a problem that could keep me from becoming the man I so desired to be. At the moment I felt naked, exposed, vulnerable. Dean waited for my response. "Yes," I answered him, "please tell me what it is that you have seen in my life."

After gently placing his hand on my shoulder, Dean said, "David, I have observed that you do not know how to participate in a conversation without bringing it back to you. You talk all the time about yourself." We continued our walk, and during long minutes Dean shared several situations where he had observed that wrong way of communicating. It was as if I had been knocked down. Tears of shame, of sorrow, and of repentance began to fall on my cheeks. I knew deep inside that what Dean had seen was true. He had put his finger squarely on an aspect of my life that I didn't like, but that I was unable to correct. And, I must admit, that it hurt.

Dean did not attempt to console me. He did not back down in front of my suffering. His goal was neither to comfort nor to diminish the importance of my error. On the contrary, he shared that what he witnessed in my conversations was only the surface sign of a deeper problem. He said that to correct the error we would need to work at different levels. On the one hand I would need to correct the way that I communicated. But on a deeper plane I would need to change the poor image that I had of myself that pushed me to seek affirmation from others by always bringing the conversation back to myself. After spending some time in prayer together, he asked, "David, do you want Christ to change this aspect of your life so that you will be more like him?"

After I had given him my positive reply to his question, Dean said, "Here is what I suggest that you do. Beginning immediately, and for the next three months, you are not allowed to use the words 'me', 'I', 'my', 'mine'. These words cannot come out of your mouth in public, or in private. Do you agree to this? Will you commit to limit your vocabulary in this way?" Once I had assured Dean that I would follow his advice, he added, "During this same time period I want you to do a study of all of the Scriptures that address the words that come from our mouths. Among those texts you will chose a few to memorize and meditate. We will meet regularly during the next few weeks to see how you are doing." We spent some more time praying together, asking the Holy

Spirit to heal me and teach me a new way of conversing. Then we separated after fixing the time of our next meeting.

Following that meeting with Dean I was completely destabilized. I spent several days without saying a word. I did not know how to formulate a sentence where the words 'I', 'my', 'me', or 'mine', are absent. Slowly, really very slowly, I learned a new way of communication. The transformation was so complete by the end of the first month that Dean said, "David, you are doing much better. You can now begin using those words once again in your vocabulary. But if I ever hear you falling back into your old habits I will not hesitate to correct you." And he did it on a couple of occasions.

Conclusions

This example of a personal accompaniment on the Way of spiritual transformation is not an absolute and exclusive model. There are other ways to place someone in a position where he experiences simultaneously the Word of God, his need, and a personal accompaniment. This example of work on my way of communication does not cover all of the areas of my life where transformation is needed. Those who follow Jesus need to be changed in their way of thinking. It is one thing to believe in Jesus, but it is altogether something else to believe what Jesus believed. Disciples must also be transformed in their relationships with others to the extent that they love as he loved. They must be transformed in their habits. This means that they must learn to practice spiritual exercises like silence (Luke 2:41–52), solitude (Mark 1:35), fasting (Matt 4:1–11), frugality (Luke 9:58), prayer (Luke 6:12), secret keeping (Matt 6:1–7; Mark 4:1), submission (John 5:8–37), humility (Phil 2:5–8), fellowship (Luke 22:14), confession (Mark 8:31; 14:36), and worship (John 4:21–24). They need also to be transformed in their acts of service so that they minister as Jesus ministered. Finally, they must be transformed in the way that they influence others, by learning to accompany others as Jesus accompanied his disciples.

That transformation touches all of the areas of human life. And since it is a deep change that occurs under the supervision of a companion, a mentor or spiritual guide, that relationship implies a nourishing *relationship*, an *apprenticeship* in various skills, personal *responsibility* for one's acts, *submission* to a trainer, and *wisdom* in choices. This particular kind of relationship between a believer and someone who serves as a sort of guide who is helping him or her to become a better disciple of Jesus carries a serious risk that we will examine in the following chapter.

Questions to Think About:

1. What do you think of the description that is made in this chapter of the Way of spiritual transformation? Among the elements composing spiritual transformation mentioned by the author, which are in your opinion the most important?

2. Think of one time in your life when your way of thinking or acting was transformed by Christ. In what ways does that experience reflect the model of transformation developed by Lifeway Research?

3. In your experience, what could be some of the brakes that slow down deep transformation in the lives of those who claim to be followers of Christ? What might be done to change that situation?

6

Two Major Objections

In the last chapter I argued that the situation that favors spiritual transformation happens when three elements take place at the same time: (1) hearing the Word of God, and more specifically the example and teaching of Christ; (2) an attitude of weakness, of vulnerability or of openness on the part of the individual who is confronted by that Word; (3) a personal accompaniment of that same individual. I already insisted in chapter 4 that most people do not wish to enter into a relationship of spiritual accompaniment that allows another person to look into their private life. Yet, evidence seems to indicate that such a relationship is necessary for deep spiritual transformation. I have already insisted as well on the notion that a disciple of Jesus seeks actively to accompany others in this kind of relationship.

After examining closely the Great Commission that Jesus gave to those who follow him, I insisted that Jesus meant exactly what he said, and that he said exactly what he meant, when he sent his disciples to make disciples of all nations. When Jesus commands us to make disciples, that is precisely what he wants us to understand. Yet in chapter 2, in spite of this very clear command, I painted a picture of the American, French and African churches that would lead us to conclude that in reality, instead of making disciples of Jesus, we are happy to make 'converts', 'faithful attendees', and 'members' for our assemblies. The testimony of one of my African students illustrates this point:

> I come from a Catholic background, and I received new birth through the Emmaus Bible studies series. Following my new birth, I began attending the Pentecostal Church. Eight years later, I found myself involved in what some people call a ministry of 'spiritual warfare'. I continued in that ministry for thirteen years, and my entire family followed me. I finally came to realize

that I was 'dying of thirst'. I felt a lack of inner peace and even began doubting my salvation. Worse yet, in the midst of these ministries, there began to develop an atmosphere of conflict that was manifested in divorces, broken relationships within couples, between children, brothers and sisters, parents, grandparents and friends. (personal communication, 1 March 2014)

Other African seminary students often describe the faithful in their churches as 'immature', 'immoral' and 'syncretistic'. While these descriptions might seem exaggerated or too severe, they do lead us to wonder how many true disciples of Jesus are making other disciples of Jesus in these churches. In spite of these troubling observations, some believers do not think that every believer is called to be a disciple of Jesus. These people recognize, of course, that Jesus made disciples, but they do not find that same pattern in either the Acts of the Apostles or the Epistles. In their opinion the coming of the Holy Spirit and the birth of the church have replaced the model of the disciple by that of the 'believer', the 'faithful attendee', the 'baptized', the 'saint', the 'brother and sister', etc. This is then the first major objection to my argument that we are called to make disciples of Jesus. These individuals would answer: "But Paul (and the other apostles) didn't try to make disciples of Jesus. They worked, rather, to establish communities of faith."

Other people maintain that we cannot make disciples of Jesus, and that when we attempt to do so it only results in spiritual abuse (Buckingham 1990; Moore 2003). These individuals remind us of the example of people who overemphasize certain biblical principles, and therefore do not hesitate to demand that their 'disciples' submit to them (like sheep are submitted to the authority of their shepherd), to the point that they require that their disciples obtain the approval of their 'spiritual guide' before making any important life decisions. Some of these 'men of God' have gone so far as to require that their 'disciples' show them their pay slips in order to establish together the appropriate 'tithe' they have to give before any other spending. Others call their 'disciples' to follow a very strict code of conduct, insisting that they meet a series of moral and religious conditions in order to be 'certain of their salvation'. These kinds of spiritual abuses lead some believers to reject the notion of making disciples.

In this chapter I will respond to these objections. I will begin by looking at the question of whether or not the apostle Paul was himself a disciple of Jesus, and if he formed disciples of Jesus. I will then argue that we can make disciples of Jesus without falling into the trap of spiritual abuse. I will also mention several signs that indicate that the relationship of spiritual accompaniment has begun moving in a wrong direction.

Was the Apostle Paul a Disciple of Jesus?

A careful reading of the biblical text reveals that Acts 21:16 is the last use of the word 'disciple' in the New Testament. Not only does it seem that Paul and his co-workers did not use this word, biblical scholars also note that Paul only rarely appears to refer directly to the teaching of Jesus. Apart from the events tied to salvation, such as the death and the resurrection of Jesus, which are constantly present, not one time does Paul quote the words of Jesus like those found in the Gospels (Benetreau, 1997). I do not want to enter into the debate that has raged between biblical scholars since the nineteenth century concerning the place of Paul and his relationship to Jesus. What is important is that we keep in mind the words of Jesus to his disciples on the eve of his betrayal and crucifixion. In that conversation he warned them that his relationship with them was going to change. They would soon no longer know that physical presence from which they had been profiting. The 'Spirit of Truth' would soon be taking the baton and would help them to progress in that relationship (John 16:13). Leaning on that affirmation, I maintain that Paul is the prototype of the disciples of Jesus who have known their Master, in spite of his physical absence, during the past two thousand years.

We will examine successively two major components of that perspective: (1) Paul was a disciple of Jesus through the witness of the faith community, and (2) Paul was a disciple of Jesus through the witness of the Spirit of Jesus.

Paul Was a Disciple of Jesus through the Witness of the Faith Community

The apostle Paul was a disciple of Jesus even though he did not walk beside him on the roads of Galilee, as had been the case for Peter, James, John, and the others. Nevertheless, he refers to the events that took place during the ministry of Jesus, and affirms that he faithfully transmits a tradition which he had himself received from the Lord (1 Cor 11:23ff.). Moreover, it is obvious in what he has written, that Paul knew many occasions that permitted him to receive information about Jesus.

> As a Pharisee who opposed and persecuted the followers of the Messiah Jesus, and who found himself in Jerusalem shortly after

the events, he surely had to acquaint himself at least minimally with Jesus before his conversion. After his conversion, Paul lived in the faith communities located in Damascus, and Antioch in Syria, villages not far from Palestine that hosted a number of Jews from Jerusalem who had been marked by the Jesus traditions. (. . .) The visits that the apostle made to Jerusalem, along with the presence of co-workers who could share information with him (Barnabas, Silvanus, John Mark), offered him numerous opportunities to know Jesus (Benetreau 1997).

The fact that Paul traveled to Jerusalem after his conversion in order to "get acquainted with Peter" (Gal 1:18) speaks to his desire to learn all that Jesus had taught (cf. Matt 28:19). Notice that Paul did not value the direct revelations that he received (his conversion experience on the way to Damascus, and Gal 1:11–12), to the detriment of the witness of the other apostles. On the contrary, he was conscious of the fact that he preached the same gospel (Gal 1:23). In this we can say that Paul is a reference for us. Like him, we cannot count exclusively on our own experiences and spiritual revelations in order to become disciples of Jesus! We must enter into a chain of transmitters which began with the original eye witnesses, those who consequently were in immediate contact with Jesus (Luke 1:1–4). Like the apostle, if we wish to be his disciples, we must continually learn about his life and his teaching through a diligent study of the Gospels.

The second lesson that we can learn from the example of Paul is that he apparently did not find it necessary to have exactly the same relationship with Jesus as the first disciples enjoyed. The first disciples profited from a direct, physical relationship with the Master. Their eyes had seen him, their ears had heard the sound of his voice, and their hands had touched him (cf. 1 John 1:1–3). Paul had not known this kind of physical intimacy with Christ, and he was conscious of the fact that he carried a new view of Jesus: "From now on we regard no one from a worldly point of view" (2 Cor 5:16).

A new view of Jesus certainly, but it is the same Jesus. Paul did not know Jesus in the same way in which the others had known him, nevertheless he knew the same Jesus. I would like to illustrate this point by reminding you of the extraordinary diversity of the image of Jesus in the New Testament. We needn't look any further than the representations associated with the titles that are attributed to him in those Scriptures: teacher, Messiah, king, prophet, priest, Lord, Son of man, Son of God, First-born from the dead, the Amen, Savior, redeemer, servant, righteous, Son of David, Word, judge, advocate, witness, friend, etc. There are also a multitude of metaphors and metonyms which apply to Jesus – lamb, shepherd, door, vine, light, bread, living water, blood, temple, stone, builder. It is impossible to choose one of these titles or metaphors as more central or meaningful than the others. Each of them contributes to our total understanding of Jesus. None of them summarizes alone all that Jesus is. We are unbelievably enriched by their abundance and by their diversity. We would be all the poorer were any of them were lacking.

> There is a very real diversity of witness to and interpretations of Jesus. On could almost say that there is a different portrait of Jesus in each of the New Testament Scriptures. The portrait of Jesus painted by Paul, and that of the book of Revelation, each possesses distinctive features. The Jesus of the epistle to the Hebrews is not in every point the same as the picture of Jesus that we find in the epistle attributed to James. Mark and John do not witness to Jesus in exactly the same way. The interpretations of Jesus that we find in Matthew are dissimilar to those of John. Every effort on our part to eliminate or diminish that diversity in order to simplify our understanding of Jesus' identity would be a violation of the texts that witness to him. In all these portraits, however, the humanity of Jesus is seen as the measure of the life of the disciple. His words are the injunctions that his disciples seek to obey. And above all, whatever their particular experience of his presence, his character remains the norm for all his disciples. (Johnson 1999, 199)

What I hold on to from this observation is the conviction that for Paul, even while all must have "the mind of Christ" (1 Cor 2:16), all of his disciples do not look alike, and there is not a uniquely legitimate way of following him in faithfulness to his teaching. The evangelical theologian, Samuel Benetreau, shares this opinion as is evident when he argues that the continuity between a master and a disciple can take several forms:

> Alongside the disciple-repeater who attempts to reproduce as faithfully as possible the *ipsissima verba* (the exact words), one finds the disciple who seeks the same faithfulness, but who works above all else to let the thinking of the master penetrate him so as to influence his way of being. (1997)

Paul did not directly quote Jesus, he did not attempt to reproduce exactly each of Jesus' gestures, and it is possible that he never asked himself what

Jesus would do in the situation in which he found himself. But the mind of Christ penetrated Paul. He lived under the influence of Jesus. How did he accomplish this? Paul lived under the influence of the Spirit of Jesus!

Paul Was a Disciple of Jesus through the Spirit of Jesus

We are sometimes tempted to separate in too radical a way the person of the Holy Spirit and the person of Jesus. One of my students even attempted to convince me that the Holy Spirit is not a person. He explained that in the faith community he belongs to, the Holy Spirit is understood to be no more than the power of God. In order to avoid this kind of error, and in an attempt to understand how the apostle Paul could be a disciple of Jesus without ever knowing Jesus in the flesh, it will be helpful to begin with the way in which the gospel of John describes the tie between Jesus and the Spirit.

In the gospel of John, it is evident that Jesus plays an active role in the coming of the Holy Spirit, even if the Spirit is sent by God the Father. Jesus prays for his coming (John 14:16). The Father sends the Spirit in the name of Jesus (John 14:26). Jesus claims to be the one who sends the Spirit on behalf of the Father (John 15:26). Jesus must leave so that the Spirit can be given (John 16:7). The work of the Spirit is understood as the prolongation and the elaboration of that of Jesus. He will remind the disciples of all that Jesus said (John 14:26). He testifies to Jesus (John 15:26). The Holy Spirit declares what he has heard of Jesus, and in that way he glorifies him (John 16:13–15).

The link between the person of Jesus and the person of the Holy Spirit is even more evident when we examine an incident that John describes in John 20:19–22:

> On the evening of that first day of the week, when the disciples were together, with the doors locked for fear of the Jews, Jesus came and stood among them and said, "Peace be with you!" After he said this, he showed them his hands and side. The disciples were overjoyed when they saw the Lord.
>
> Again Jesus said, "Peace be with you! As the Father has sent me, I am sending you." And with that he breathed on them and said, "Receive the Holy Spirit."

If it is true that the Holy Spirit came at Pentecost (Acts 2:1–4), how should we understand this 'breathing' of the Holy Spirit described by John? It is evident that following the experience described in the Acts 2, the behavior of the apostles really changed. For this reason we should perhaps understand the incident described by John as symbolic. His goal was didactic. Jesus was teaching the apostles who is the Spirit. If my use of the word 'symbolic' to describe this incident seems to diminish its importance, please remember that the Spirit could not have been given at Pentecost if the apostles had not learned his identity beforehand! (Milne 1993, 301). The coming of the Spirit at Pentecost depended largely on that action that took place on the evening of the resurrection. Do we want to know who the Spirit is? He is the breath of the glorified Jesus. The resurrected Jesus "breathed on them" and said, "Receive the Holy Spirit"! "The Holy Spirit is Christ himself, in the power of his resurrection (. . .) the stretched out arm of him who has been exalted," according to Karl Barth (1956, 413).

The Holy Spirit is therefore the Spirit of Jesus. Xavier Léon-Dufour explains that Jesus, who is physically absent (because he was taken up before the very eyes of the apostles [Acts 1:9–10]), is nonetheless present with them always, to the very end of the age, as he promised them (Matt 28:20). This is possible through the presence of the Holy Spirit – but a "Holy Spirit who with the distinction of persons, is none other than the presence of Jesus" (1963, 457–458). This is why Paul could state that if anyone does not have the Spirit of Christ, he does not belong to Christ (Rom 8:9). In like fashion we read in Philippians 1:19 that it was the Spirit of Jesus Christ who helped Paul in his imprisonment. And in Acts the Spirit intervenes often to direct the apostle, even in the small details. In Acts 16:7 he is designated as the 'Spirit of Jesus'; he would not allow the apostle to enter the province of Bithynia. In other words, it is Jesus, it is the Spirit, who enables and who directs the apostle. The tie between the Holy Spirit and Jesus is so strong that the Biblical scholar, Yves Congar, could write: "Jesus is not Jesus Christ except by the Holy Spirit. (. . .) But the Holy Spirit is not given (. . .) unless Jesus is Christ and Lord" (1984, 202).

Paul was a disciple of Jesus through the testimony that he received from those who had walked with Jesus and through the Holy Spirit. But the question remains: Did Paul seek to make disciples of Jesus?

Did Paul Make Disciples of Jesus?

We have already seen that the word 'disciple' does not show up in the biblical text after Acts 21. Rather than use the word disciple (Greek: *mathetes*), Paul uses the verb *manthano* (which is the verbal form of *mathetes*) fifteen times.[1] This verb signifies 'to learn, to be instructed' (within both formal contexts and informal relationships) through experience and often with the additional idea of reflection (Louw & Nida 1989, 327). It is clear that although Paul did not call the people he accompanied 'disciples', he considered that the process of their development was disciple making (Wilkins 1988, 160).

We find a second indication that the apostle Paul made disciples when he instructed: "Join with others in following my example, brothers, and take note of those who live according to the pattern we gave you" (Phil 3:17). Or as the New Living Translation puts it: "Dear brothers and sisters, pattern your lives after mine, and learn from those who follow our example." Or in the words of the Good News Translation: "Keep on imitating me, my friends. Pay attention to those who follow the right example that we have set for you." Paul knew that believers need concrete models in order to progress. Being himself an imitator of Christ, he dared to propose that others follow his pattern of life (1 Cor 11:1). It is evident that we are to imitate Jesus. However, since the life of Jesus had become his life (Gal 2:20), he could serve as a model for those he accompanied. His goal was to make good followers of Jesus.

Following his proclamation of Christ crucified and risen from the dead, having himself 'birthed' these believers through the power of the Spirit, Paul found it legitimate to call these people to imitate himself. Had he not worked for their growth? Hadn't he served them through his many sufferings? Yes, he had given himself fully to them. He knew that in following his example these believers would become more Christ-like, more like their Master. But imitating is not copying! The Holy Spirit, the Spirit of Jesus, who makes us members of one another, stimulates us to follow the example of those who can be good models of Jesus-like living to us. If the believers of old imitated Paul, the Holy Spirit was using Paul to teach them how to better submit themselves to Jesus. None of those disciples was to be a carbon copy of the apostle (Besse, 2014).

Led by the Spirit, Paul made disciples of Jesus. He was not content to only proclaim the gospel in places where Christ was yet unknown (Rom 15:20). He cared about the salvation of souls, but he went even further. He taught his converts more than a way of worshiping God in song, more than how to pray for the sick and cast out evil spirits. In one of his letters to Timothy, for example,

---

1. Rom 16:17; 1 Cor 4:9; 14:31, 35; Gal 3 :2; Eph 4 :20; Phil 4:9, 11; Col 1:7; 1 Tim 2:11; 5:4, 13; 2 Tim 3:7, 14; Tit 3:4.

he states that Timothy had accompanied him in many different settings. He had listened to his teaching, observed his way of life, and had adopted it as his own (2 Tim 3:10). Paul praises his faithful companion for imitating his faith, patience, love, and endurance. And he compliments him on having adopted as his goal in life to believe, to love, and to endure sufferings just as the apostle did. Timothy is but one of the people who gravitated around Paul. We can count more than thirty men and women whom Paul called his co-workers (Rom 16:3). And just like Timothy, it is probable that many of those people were formed as disciples of Jesus by Paul himself.

Are we now ready to answer the question: "Does the Great Commission to make disciples of all nations apply only to the Eleven who met the resurrected Christ on the Mount in Galilee?" Did Paul (and ourselves as well) have a different assignment since he was living under the regime of the Holy Spirit? I personally do not believe so. The goal was, and remains, to make disciples of Jesus among all peoples. Those who intentionally and personally accompany others, with the goal of learning together how to better resemble Jesus, are working in synergy with the Spirit of Jesus. That is the primary work of the Holy Spirit in our world. Those who are not intentionally and personally accompanying others in that way are undoubtedly doing good things in the name of Christ. But all those activities are not accomplishing their ultimate design if they are not producing disciples of Jesus.

Some people object that we cannot intentionally and personally accompany others in this way without creating unhealthy and abusive relationships. It is to this objection that we now turn our attention.

Does the Personal Accompaniment of Others in Discipleship Invariably Give Rise to Spiritual Abuse?

In order to understand the importance of this objection, it will be helpful to look at an example of spiritual accompaniment that aimed at the formation of disciples of Jesus, but that did not live up to its promises. There are doubtless other examples that we could consider. However, I have chosen the following because it is well documented, and contains many of the elements that might be found in other places. I am referring to a group known as the Shepherding Movement that was born in 1974 in the USA.

The Case of the Shepherding Movement

In 1970 four charismatic[2] preachers coming from different Protestant traditions (Bernard [Bob] Mumford of the Assemblies of God, Derek Prince a Pentecostal, Don Basham of the Disciples of Christ, and Charles Simpson, a Baptist) decided, for various reasons to submit to each other, and to give each other an account of their actions. That experience of mutual submission became for them a supernatural experience that revolutionized their ministries. Shortly thereafter a Pentecostal Canadian, W. J. E. (Ern) Baxter joined the group which became known as the 'Fort Lauderdale Five'.

Over time, these five men began to center their teaching on subjects like authority, submission, discipleship, covenant relationships, loyalty, pastoral care, and spiritual covering. Their teaching was spread through the magazine *New Wine*, that was printed more than 90,000 copies. In his extensive study of the movement, S. David Moore summarizes in a few words the primary goal of this group:

> . . . the need for discipleship through personal pastoral care or, as they termed it, 'shepherding' care . . . a believer was to submit to a 'personal pastor' who would help the individual develop Christian maturity. (Moore 2003, 1–2)

In June of 1974 a "Shepherds Conference" was held. Almost 2,000 pastors and Christian leaders attended. One year later, in Kansas City, the "1975 National Men's Shepherds Conference" brought together nearly 5,000 charismatic leaders. A growing number of Christian communities submitted to the 'Five'. The number of adherents immediately implicated in the movement was estimated to be more than 100,000. Through the *New Wine* magazine, and the use of the new media like video and audio cassettes, the distinctive doctrines of the Shepherding Movement were spread throughout the United States and around the world. Moore indicates, supported by statistical data, that for the five years from 1979 to 1984, four and a half million magazines were distributed, one million newsletters sent out, and six hundred thousand cassettes along with fifty thousand books were circulated (Moore 2003, 7).

---

2. The Charismatic spiritual stream, also called the 'Charismatic Renewal', or the 'Charismatic Movement', was born in the second half of the twentieth century. It accentuates the persistence yet today of the extraordinary spiritual gifts that are mentioned in the New Testament (prophecy, healing, speaking in tongues, etc.). Unlike Pentecostalism, the charismatic stream is not a well-defined institutional church, but rather a movement that penetrates most Christian denominations today whether they be Protestant or Roman Catholic.

One could say that this movement had a great impact and was very influential. One could add that it was founded on legitimate concerns. The following is a short excerpt from *New Wine*: "Unfortunately, many people who have what they call a genuine conversion experience never seem to grasp what it means to be a disciple or how to live and grow in the faith" (Basham 1974, 27). Another leader of the movement criticized severely, and I think justifiably, the majority understanding of the mission that Christ has assigned us:

> A lot of what we call 'God's servants' are organizers, professional sermonizers, (much of which is based on theory) who have dived head-long into mass-evangelism, mass-literature crusades, mass-TV programs. We pretend we have discovered a short cut, a way of getting the 'job' done quickly. But we are slowly awakening to the solemn conclusion that we have been *laying bricks in the air,* and have not been "building the walls of Zion." (emphasis his) (Baker 1974, 31)

Concerning the idea of disciple making, we find many statements like those that I am making in this book:

> We may make many converts and not make any disciples. Discipleship is vastly more than making converts. In fact, we may do many religious things and yet miss his commandment to make disciples. (Simpson 1974, 4)

What is problematic in this movement is neither its analysis of the situation nor its desire to respond to that lack by the personal accompaniment of each believer with the goal of spiritual growth. No. What is a real problem, and that which in my opinion made this movement go awry, is the fact that the leaders based it on the inappropriate application of two biblical notions: that of authority and that of submission. Nevertheless, their wrong interpretation concerning authority and submission has had a widespread influence on the charismatic renewal movement. It was taught that each individual was to be submitted to another person and that all of the important life decisions had to receive the approval of a 'shepherd' or a 'pastor'. The movement was quickly changed into a system in which the elders or 'shepherds' acted like the spiritual leaders who were responsible for the entire faith community. Every member of the community was to submit to an elder to whom they gave an account of all they did or experienced. Very early there were reports from some members of an abusive use of authority, of unhealthy demands for submission and of manipulation. In 1976 the 'Five' published a brief note in which they expressed their regrets:

> We realize that controversies and problems have arisen among Christians in various areas as a result of our teaching in relation to subjects such as submission, authority, discipling, shepherding. We deeply regret these problems and, insofar as they are due to fault on our part, we ask forgiveness from our fellow believers whom we have offended. (quoted in Moore 2003, 102)

In 1980, it was evident that many people had been hurt by this movement. In 1984 Derek Prince publically withdrew. Don Basham died in 1989.[3] In November of that same year Bob Mumford read a declaration during the meeting of the Christian Believers United that was held in North Carolina. That declaration made the front page of the January/February 1990 edition of the magazine, *Ministries Today*. It reads as follows: "Discipleship was wrong. I repent. I was wrong. I ask for forgiveness. – Bob Mumford" (Buckingham 1990, 46). Mumford repented publically of his involvement in the Shepherding Movement, admitting that "some families were split up and lives turned upside down. Some of these families are still not back together." There was an admittance that the movement had caused "an unhealthy submission resulting in perverse and unbiblical obedience to human leaders" (Buckingham 1990, 48).

Does an Experience Like That of the Shepherding Movement Show That Discipleship is Not Appropriate for Us Today?

I am not in agreement with Mumford's declaration that discipleship is wrong. I would say instead that his way of making disciples was inappropriate. Contrary to his thinking, he was not wrong about the need to put in place a personal accompaniment with the goal of the deep life transformation of those who were converted to Christ. On the other hand, he was misled in seeking to accomplish that based on his defective understanding of authority and submission in the faith community.

Let us not shut our eyes to the truth. We sometimes encounter this same kind of problem in Christian communities that do not underline the notion of disciple making. It is not uncommon, for example, to come upon a faith

---

3. Ern Baxter died in July 1993 and Derek Prince in September 2003.

community that is led by a single person (called Pastor, Elder, Bishop, or Apostle, etc.). Sometimes it is the founder of the group, who is supported by a small group of elders or deacons who are entirely devoted to him. Inside his group, that man often does not account to anyone for his actions. He leads the group with an iron fist, imposing his opinions and allowing no one to question his decisions. In such a setting, the notion of disciple making is frequently absent, nevertheless spiritual abuse abounds.

There are other Christian settings where the authority of the leader is reinforced by the fact that he or she is certain to have received 'divine inspiration'. Those who contest this person's authority are considered 'rebels', like Jannes and Jambres who resisted Moses (2 Tim 3:6–8). One rarely hears this kind of leader say, "It seems to me that . . .", or "I think that . . .". The favorite expressions are rather, "God showed me that . . .", or "The Lord said to me that . . .".

I remember also an experience that my wife and I had in a Christian community in Cameroon that we attended for several months. For professional reasons I had to miss a couple weeks of meetings. On my return, the pastor bawled me out, saying that I should have informed him that I was going to travel. His comments were undoubtedly motivated by his pastoral concern for me, which I appreciate. Sometimes it is wise to ask the advice of a man of God before making a major decision. But this can lead to serious abuse on the part of pastoral authorities. I repeat, this is not only a problem that is encountered by those who seek to accompany others in Christian discipleship.

By What Authority?

At this point in our discussion, it will perhaps be helpful to look at a biblical text that is often wrongly used to support the idea that the faithful must be obedient to their pastor, or that a disciple must be submitted to the person who is accompanying him or her in the journey of faith. I am referring to the text of Hebrews 13:17 that reads: "Obey your leaders and submit to their authority. . ." (NIV). Other translations read: "Obey them that have the rule over you, and submit yourselves . . ." (King James Version). "Obey your leaders and follow their orders . . ." (Good News Translation). "Obey your spiritual leaders and do what they say . . ." (New Living Translation). This text seems very clear. It is understood as a biblical command to obey those who lead us in the faith, to be submit to them, to do as they say (Bevere 2002, 131).

It is not without interest to note that in the Greek text of this verse, the word translated in English 'obey' is *pitho*, which normally means to 'persuade'.[4] One of the commentators of this verse recognizes that by its use here, the word can legitimately be translated with the English word 'obey'. This explains why that is the translation that is the most often used in our Bibles. However, the same commentator also underlines the fact that this word "always carries the notion of obedience that is obtained through persuasion, rather than obedience that is obtained by appealing to authority" (Leighton, 2008). In his commentary on the epistle to the Hebrews, Ray C. Stedman writes:

> About the texts of Hebrews 13:17 and 1 Thessalonians 5:12, notice that the word 'obey' comes from the Greek *pitho*, 'persuade'. The form of the Greek that is used here, (present, imperative, middle), signifies "let yourself be persuaded", or "let yourself be convinced". This in no way signifies that we should blindly follow orders. The phrase "your leaders" does not contain the ideas of someone who is 'above' another, nor does it signify someone who us under the domination of a leader. The authority of a Christian leader is not the authority of one who orders. It is rather the authority that expresses itself in service. As Jesus said, a servant has authority because his charitable service gives others the desire to follow him. Or perhaps he persuades by his logic or by his knowledge. (Stedman, 1992)

If we are exhorted to allow ourselves to be persuaded by those who accompany us in the faith it is because they 'keep watch over us'. Steven Lambert underlines that,

> this Greek word *pitho*, translated by *obey* in many versions, is closely tied to the word *pisteuo*, which means to trust . . . the difference of meaning between these words is that *pitho* (persuasion/obedience) is produced by *pisteuo* (trust). In the original language, the obedience referred to here is a docility and cooperation that results from assurance and confidence. (Lambert, 2003)

There is an authority to which one must submit in discipleship, but it is an authority of service and of confidence. This is the error committed by the men who launched the Shepherding Movement. Having wrongly understood

---

4. In fact, in ancient Greek culture, *Pitho* was the goddess of persuasion.

the nature of biblical authority, they insisted on a kind of obedience and of submission that was inappropriate. The problem was not their desire to make disciples of Jesus! If their efforts did not produce the results they hoped for, it is simply because they went about it in the wrong way. What they apparently did not understand is that the accompaniment that produces disciples of Jesus is based upon *trust*, and not upon *authority*. Doesn't Jesus himself indicate this when he said to his disciples, "I no longer call you servants (. . .) I have called you friends" (John 15:15)?

It seems also that in their attempt to make disciples of Jesus, the founders of the Shepherding Movement didn't apply the principle of Ephesians 5:21. According to this verse, within the faith community, all are to be submitted to each other out of reverence for Christ. No one obliges the other. All freely accept that discipline. Philippians 2:3–5 suggests that in that mutual submission, all illusion of superiority is banished, no one is considered superior to the others.

One could say that Paul was this kind of model in his relationship to those he accompanied in obedience to Christ. Although he was an apostle, Paul did not treat Timothy as his subordinate! Rather, he let him observe his teaching, his conduct, his projects, his faith, his patience, his love, his perseverance, etc., with the unique goal of forming him as a disciple of Jesus. He also did it, undoubtedly, for his own spiritual progress, since he was also himself a disciple of Jesus. Although he had begun his journey following Christ earlier than was the case for his "son in the faith", he knew that in this way, like iron sharpens iron, he would himself become more like Jesus in the process (Prov 27:17).[5] He recognized that even an apostle can lack discernment and act wrongly. He had been forced to 'correct' Peter, the 'prince of apostles' (Gal 2:11–16). Conscious of his own weaknesses and limitations (cf. Rom 6–7), Paul entered actively and intentionally into this kind of accompaniment.

To Finish Well

When I was a seminary student I had a class with Dr Robert Clinton.[6] One day he said to us: "Look at the person sitting on your right, and at the person on your left. If the statistics of my research are trustworthy, only one of you

---

5. Paul was between 65 and 70 years old when he wrote to Timothy, and Timothy was somewhere between 30 and 35 years old.

6. Class titled "Christian Leadership" given at Fuller Theological Seminary School of World Mission, Pasadena, CA, 1994–1995.

will finish well his life with Christ!" He explained, "That is approximately the ratio of those who finish their life well as compared to those who don't. One biblical leader out of three finished well – and we are not doing any better than they did." Those words continue to speak to me today, for I want to be one of those who finishes well with Christ.

Dr Clinton continued his lecture by explaining that the Bible mentions nearly one thousand leaders. Some of those are only named, others are known for the role they played. Others yet occupy an important place. The description of the life of leaders such as Moses, David, Paul and Jesus gives us many more details that we can analyze. And Dr Clinton alerted us to the fact that even when the biblical text gives us a lot of information about the life of a leader, it doesn't always tell us how he ended up. Having said all this, he said that he had enough biblical information about forty-nine of those leaders to be able to do a serious analysis.

I cannot give you here all of the details of that study. I will only briefly mention six of the barriers or obstacles that his study identified that often keep leaders from finishing well (Clinton 1993, 93). When Dr Clinton speaks of finishing well, he means that the person walked with God up to the end of his life, and that he probably contributed significantly to the progress of God's projects. We will also look at one detail, one of the five qualities that according to the study done by Dr Clinton, characterize the lives of those who finish well with Christ that has a direct bearing on our discussion.

Six Barriers

Barrier 1 – Finances

Among leaders, especially those who occupy privileged positions of power and who therefore make financial decisions, some fall into the trap of using practices that encourage dishonesty. For instance, they sometimes insist too much on the need for others to give, notably the tithe. Often they go so far as to argue that this is a necessity for obtaining the blessings of God. It is surprising that these same leaders are often hesitant to give an account of the ways in which those funds are spent. Greed, the desire to possess wealth, is a character trait that will inevitably open the door to financial irregularities. Many leaders have fallen over financial questions (biblical example: Gideon's Ephod [Judg 8:22–32] and Ananias and Sapphira [Acts 5:1–11]).

Barrier 2 – Power

Leaders who exercise a successful ministry for Christ, increase in so doing, their power over others. Often very strict rules are imposed on the members of the congregation, while the behavior of these leaders lies beyond all censure ("Don't touch the Lord's anointed!") These leaders sometimes allow themselves to begin doubtful practices, most often in private. When those practices are brought to light they justify themselves by claiming a "special indulgence from the Lord", or a "greater spiritual maturity", that permits them to do these practices without being affected (unlike the weak in the faith who would be destroyed by the Evil One were they to follow their example). This sometimes leads to serious abuses by pastoral leaders, mainly in the areas of finances or sexual practices (biblical example: Uzziah [2 Chr 26]).

Barrier 3 – Pride

Leaders who are too proud often begin criticizing others for their 'compromises' or their 'lukewarmness'. Compared to those around them, these leaders claim to be the only ones who are truly faithful to Christ; when they are themselves criticized by other leaders, they sometimes invoke a 'special revelation from the Lord' to justify their differences. They encourage their faithful to 'come out from among' the others, so as not to spiritually fall along with those who 'have not received the light'. One begins by cultivating a spirit of exclusion, pretending to be 'closer to God' than the other groups. Soon they begin to think that their divine calling is to show others the error of their ways (biblical example: David's numbering of the fighting men [1 Chr 21]).

Barrier 4 – Sex

Illicit sexual relationships have been the downfall of many important leaders whose life is detailed in the Bible, and also for many contemporary Christian leaders. When one speaks of sin in the area of sex, the classical model of integrity should be the ideal that is actively pursued by all leaders (Gen 39). Every Christian leader should also be on his or her guard against pornography.[7] Pornography is not only accessible, it is also promoted and spread through the internet. No one – no adult – no Christian leader – no

---

7. Pornography can be defined as any amusement that relies on indecent or obscene images to stimulate sexual impulses.

one, is sufficiently mature enough to be able to run the risk of intentional exposure to this poison. The leader must be careful to avoid pornography at all times, for pornography is a powerful drug. Scientific research, notably the new techniques of scanning brain waves, is beginning to indicate that pornography can cause physical and chemical changes to the brain that are not unlike those caused by illicit drugs (biblical example: The sin of David with Bathsheba [2 Sam 11-12] marks a turning in his role as leader. He never fully recovers from that sin).

Barrier 5 – Family

Problems between spouses, between parents and their children, between brothers and sisters, can also destroy the ministry of a leader. We must notice, however, that voluntarily or involuntarily, certain faith communities isolate their members from their families and close friends out of a desire to keep them from 'bad influences'. That isolation can also be the result of too much participation in the meetings and religious activities of the group. To insure the total participation of the members, some leaders do not hesitate to tell their faithful either explicitly or implicitly that the time they spend in the faith community is more important than the time spent with family (biblical example: The family of David [Amnon and Tamar, 2 Sam 13] and the revolt of Absalom [2 Sam 15]).

Barrier 6 – Plateauing

Competent leaders tend to go through phases of plateauing. In these instances their strengths become a cause of weakness because they begin to feel that they can continue their ministry without being intimately renewed by the Holy Spirit. Most Christian leaders will go through these phases of plateauing or stagnation several times in their life. The problem comes when they do not realize their need to continue to grow, and they begin to be content with the *status quo* in their personal life and in their ministry (Clinton 1989, 177, 213) (biblical example: David at the end of his career, right before the revolt of Absalom [2 Sam 14]).

These then are the six barriers that trip up two out of three leaders who begin following after Jesus. They were identified through the study of dozens of biblical examples, and confirmed through the examination of the lives of hundreds of Christian leaders. However, we can be comforted by the fact that we also have the possibility of studying the example of those who went successfully all the way in their commitment. Dr Clinton has uncovered five elements that are often found in the lives of those believers who finish well. All five of the elements are not found in the life of each individual, but there are always several of them. I will only look at the one element that is connected to our reflection on personal accompaniment in discipleship.

The Importance of Finding Someone Who Can Accompany You in Your Spiritual Life and in Your Ministry

According to Dr Clinton, a comparative study of Christian leaders reveals that other people frequently play a significant role in their lives, questioning them, encouraging them, and counseling them. Christian leaders who bear spiritual fruit and who finish well their life with Christ are accompanied an average of between ten and fifteen times in their lifetime. These people influence them in a significant way through their accompaniment.

I think that Timothy, and his other c-oworkers, played a significant role in the life of Paul. At the same time that the apostle communicated his life to them, his friends and co-workers brought him encouragement, counsel, moral and spiritual support, and raised questions that enabled him to progress. We do not make disciples only to obey the Great Commission. Nor do we make disciples only so that their lives will be transformed into the image of the Master. We also make disciples of Jesus because our own spiritual health needs it. Do you want to go all the way with Christ, and not trip up on one of the barriers that cause so many to fall (two out of three)? If you really want to finish well, enter intentionally and actively into this kind of accompaniment. If you do so, there is a great possibility that one day you will be able to say with the apostle Paul: "I have fought the good fight, I have finished the race, I have kept the faith" (2 Tim 4:7).

Some Warning Signs

Drawing from our study of the Shepherding Movement and the barriers that Dr Clinton has identified, I will now mention some warning signs that indicate that a relationship of personal accompaniment is heading in the wrong direction. This list is not exhaustive, but sheds light on some of the most common elements.

1. When one of the individuals begins telling the other what he or she should do because: "God showed me that . . .", or "The Lord told me that . . .". The accompaniment in discipleship is not directive. It does not authorize one person to tell the other what he or she must do.

2. When one of the individuals begins to order the other to give an account of all of his or her actions. The accompaniment in discipleship is a voluntary relationship, founded on trust and confidence, and not on this kind of submission.

3. When one of the individuals begins to order the other to show loyalty by all kinds of personal sacrifices. The accompaniment in discipleship consists in two people learning together how to deepen their attachment to Christ. Their relationship to each other is secondary.

4. When one of the individuals begins imposing opinions on the other and does not allow questioning. The accompaniment in discipleship is an apprenticeship relationship that is marked by constant self-examination.

5. When one of the individuals begins trying to force a strict code of conduct on the other. The accompaniment in discipleship recognizes that there is not a single legitimate way to follow Jesus, and that the disciplines that one person finds helpful might not be appropriate for the other at this particular moment in his or her progression.

6. When one of the individuals begins looking for inappropriate physical signs of affection (hugs, kisses, etc.) The accompaniment in discipleship is an expression of Christian charity that excludes this type of relationship.

7. When one of the individuals seeks to isolate the other from deep relationships with other disciples of Jesus through the use of formulations such as: "we are right," or "the others are wrong," or "the others have been seduced by demons." The accompaniment in discipleship is not an exclusive relationship which separates the disciple from his faith community. Nor does it isolate him or her from non-believers.

Questions to Think About:

1. What would you answer the person who claims that discipleship is not for everyone because even though Jesus left us a model for discipleship, the word disciple does not appear after the book of Acts?

2. What would you answer the person who argues that personal accompaniment in a disciple-making relationship inevitably produces spiritual abuse?

3. What lessons do you draw from the study done by Dr Clinton?

4. What are the most important 'warning signals' in your context that a personal accompaniment in discipleship is beginning to move in the wrong direction?

7

The Disciple of Jesus and the Glory of God

If we were to do a survey asking Christians what is the most important goal of a believer, many people would respond: "We must live to bring glory to God." That conviction is in line with what Paul wrote to the Corinthians: "So whether you eat or drink or whatever you do, do it all for the glory of God" (1 Cor 10:31). The assurance that the believer is called above all else to bring glory to God is also put forward in the Westminster Shorter Catechism which begins with the question: "What is the chief end of man?" To which the response is given: "Man's chief end is to glorify God, and to enjoy him forever."

The word 'glory' is frequently used in Christian circles and in multiple ways. It is a word that is sung, that shows up in sermons, that is read in numerous biblical texts, and is repeated in Christian literature (Viguier 2014, 18). It is often used to designate divine splendor. When we celebrate that splendor we frequently cry out "Glory to God!" We commonly speak of "giving glory to God." But what does that mean? Is it simply a fashionable form of speech in Christian language (like the use of the word 'disciple')? Or is it rather an expression with a unique and precise meaning?

I will attempt to respond to these questions in this chapter. Since it is widely assumed that the chief end of man is to live for the glory of God, and since Jesus sends us out to make disciples of all nations, I propose that there exists a link between the glory of God and the act of making disciples of Jesus Christ. Jesus himself suggested that this is the case when he affirmed: "This is to my Father's glory, that you bear much fruit, showing yourselves to be my disciples" (John 15:8). My goal is therefore to demonstrate why the act of making disciples of Jesus is the best way to give glory to God.

The Concept of Glory in the Old Testament

Few notions are more important to the ancient world that those of honor, distinction, esteem, and glory (Burge 1992, 269). For this reason we shouldn't be surprised to learn that in Hebrew there are a few words that communicate the idea of 'glory'. However the most important of these, and also the most often used in the Old Testament (nearly 200 times) is the word *kabod*. Its root is the word signifying 'weight' and it indicates 'to be heavy'. It is used to designate someone who is honorable, impressive, worthy of respect.

This word when applied to people often describes their wealth, position or power (Gen 31:1; 45:13; Isa 8:7). But it is when *kabod* is used to describe God that takes on its most surprising and distinctive meaning. Forty-five times this word is used as descriptive of God in the Old Testament. John Oswalt says that it always refers to the *heavy presence* of God. More than a simple characteristic, this word implies the very presence of God (1980, 427). Other biblical scholars underline the visibility of that manifestation (Brown, Driver, & Briggs 1955, 458–459; Unger 1977, 409). And others yet insist that when this word is used it does not refer to one of God's attributes in particular, but indicates rather the presence and the grandeur of his entire nature (Ramm 1963, 18).

This notion that the glory of God implies the greatness of his presence, as it is both *felt* and *recognized*, is contrasted in the Scriptures. Sometimes the Bible indicates that his presence is discreet. And while it is true that God is present everywhere, that his eyes observe all people everywhere and all that takes place under the heavens, his intervention is not always evident (Ps 11:4; 139; Matt 10:29). He can even be present in the midst of his people without intervening or manifesting himself openly.[1] All this leads us to believe that we should understand his glory as his 'active' and 'recognizable' presence. Not only when he is present, but above all when he manifests his presence. We have numerous examples of God's active and recognizable presence in the Old Testament of the Bible. We will look quickly at four of them: (1) the glory of God in the garden of Eden, (2) the glory of God among the people of Israel, (3) the glory of God in the tabernacle, and (4) the glory of God in the temple.

---

1. The active presence of God was the exceptional privilege of Israel, but it could be lost as when the sons of Eli lost the Ark of the Covenant to the Philistines (1 Sam 4). 'Ichabod' (1 Sam 4:21–22), the name of one of Eli's grandsons, means 'the glory has departed'.

In the Garden of Eden

Life With the Glory of God

In Genesis 3:8 we read that Adam and Eve "heard the sound of the LORD God as he was walking in the garden in the cool of the day." Before the fall of man, the great reality in the life of Adam and Eve in the garden was the fact that they lived in the active and recognizable presence of God. To speak of that active and recognizable presence the Hebrews used the word *shekinah*, which signifies 'to live, to reside' (associated with fire, lightning and brilliant light [Ezek 1:27]).[2] Adam and Eve lived with the *shekinah* of God.

According to John 4:24, God is Spirit, which means that in the garden of Eden he did not have a physical body. How did he manifest himself? I think that he probably appeared as a glorious translucent and brilliant light. In other places in the biblical text he appears in that way. The active and recognizable manifestation of his presence (in other words his infinite and eternal glory) rested with Adam and Eve in the garden. In that way they could communicate with him.

The Loss of the Glory of God

Immediately following the sin of Adam and Eve, they were chased out of the Garden, driven from the glory (the active and recognizable presence) of God (Gen 3:23–24). Fallen humans cannot experience the glory of God, they cannot live in his active presence, nor can they even recognize that presence. "No one has ever seen God . . ." states the gospel of John (1:18).

In the midst of His People

In Leviticus 26:11–12 God makes an extraordinary promise to his people Israel: "I will put my dwelling place among you, and I will not abhor you. I will walk among you and be your God, and you will be my people." The promise of the active and recognizable presence of God among his people was the most foundational and precious element of the alliance that he made with them (Exod 19:4–6).

---

2. In the *Mishna*, the *Shekinah* represented the divine presence in *Sanhedrin* 6,5 and *Aboth* 3,2 (Danby 1933).

The Presence of God in the midst of His People, and the Restoration of Eden

The biblical scholar and Old Testament specialist, Christopher Wright, points out that in Leviticus 26, which is home to the verses that we just read, we find numerous "echoes of the Genesis portrait of creation under God's blessing". He sees these echoes in the notions of fruitfulness and increase, in peace and the absence of danger. More importantly, he specifies that even the phrase "I will walk among you" uses a very rare form of the verb *halak* (the *hithpael*), which is also used in Genesis 3:8 to describe God's habit of spending the cool of the day just strolling with Adam and Eve in the garden (Wright 2006, 334). The covenant presence of God among his people would therefore be a return to the intimacy of Eden.

The Presence of God in the midst of His People, and Their Identity

More than the Torah, or other distinguishing elements of their identity like circumcision, food laws or the observance of the Sabbath, it was the active and recognizable presence of God in their midst that would set his people off from the rest of humankind. However, after their apostasy (Exod 32–34), God proposed that one of his angels replace his presence in their midst (Exod 33:1–5). Moses refused categorically that substitution saying: "What else will distinguish me and your people from all the other people on the face of the earth?" (Exod 33:16). Then Moses asks of God to show him his glory (Exod 33:18).

Let's remember that the glory of God can be understood as the active and recognizable manifestation of his presence. In Moses' day that active presence was so central and significant that three other expressions were used to designate it: the 'face', 'appearance', or 'presence' of the LORD (Hebrew: *panîm*); the 'Angel of the LORD' (Hebrew: *malak YHWH*); and his 'name' (Hebrew: *sem*). Most of these elements are found in Exodus 33 where Moses had asked God to show him his glory (Kaiser 1978, 120).

In the Tabernacle

In the Old Testament, the word *shekinah* is frequently used in connection with the tabernacle and most often designates the visible manifestation of the presence of God. When the tabernacle had been built, the text of Exodus 40:34 says: "Then the cloud covered the Tent of the Meeting, and the glory of the LORD filled the tabernacle." The tabernacle had been built to be a temporary sanctuary for God (Exod 25:8), the place of his proximity and active presence (Cross, 1961). It was a concrete manifestation of God's desire to reveal himself and to dwell among men and women (Exod 29:46).

In the Temple

After having settled in the Promised Land, it was the temple which became the place of the visible and active presence of God among human beings. Remember that God did not give in immediately to David's request to build him a temple. In fact, God's immediate response seems to have been negative for fear of too great a materialization of his presence. However, when Solomon finished the construction of the temple, "the glory of God filled the temple like a dark cloud," to the extent that the priests could not perform their service at the altar (1 Kgs 8:10–11).

The temple was the place for rituals and sacrifices. But what made it so important for people was the fact that God was actively and visibly present. This explains why the destruction of the temple was such a catastrophe for the people of Israel. It was an event that touched the Israelites to the core. Not only did they become slaves, more importantly they also became a people among whom the visible and active presence of God disappeared.

The New Testament Concept of the Glory of God

To speak of the glory of God, the New Testament authors use the Greek word *doxa* (or *doxazein*). In a few cases this word refers to the honor given to men (Matt 4:8; 6:29), but in the majority of cases it is used to describe the revelation of the *active presence* of God (Nixon 1994, 424). Note well that the manifestation of the active and recognizable presence of God, once known in the garden of Eden, then in the midst of the people of Israel, in the tabernacle and in the temple, is now inseparably tied to the person of Jesus of Nazareth.

It is in the gospel of John that this theme is the most developed. In his gospel, John never associates the glory of Jesus with some sort of future "Son of Man." Rather, he uses this word to describe Jesus' earthly work. In fact, glory is one of John's favorite concepts. He uses the words *doxa* or *doxazein* forty-one times (as compared to eleven times in Matthew, four times in Mark, and twenty-one times in Luke). Sometimes he even picks up the manifestations of the 'glory' of God from the Old Testament and associates them with Jesus.

Jesus Was the Manifestation of the Glory of God

Right at the beginning of his gospel, where he writes, "The Word became flesh, *and pitched his tent among us*, . . . and we have seen his glory, the glory of the One and Only who came from the Father" (John 1:14, emphasis mine). John does not hesitate to associate Jesus with the manifestation of the active and visible presence of God. According to John, the uncreated and creative Word entered fully into the human condition in the person of Jesus of Nazareth. John claims that the Word became 'a man'. And that man would know fatigue and hunger. He would be deeply troubled at times and would even weep at the death of a friend. John goes even further when he states that the Word "made his dwelling among us".

You certainly have noticed that I translated the phrase "made his dwelling among us" with the words "*pitched his tent among us*". The verb *skenoo*,[3] which John uses in this verse and which is often translated by the word 'dwell', not only aims to communicate a real abiding of the Word among men. It is more likely that John is making allusion to the 24th chapter of the Book of Ecclesiasticus[4] which praises Wisdom who came out of the mouth of the Most High (v. 5). She was created from the beginning and before the world, and she shall not cease to be (v. 14). Upon the order of God she came to "pitch her tent" in Israel and then the "Creator of all things . . . rested in her tabernacle" (v. 12). The Creator full of wisdom has come to dwell among his people. He has pitched his *tabernacle* or *tent* among us. In the book of Ecclesiasticus, the word that is translated 'tabernacle' is the same word that John uses to say that "the Word has become flesh, and dwelt (*tabernacled*) among us" (1:14). So John is alluding undoubtedly to the tabernacle in the desert, place of the active presence of God in the midst of his people, and perhaps as well to this image from the book of Ecclesiasticus. This is the place where he manifests his glory (Exod 40:34–38). However, instead of this manifestation taking

---

3. Charles L'Eplattenier observes also that the verb *skenoo* is phonetically close to *Shekinah*, which in later Judaism designated the 'divine presence' (1993, 28).

4. Ecclesiasticus, more properly known as The Wisdom of Sirach, was well known and widely read in New Testament times, but it was not always viewed on a par with other Old Testament books. The common title of the book comes from the fact that it was used in ancient synagogue services, and it even had popular use in early church meetings. The Book of Ecclesiasticus was included in the Septuagint, a Greek translation of the Old Testament written around 250 BC, as well as Codex Vaticanus and Codex Sinaiticus (both from the 4th century AD). Despite its inclusion in the Septuagint and its widespread use in the early centuries, it was not included in the Hebrew canon, and no early church father included it in the canon until Augustine in AD 397.

place in a tent, it happens in a human being. It seems that the expression was carefully chosen to suggest a truth that John would declare openly in verse twenty-one of the second chapter of his gospel: "But the temple he had spoken of was his body."

You have already undoubtedly noticed that John's gospel has few incidents in common with the other three Gospels. Strangely, one of the incidents that he shares with the others he places right at the start of his account while the others place it at the end of theirs (John 2:13–22). Jesus has traveled to the temple in Jerusalem. There he drives out the money-changers with a whip of cords. The Jews demanded what miraculous sign he could show to prove his authority to act in that way. And Jesus responded: "Destroy this temple, and I will raise it again in three days" (v. 19). The Jews didn't understand Jesus' answer, but John explains that the temple he had spoken of was his body (v. 21).

We have seen that for the Jews, the temple was the place where the One True God had promised to dwell. The temple was therefore, in their eyes, the place where earth and heaven came together. It was the place where one went to encounter God. It was also the place of sacrifices, the place where atonement for sin was made. And, finally, it was the place where celebrations were held since it was uniquely in that place that one could experience the presence and love of God.

John says constantly that Jesus thought and acted as if he considered himself to be the replacement for the temple. When he went up to Jerusalem for the various celebrations he took on their meaning. He did this when he went to the Feast of Tabernacles in chapter seven, at the Feast of Dedication in chapter ten (v. 22–39), and three times with the Passover Feast (chapters 2, 6, 12 and 19). And to cap it all off, he dies as "the Lamb of God who takes away the sin of the world" (John 1:29).[5]

In John's view, Jesus is both the sacrifice and the temple, and in chapter 17 he is the High Priest who sanctifies himself in order to present his people

---

5. There are at least five notions associated with the title 'Lamb of God': (1) the lamb given by God to Abraham (Gen 22:8, 13); (2) the lamb of Jewish Passover (John 2:13, cf. Exod 12:11–13 and 1 Cor 5:7); (3) the lamb that was sacrificed every morning and every twilight as a 'perpetual atonement' for the sins of the people (Exod 29:38–42); (4) the gentle family lamb that was led to be butchered (cf. Jer 11:19 and Isa 53:7); and (5) the lamb of a tradition attested to by apocryphal or deuterocanonical literature, sometimes represented as a young horned ram, the symbol of a powerful king, or of a victorious liberator. That image is picked up in the Revelation of John. The title of Lamb is attributed 28 times to the glorious Christ in that book; he is the "Lamb who was slain", yet remains the Lamb who will overcome all his foes because he is Lord of lords and King of kings (Rev 17:14).

to God (17:17) and to bring them into the same intimate relationship with God that he enjoys (17:20–21). According to John we no longer need to go to Jerusalem to "gaze upon the beauty of the Lord" (Ps 27:4). Everything that this psalm affirms has been accomplished in Jesus. He is fully the new temple in whom we are invited to meet God and gaze upon his beauty!

In his detailed study of this text, Charles L'Eplattenier underscores the fact that when Jesus compares his body to the temple (John 2:18–22) and declares, "Destroy this temple, and I will raise it again in three days!" he replaces the word *hieron* (temple) by that of *naos* (sanctuary). And he points out that we could have expected him to use *hieron* since it shows up twelve times in the gospel of John. Instead the word *naos* is used, and it is precisely this word that Paul will use to argue that the believers are the 'temple of God', or that their 'body is the temple of the Holy Spirit' (1 Cor 3:16, 6:19). So we have the visible presence of God in the *naos* (sanctuary) of a human body, the person of Jesus, the Word made flesh (L'Eplattenier 1993, 75).

Once again, John associates unceasingly the glory of God (his active and recognizable presence) with the person of Jesus of Nazareth. His entire life was a manifestation of the active presence of God. When he transformed water into wine at Cana in Galilee, John says that he manifested the active presence of God, his glory, to his disciples and that they believed in him (John 2:1–11). Throughout his gospel, John wants us to look at Jesus and witness the active presence of God (John 1:18; 10:30; 14:9–10). To discover God, one must look at Jesus. And to discover who God is, one must learn to understand the miraculous sign that is Jesus.

The glory that Jesus manifested was the active presence of God. It did not come from men (John 5:41). Jesus did not seek his own glory (to manifest his own active presence), but that of the One who had sent him (John 7:18). It is the Father who glorified Jesus (John 8:50, 54). Jesus opposed the manifestation of the active presence of God to the death of his friend Lazarus (John 11:4, 40). The glory that was on Jesus, that clung to him, that shone through him, that acted in him, is the active presence of his heavenly Father (Barclay 1975, 69). That glory was at the same time his own. Toward the end of his life he prayed: "And now, Father, glorify me in your presence with the glory I had with you before the world began" (John 17:5).

The Ultimate Manifestation of the Glory of God in the Person of Jesus

When at the beginning of his gospel John claims to have 'beheld' the glory of Jesus (John 1:14), we might think that he is referring to the incident that took place on the Mount of Transfiguration where he saw the appearance of Jesus' face change, and "his clothes became as bright as a flash of lightening". But this is not the case. In his gospel, John does not give an account of the Mount of Transfiguration as the other gospel writers do.[6] That is surprising since John was himself one of the three disciples, along with Peter and James, who personally witnessed the event, and he explicitly says here that, "We have seen his glory." All of the mentions of Jesus' glory in John's gospel lead us to think that he is inviting us to look at the human face of Jesus of Nazareth, and there to discern the face of the living God.[7] And as the biblical scholar N. T. Wright has pointed out, John invites us to enter even more deeply into that reflection. He suggests that it is specifically the face of Jesus on the cross, crowned with thorns, that is the expression of the glory (active and recognizable presence) of the living God. According to John, it is in the death of Jesus on the cross that we see the ultimate manifestation of the active presence of God, the supreme revelation of his glory! Hence Wright suggests that John is inviting us to see the Mount of Golgotha as the Mount of Transfiguration (Wright 1994, 33–41).

In order to better appreciate John's invitation to look on the human face of Jesus and discern there God's glory, it will be helpful to examine John 3:14–16:

> Just as Moses lifted up the snake in the desert, so the Son of Man must be lifted up, that everyone who believes in him may have eternal life.
>
> For God so loved the world that he gave his one and only Son, that whoever believes in him shall not perish but have eternal life.

How should we understand the words, "the Son of Man must be lifted up"? At first glance these words clearly refer to the cross. On the cross Jesus is lifted up above the earth, lifted up in a position or place of shame, cruel suffering, and judgment. It is a place that represents everything that is wrong with our world. However on a different level, that elevation is closely

---

6. Matt 17:1–9; Mark 9:2–10; Luke 9:28–36.

7. This mystery is the central theme of the gospel of John. If the old theological maxim is valid: *Deus comprehensus non est Deus* (a God who is understood is not God), then one could also claim, *Christus comprehensus non est Deus* (a Christ who is fully understood is not God).

1 with glory, a powerful manifestation of the active and recognizable p.~~~~ of God. On the cross, Jesus is lifted up as the true revelation of "the compassionate and gracious God, slow to anger and abounding in love and faithfulness, maintaining love to thousands, and forgiving wickedness and rebellion and sin" (Exod 34:6–7).

But those words also draw our attention back to another incident: "Just as Moses lifted up the snake in the desert . . ." What does that mean? In the Old Testament book of Numbers we read the account of the people of Israel who sinned by speaking against God and against Moses (Num 21:4–9). "Then," the text explains, "the LORD sent venomous snakes among them; they bit the people and many Israelites died" (Num 21:6). After the people had recognized and confessed their sin, and Moses had prayed for them, God said, "Make a snake and put it up on a pole; anyone who is bitten can look at it and live" (Num 21:8).

This ancient story was well known by the original readers of John's gospel, however John will give it a new twist. When Jesus is lifted up on the cross, he who is the ultimate manifestation of the active presence of God, anyone who looks at him and believes in him will have eternal life!

John will come back to this image in chapter 12 of his gospel to explain how Jesus is the Savior of the world through his 'lifting up' on the cross. Jesus has just arrived in Jerusalem accompanied by a great crowd that was shouting, "Hosanna! Blessed is he who comes in the name of the Lord!" (John 12:12). There were some Greeks among the crowd who wished to see Jesus. Jesus responds to their request with these words:

> The hour has come for the Son of Man to be glorified. I tell you the truth, unless a kernel of wheat falls to the ground and dies, it remains only a single seed. But if it dies, it produces many seeds. The man who loves his life will lose it, while the man who hates his life in this world will keep it for eternal life. Whoever serves me must follow me; and where I am, my servant also will be. My Father will honor the one who serves me.
>
> Now my heart is troubled, and what shall I say? Father, save me from this hour? No, it was for this very reason I came to this hour. Father, glorify your name!
>
> Then a voice came from heaven, "I have glorified it, and will glorify it again." The crowd that was there and heard it said it had thundered; others said an angel had spoken to him.

Jesus said, "This voice was for your benefit, not mine. Now is the time for judgment on this world; now the prince of this world will be driven out. But I, when I am lifted up from the earth, will draw all men to myself." (John 12:23–32)

In this passage we have nearly all of the images that John develops in his gospel to speak of the passion of Christ. The grain of wheat must fall to the ground and die. This is the hour for which Christ has come into the world. His death was not a sad accident that put a premature end to what was a promising life. On the contrary, his death was the climax and goal of all of his existence. In that unique event God glorified his name (in other words he manifested his active presence). And when Jesus was finally 'lifted up' – glorified, crucified – he began drawing all men to himself. And how could it be otherwise, if the cross was the ultimate, true manifestation of the active presence of the true God?

If the 'miraculous signs'[8] of John's gospel lead to the new creation through the cross, the 'lifting up' of Jesus underlines the fact that the crucifixion is itself the moment of supreme glory, the instant when God actively embraced an agonizing world. The lifting up of Jesus, or his glorification, is the absolute revelation of the glory of God, the ultimate manifestation of his active presence.

The Glory of God and the Disciple of Jesus

Now we are ready to understand how, in what we do, we can bring the most glory to God. If the glory of God is, as I have claimed, the manifestation of his active presence, what might we do to bring him glory, reveal his activity, or make his presence more noticeable? We all want God to be "truly in our midst." We desire him to work, act, speak and display his power and his gifts among us. Our faith communities have probably never known such agitation, so many gesticulations, projects and strategies that aim at "making God's presence visible." The 'Hallelujah!' and the 'Amen!' punctuate our meetings. The faithful try to outdo each other in their expressions of earnestness and zeal for God. Yet, I believe that the manifestation of the active presence of God does not depend on the ambiance of the meeting, or on the volume of the

---

8. John systematically and methodically calls the remarkable interventions of Jesus 'signs' (John 2:11; 4:54; 6:2, etc.). Their purpose is to make known the real identity of Jesus (John 12:37).

music, or even on the amount of energy that we expend in our gesticulations. Neither the strength of our voice nor the length of our sermons makes the presence of God more perceptible. Drawing from the example and the teaching of Jesus, I suggest that this does not depend on our 'worship', our 'praise', or our 'songs of adoration', as much as it is the result of our 'giving weight' (from the Hebrew root *kabod*) to Jesus in our lives. This is what the disciple of Jesus learns to do day after day.

Four Lessons Drawn from the Life of Jesus

1. **Jesus 'gave weight' to God the Father in his life by not seeking his own glory** (cf. John 12:28; 13:31).

   To 'give glory to God' means to put him in the limelight. For that to happen we must abandon our natural tendency to center our world around ourselves (John 5:41; 7:18). During his lifetime Jesus always drew attention to God the Father (John 13:31). He demonstrated time and again that he was seeking to know and accomplish the will of his Father (John 4:34).

   In like fashion, in his daily life the disciples of Jesus seek to draw attention to their Master. They want Jesus Christ to be known, loved, listened to, and obeyed. For this reason when one person is accompanying another on the Way of transformation, following Jesus, it is Jesus, and no one else, who occupies the center of that relationship. The most important aspect is not the privileged relationship shared by the two disciples. That relationship is meaningless apart from the fact that it focuses on Christ and 'gives him weight'. For this reason I find it awkward, for example, to speak of someone with the words, "Here is my disciple". Or to say, "I am the disciple of this or that person". All that we are doing is walking together for a period of time in the footsteps of Jesus. Both of us are his disciples. We belong to him, we are not inappropriately attached to each other as seems to have been the case for the believers in Corinth who said, "I follow Paul"; another "I follow Apollos"; another, "I follow Cephas" (1 Cor 1:12).

   Moreover, one does not accompany others on the path of discipleship in order to demonstrate one's superiority. On two different occasions the disciples who followed Christ on the roads of Galilee argued among themselves about which of them was the greatest (Luke 9:46, 22:24). Jesus had to correct them. We do not accompany others with the goal of showing our own greatness, our intelligence or even our spirituality. It is rather an act of obedience and of service that we render to Christ and to the Father.

2. **Jesus 'gave weight' to God the Father by embracing the cross** (John 12:24).

Jesus was glorified by going through death. He is the grain of wheat that needed to fall to the ground and die in order to produce fruit for the Father. The link between the crucifixion and glorification is therefore fundamental. Perhaps you find that thought shocking. Is it not true that the disciples saw the cross as the ultimate degradation, and so much so that it scandalized them and made them doubt the 'glory' and divine makeup of the mission of their Master? "Unless a kernel of wheat falls to the ground and dies, it remains only a single seed. But if it dies, it produces many seeds" (John 12:24). These words allow us to understand that the "glorification of Christ is in his death, *insomuch as his death produces much fruit*" (Grossouw, W. 1958, 136, emphasis mine).

We cannot separate the death of Jesus (understood as a defeat), from his resurrection (understood as a victory) for the simple reason that his death continues to bear fruit. The *doxa* divine of Jesus is manifested in his passion, for it is in his death on the cross that God accomplished the act that opens salvation to us. So we can say that the death of the Savior on the cross, *and* his resurrection form one single event in which he revealed the active presence of the Father. It follows that if we can say that the *doxa* of God is revealed in the resurrection (John 13:31–32; 17:1, 5), the essence of that glory is found in the fact that Jesus voluntarily embraced the cross (John 1:14; 8:50, 54; 12:28; 13:31–32).

If the extraordinary presence of God is tied to the death of Jesus on the cross, then it is not really a sign of spiritual maturity to focus exclusively on the resurrected Christ who is seated at the right hand of the Father, as is the case for many believers in our worship services. Even when the cross is not ignored in these services, the gaze of the faithful is fixed in a different direction. Here in Africa, and around the world, we hear preachers claim that a child of God should not be poor or suffer. The cross of Christ is honored as the means of our salvation. But the glory of God, his active presence, is more recognized in the idea that once Christ has been accepted by faith, the Christian has found the answer to all the evils of this physical world. So believers seek after, and celebrate, a victorious God. They rejoice in the idea of a God who is gloriously powerful, who blesses his children with health and wealth. To obtain those blessings the believers are invited to make positive statements of their faith. With the prevalence of this kind of teaching it is not surprising that the glorification of Jesus in his death on the cross is largely ignored.

Be that as it may, the fact that God is glorified in the fecundity of death is not a reality that is unique to the experience of the Savior. It is also the case for the disciple of Jesus. Christ claimed that just as the kernel of wheat which falls to the ground must die to bear fruit (John 12:25) the disciple must follow his example of 'detesting his life in this world' if he wants to be 'honored' by the Father (John 12:26). The principle of life and honor in death is the law of the kingdom of God (Beasley-Murray 1987, 211). Fruitfulness is costly. It is in dying to ourselves that we bring life to others.

Jesus offered the Jews of his time a new vision of life. The glory of God was, in their understanding, to be seen in conquests, acquiring wealth, and in power. Jesus, on the other hand, saw it in the cross. He taught that life is born only in death, and that the one conserves his life only in giving it for others (John 12:25; Mark 8:35; Matt 10:39; 16:25; Luke 9:24; 17:33). Paul made the same claim in these words: "For we who are alive are always being given over to death for Jesus' sake, so that his life may be revealed in our mortal body. So then, death is at work in us, but life is at work in you" (2 Cor 4:11–12). Like the apostle, disciples of Jesus learn to give themselves over to death day after day (1 Cor 15:31) in the inner battles that are waged, in the difficult experiences that take place, in the opposition of those who are enemies of the gospel, and in the suffering that God allows that spring from their weaknesses. In order for the harvest to happen, the kernel of wheat must die.

3. **Jesus 'gave weight' to God the Father in his life by doing the Father's will** (John 12:27–28).

John does not give us the details of the agony of Jesus in the place called Gethsemane.[9] Instead, he quotes Jesus: "Now my heart is troubled, and what shall I say? Father, save me from this hour? No, it was for this very reason I came to this hour. Father, glorify your name!" (John 12:27–28). We can say that this prayer of Jesus is the equivalent of the words of Gethsemane: "Yet not as I will, but as you will" (Matt 26:39). And it corresponds also with the prayer that Jesus taught his disciples: "Our Father in heaven, hallowed be your name" (Matt 6:9). The biblical scholar, Raymond Brown, goes even further in his analysis and suggests that the first three requests of the Lord's Prayer are all synonymous (Brown, R. 1966, 476). If he is correct, the hallowing of God's name, the coming of his kingdom, and his will being done "on earth as it is in heaven" are truly the realities that demonstrate his active presence.

For this reason, disciples of Jesus 'give weight to God' in their lives when they pray in all sincerity, "Lord, in the situation in which I find myself at this point in my life, happy or miserable, show me your will so that I can do it, in the power of your Spirit." We must admit that more often than not we ask things of God, we call him to serve our purposes, to do this or that to help us in our current situation. And even when it is not exclusively for ourselves that we ask things of God, we hope that he will act according to what we desire. Sometimes we even fall into the trap of thinking that if we spend long hours in prayer on our knees, if we fast, and if we are faithful attendees of church activities, we will somehow convince God to intervene in our situation. This attitude looks strangely like an attempt to turn God into our servant. All the time we know that we should not put our own will ahead of that of God, or try to manipulate him even through

---

9. Matt 26:36–56; Mark 14:32–50; Luke 22:39–53.

our spirituality. Jesus teaches us that we glorify God when we submit our will to his will.

One last observation at this point. To pray "Our Father in heaven, hallowed be your name" is insufficient. Jesus not only wants to do the will of the Father, he did it! (John 5:30; 6:38). In like manner, Jesus does not send us to make disciples who want to do his will. We cannot be his disciples, nor can we accompany others in discipleship without doing his will. A disciple is not only someone who has received the gospel, or who has been baptized; a disciple is an individual who obeys all that Jesus taught. And our Lord Jesus identifies himself intimately with his disciples who honor him in that way (Matt 12:49–50; Luke 11:127; Mark 3:34–35).

4. **Jesus 'gave weight' to God the Father in his life by finishing the work that God had given him to do** (John 17:4).

Just hours before being betrayed and then suffering his passion on the cross, Jesus prayed using these words: "I have brought you glory on earth by completing the work you gave me to do" (John 17:4). Notice how Jesus ties the revelation of the *doxa* of God on earth to the work that he had accomplished. If our chief aim is to glorify God (give him weight) and enjoy him forever, then, according to the prayer of Jesus, we know that this is accomplished by fulfilling the mission that he has given us. This eliminates all opposition between worship and the act of accompanying someone in discipleship. All worship which does not lead to the formation of disciples of Jesus is sterile, and does not really 'give weight' (or glorify) to God. The act of accompanying someone on the path of discipleship in the footsteps of Jesus is in itself an act of worship, a glorification of the Father and the Son. In order to strengthen my argument in this sense, I want to examine more closely this text.

Here Jesus speaks of glorifying God *on earth*. In heaven there will be a different way of 'giving weight' to God that will not include what we are doing in this sense today. The missionary mandate that we have received from the Lord Jesus, we can only fulfill in making disciples of Jesus during our days on earth. Jesus warned us: "As long as it is day, we must do the work of him who sent me. Night is coming, when no one can work" (John 9:4).

This text also speaks of a *specific limitation*: ". . . the work you gave me to do." The work of Jesus Christ was limited from several standpoints. First from the geographic perspective, since his entire career was limited to the interior of Palestine. He saw neither Rome, nor Athens, nor Alexandria. His ministry was also limited by his human experiences. He never knew the intimacy of marriage, the joys and trials of fatherhood, or even the challenges of old age. His teaching, healing and deliverance ministry was also limited. There were multitudes of needy people in Palestine who never benefitted from his ministry in word or in act. Yet, in spite of these limitations, his ministry was complete and perfect since he had done all that the Father had given him to do. He could therefore say, in complete honesty, "I have completed the work you gave me to do." And like Jesus, every disciple is limited in his or her ministry! We are neither called to evangelize the entire world, nor to intervene to alleviate all human suffering, nor to plant churches where they are absent. We are called to do one specific work – make disciples of Jesus!

Finally, this text speaks of a *necessary accomplishment*. The glory of God, his active presence, is not manifested only in the enthusiastic undertaking of the work that he has given us to do, but also in its completion. But isn't there something shocking in these words of Jesus? In his prayer, Jesus claims that at the moment he is speaking to God he *has already* finished the work that the Father had given him to do! How could he make this claim? This is prior to his death on the cross for our sin! How could he say that he had already finished his work? He prays, "I have brought you glory on earth, by completing the work you gave me to do." In the rest of his prayer, Jesus prays for his disciples (John 17:6–26). The interpretation is clear. The disciples were the work his Father had given him to do! Accordingly, he revealed the Father to them (v. 6). He had given himself entirely to the Father on their behalf, so that they would also be truly his (v. 19). The work that the Father had given him was to make disciples. The work that he gives us today is also to make disciples. "As the

Father has sent me," Jesus would say shortly after his resurrection from the dead, "I am sending you" (John 20:21).

We will return to the prayer of Jesus recorded in John 17 in the last chapter of this book. But for now I want to close our reflection with one small phrase from the mouth of the Master. In verse 10, speaking of his disciples, Jesus claims: "Glory has come to me through them." In other words, Jesus certifies that his disciples revealed his active presence on earth! Later, Paul would say something similar when he writes that God makes the light of his active presence in the face of Christ shine in the heart of the disciple (2 Cor 4:6). Because the disciple learns how to give Jesus his 'weight', his appropriate place in his life, the *doxa* of Jesus and of the Father shines for all to see. For this reason Paul could attest that the presence of Christ in the life of the disciple is his "hope of glory" (Col 1:27). And to the believers in Ephesus he could speak of the fullness of God that fills the disciple and that is at work powerfully in him (Eph 3:19–20). The disciple of Jesus is the place where the *shekinah* of God is to be found today. He is the 'sanctuary' of the Spirit of Jesus!

Questions to Think About:

1. The author began this chapter with a quote from the words of Paul to the Corinthians, "whatever you do, do it all for the glory of God." After reading this chapter, how would you interpret these words?

2. Jesus certified in his prayer of John 17 that his disciples showed his glory (John 17:10). Yet, shortly after that prayer, his disciples would abandon him, Peter would deny him, and Judas would betray him. What relationship do you see between the weaknesses and failures of his disciples and the glory of Jesus in their lives?

3. The author argues that Jesus was crowned with glory when he received the crown of thorns on his head and was crucified. Why might some people find that teaching to be scandalous today? What is your own reaction to this perspective?

8

How to Begin and Sustain a Disciple-Making Accompaniment

Jesus was a great communicator. Mark tells us that "the large crowd listened to him with delight" (Mark 12:37). And the Gospels speak of several incidents when large crowds followed him into deserted places, far from the ordinary tumult in order to listen to him and profit from his ministry. People pressed so hard on him that at times he had to get away to avoid being crushed (Mark 3:9). From time to time he could not even take the time to eat (Mark 3:20). But John tells us that Jesus did not measure the success of his ministry by the size of the crowd that he attracted. He did not trust those people who followed him because he knew they only enjoyed the sound of his voice or were attracted to the miraculous signs that he performed (John 2:24).

We can say today that the crowd looks a lot like the multitude that surrounded Jesus in his day. It is much more interested in seeking the works of God than it is in seeking God himself. All around us in Africa, where the churches are full, we witness crowds that love motion, noise, excitement and spectacular occurrences. That which is emotional and fantastic receives its approval. The crowd follows Jesus uniquely out of self-interest. It is focused on itself. In spite of this fact, isn't it true that we measure success by the number of people we draw? Jesus did not trust large crowds, for he knew the real motivation of the multitudes that surrounded him (John 2:25).

One particular incident can help us to understand what interested Jesus and his way of measuring success. In Luke 19, we read how Jesus, surrounded by a large multitude of people, noticed the presence of a small man who had climbed a sycamore-fig tree to see him. A few minutes of special attention given by Jesus to this man named Zacchaeus was enough to change his life. If we had been in the place of Jesus, we would have undoubtedly fixed our eyes on the size and enthusiasm of the crowd that was "praising God" (Luke 18:43). Instead, Jesus focused on a desperate individual. We are happy to gather a multitude who will listen to the Word of God. Jesus sought disciples rather than to settle for a crowd of people who are really only interested in hearing a pleasant speech, or witnessing miracles or marvelous phenomenon.

In this chapter I will explain how we can enter into and maintain a relationship of personal accompaniment in the footsteps of Jesus. You have undoubtedly noticed that from the beginning of this book I have not used the usual expression, 'make disciples', but I prefer to speak of a 'personal accompaniment'. I attempted to demonstrate in chapter 5 that only God can 'make disciples of Jesus', since he alone can deeply transform lives. Our role, I claimed, is to work in synergy with the Holy Spirit, in *accompanying* the individuals who find themselves confronted by the teaching of Jesus, in a position of vulnerability and openness.

According to the Oxford American Dictionary, 'accompaniment' is the action of going with or traveling with as a companion or helper. It is the act of being present with, of escorting or guiding. In the context of our study, this expression contains the notions of help and support. This personal assistance can take several forms. The help that I am advocating in this chapter is more *informal* than formal. This accompaniment is also more *reciprocal* than hierarchical. It is also a way of traveling with someone in the footsteps of Jesus that is more *suggestive* and *evocative* than directive. The accompaniment that I am describing here is more *unofficial* than official, more the practice of *laypeople* than that of their pastors or other 'Christian professionals'. This way of going with someone who wants to better follow Jesus is more *individualized* and *private*, than it is public and predetermined. Above all, this accompaniment is *relational*!

How to Initiate a Personal Accompaniment in the Footsteps of Jesus

It all starts by the act of accompanying someone in a prayer in which he acknowledges his sinfulness, and casts himself on the grace of God for forgiveness. It is a prayer wherein the person renounces his sin and expresses his faith in Jesus who has entirely paid his debt through his death on the cross. In this prayer the person also expresses his confidence in the resurrected Christ and welcomes him as the Lord and Master over his life. After leading an individual in such a prayer of conversion, I have developed the practice of inviting that person to meet with me for a few minutes the following day.

Before going to the place of meeting, I ask God to guide the time that I will spend with the new convert. I ask him to grant me discernment so that I will know how best to respond to the questions that the individual will inevitably ask. I pray that he will grant me the grace to listen actively, so that I can understand what is going on that does not show up on the surface – the motivations, the fears, the needs, the desires and the goals of this person. Finally, I ask that God will reveal to me what he is doing exactly in the life of that person.

When the new believer arrives at our meeting place, I welcome him and ask how the first hours of his new life with Jesus have been, what he feels, and if he has shared with anyone else the conversion experience that has just taken place. If the person affirms that he has indeed shared his conversion experience, I ask him to explain how he described the event and the reactions of the person with whom he has shared. After those minutes of discussion, I invite my friend to pray with me that our heavenly Father would guide us as we meditate on his Word.

Then we read together Luke 10:38–42:

> As Jesus and his disciples were on their way, he came to a village where a woman named Martha opened her home to him. She had a sister called Mary, who sat at the Lord's feet listening to what he said. But Martha was distracted by all the preparations that had to be made. She came to him and asked, "Lord, don't you care that my sister has left me to do all the work by myself? Tell her to help me!"
>
> "Martha, Martha," the Lord answered, "you are worried and upset about many things, but only one thing is needs. Mary has chosen what is better, and it will not be taken away from her."[1]

---

1. This method of accompaniment can also be used with illiterate people, or among those who live in cultures that are oral-based. In this case, one reads the text, and then asks the person who is being accompanied to give the contents of the text in his or her own words. If the person does not furnish the important elements of the text in his or her rendition, you can give an instruction such as: "Listen once again to the text, but this time give special attention to (. . .)" (Terry 2008, 96–97). Repeat the process until the person can express the message of the text accurately. Then move on to the stage of asking questions that I propose in this chapter.

After reading this text aloud, I ask several questions like: What is happening in this incident? What do you think might have motivated Martha to act as she did? What might have motivated Mary? What does the fact that Mary was sitting at Jesus' feet listening to him suggest? How did Jesus evaluate the situation? In your opinion what did Jesus mean when he said, "Martha has chosen what is better?" What can we learn from this incident about our own relationship to Christ? In what ways will you apply these lessons to your own life?

We end our time together with a prayer asking that our heavenly Father enable us by his Spirit to put into practice the lesson that we have learned through our meditation on the life of Jesus. Then we set up the time and place of our next meeting.

This example illustrates one way to begin a relationship of personal accompaniment as disciples of Jesus. When you are accompanying a new convert it is true that she has much to learn. In the Great Commission Jesus clearly said that we are to teach others to 'obey everything' that he has commanded. For that reason one cannot accompany a person in discipleship who is unwilling to learn how to live according to the Word of God.

We can understand that the apostles followed the pattern that is spelled out in the Great Commission because it is said of the new believers in Jerusalem that they "devoted themselves to the apostles' teaching" (Acts 2:42). They were immediately instructed in scriptural truth about Jesus. "Like newborn babes," writes Peter, "crave pure spiritual milk, so that by it you may grow up in your salvation, now that you have tasted that the Lord is good" (1 Pet 2:2–3).

Notice the Form of that Accompaniment

No one can deny the importance of solid biblical instruction in the process of the spiritual edification of believers. Any mission or ministry that does not give healthy instruction in the Word of God does not fit the New Testament model. This being the case, we should also note that the form of that instruction varied greatly. However, this is not the impression that we get when we observe Christian gatherings today. On the contrary, we see all around us a communicational uniformity. It is as if we are convinced that our televangelists and our preachers are imitating the way that Jesus communicated. However, this is simply not true.

It is consternating to see just how poorly we have understood Jesus' way of communicating! In the name of Jesus Christ, who very rarely used monolog, we wrongly advocate preaching (a monolog) as the most appropriate way of communicating. Our misunderstanding comes primarily from the fact that Catholic and Protestant preachers have been formed by the university training that they have received. And that training is based on the presence of a professor who shares his knowledge with an auditorium full of students. Keep in mind the fact that the reformers, Luther and Calvin and the others, were all academicians. They were trained through the process of listening to lectures. And while they correctly judged that their faithful needed more teaching, they unfortunately used the same model that dominated the society of their time. For this reason they made preaching the center of the meetings they held. But perhaps there is yet another reason why we think that preaching is the most appropriate way to communicate the gospel message. I am referring to a poor translation of the biblical text:

> It seems to me utterly inexcusable for our Bible translators to reduce the nine or more Greek words used in the New Testament for communication to two words in English: preach and proclaim. But this is what has been done in most of our English translations, in spite of the fact that in New Testament times these words were used to cover a much wider area. The main word, *kerusso*, for example, signified to put across a message given by someone else to the communicator in whatever way was appropriate in the given context (see Kittel on *kerusso*). If one term is to be used in English, that term should be 'communicate', not preach or proclaim, both of which signify monolog presentation. I am afraid we have not imitated Jesus in church communication nearly so much as we have imitated the Greek love for oratory. Jesus seldom, if ever, monologued. He interacted. (Kraft 1991, 25)

This observation concerning the poor translation of the word *kerusso* in the English versions of the Bible also apply to the French translations of the New Testament text. This misunderstanding of the way in which Jesus communicated undoubtedly influences our manner of passing on to others what we have ourselves received. For instance, on occasion a friend or seminary student will inform me that he 'preached the gospel' to the taxi driver, or to another person that he just happened to encounter. Another example comes to mind. Look at what takes place in our Sunday school classes or Bible studies. More often than not, they look like 'mini worship services', complete with teaching that is dispensed in monolog.

I began this chapter with the statement that Jesus was a great communicator who drew crowds. We might think that what made his teaching so attractive and effective was his way of telling parables, or the strength of his preaching. But this conclusion would ignore the importance of the questions that he asked before, during, and after those times of teaching (Stein 1978, 23). He asked questions with a precise goal in mind, with the purpose of drawing a response, exposing error, and bringing to the forefront deep truths. For Jesus, the crucial questions dealt with attitudes, relationships, values and the responses of the heart. Jesus sought deep understanding that would bring life transformation. For that reason he asked pertinent questions (Willis Jr. & Snowden 2010, 66–67). In order to better understand Jesus' way of communicating let's look at some of the questions that he asked:

Questions Jesus Asked

If you love those who love you, what reward will you get? (Matt 5:46)

If you greet only your brothers, what are you doing more than others? (Matt 5:47)

Who of you by worrying can add a single hour to his life? (Matt 6:27)

Why do you worry about clothes? (Matt 6:28)

Why do you look at the speck of sawdust in your brother's eye and pay no attention to the plank in your own eye? (Matt7:3)

Do people pick grapes from thornbushes, or figs from thistles? (Matt 7:16)

Why are you so afraid? (Matt 8:26)

Why do you entertain evil thoughts in your hearts? (Matt 9:4)

Which is easier: to say, "Your sins are forgiven," or to say, "Get up and walk"? (Matt 9:5)

How can the guests of the bridegroom mourn while he is with them? (Matt 9:15)

Do you believe that I am able to do this? (Matt 9:28)

What did you go out into the desert to see? (Matt 11:7)

To what can I compare this generation? (Matt 11:16)

If any of you has a sheep and it falls into a pit on the Sabbath, will you not take hold of it and lift it out? (Matt 12:11)

How can anyone enter a strong man's house and carry off his possessions unless he first ties up the strong man? (Matt 12:29)

You brood of vipers, how can you who are evil say anything good? (Matt 12:34)

Who is my mother, and who are my brothers? (Matt 12:48)

Why did you doubt? (Matt 14:31)

Why do you break the command of God for the sake of your tradition? (Matt 15:3)

How many loaves do you have? (Matt 15:34)

Do you still not understand? (Matt 16:9)

Who do people say the Son of Man is? (Matthew 16:13)

Who do you say I am? (Matt 16:15)

What good will it be for a man if he gains the whole world, yet forfeits his soul? Or what can a man give in exchange for his soul? (Matt 16:26)

How long shall I stay with you? How long shall I put up with you? (Matt 17:17)

From whom do the kings of the earth collect duty and taxes – from their own sons or from others? (Matt 17:25)

What do you think? If a man owns a hundred sheep, and one of them wanders away, will he not leave the ninety-nine on the hills and go to look for the one that wandered off? (Matt 18:12)

Why do you ask me about what is good? (Matt 19:17)

What is it you want? (Matt 20:21)

Can you drink the cup I am going to drink? (Matt 20:22)

What do you want me to do for you? (Matt 20:32)

John's baptism – where did it come from? Was it from heaven, or from men? (Matt 21:25)

What do you think? (Matt 21:28)

Have you never read in the Scriptures? (Matt 21:42)

Why are you trying to trap me? (Matt 22:18)

What do you think about the Christ? Whose son is he? (Matt 22:42)

Which is greater: the gold, or the temple that makes the gold sacred? Which is greater: the gift, or the altar that makes the gift sacred? (Matt 23:17, 19)

How will you escape being condemned to hell? (Matt 23:33)

Why are you bothering this woman? (Matt 26:10)

Could you men not keep watch with me for one hour? (Matt 26:40)

Do you think I cannot call on my Father, and he will at once put at my disposal more than twelve legions of angels? (Matt 26:53)

But how then would the Scriptures be fulfilled that say it must happen in this way? (Matt 26:54)

Am I leading a rebellion, that you have come out with swords and clubs to capture me? (Matt 26:55)

My God, my God, why have you forsaken me? (Matt 27:46)

Why are you thinking these things? (Mark 2:8)

Do you bring in a lamp to put it under a bowl or a bed? Instead, don't you put it on its stand? (Mark 4:21)

What shall we say the kingdom of God is like, or what parable shall we use to describe it? (Mark 4:30)

Why are you so afraid? Do you still have no faith? (Mark 4:40)

What is your name? (Mark 5:9)

Who touched my clothes? (Mark 5:30)

Why all this commotion and wailing? (Mark 5:39)

Are you so dull? (Mark 7:18)

Don't you see that nothing that enters a man from the outside can make him 'unclean'? (Mark 7:18)

Why does this generation ask for a miraculous sign? I tell you the truth, no sign will be given to it. (Mark 8:12)

Why are you talking about having no bread? Do you still not see or understand? Are your hearts hardened? Do you have eyes but fail to see, and ears but fail to hear? And don't you remember? (Mark 8:17–18)

When I broke the five loaves for the five thousand, how many basketfuls of pieces did you pick up? (Mark 8:19)

When I broke the seven loaves for the four thousand, how many basketfuls of pieces did you pick up? (Mark 8:20)

Do you still not understand? (Mark 8:21)

[To the blind man] Do you see anything? (Mark 8:23)

Why then is it written that the Son of Man must suffer much and be rejected? (Mark 9:12)

What were you arguing about on the road? (Mark 9:33)

Salt is good, but if it loses its saltiness, how can you make it salty again? (Mark 9:50)

What did Moses command you? (Mark 10:3)

Why do you call me good? (Mark 10:18)

What do you want me to do for you? (Mark 10:51)

Why are you trying to trap me? (Mark 12:15)

Do you see all these great buildings? (Mark 13:2)

Are you asleep? (Mark 14:37)

Could you not keep watch for one hour? (Mark 14:37)

Why were you searching for me? (Luke 2:49)

Didn't you know I had to be in my Father's house? (Luke 2:49)

Why are you thinking these things in your hearts? (Luke 5:22)

Which is easier: to say, "Your sins are forgiven", or to say, "Get up and walk"? (Luke 5:23)

Why do you call me, "Lord, Lord", and do not do what I say? (Luke 6:46)

Where is your faith? (Luke 8:25)

What is your name? (Luke 8:30)

Who touched me? (Luke 8:45)

Will you be lifted up to the skies? (Luke 10:15)

What is written in the Law? How do you read it? (Luke 10:26)

Which of these three do you think was a neighbor to the man who fell into the hands of robbers? (Luke 10:36)

Did not the one who made the outside make the inside also? (Luke 11:40)

Who appointed me a judge or an arbiter between you? (Luke 12:14–15)

Who of you by worrying can add a single hour to his life? (Luke 12:25)

Why don't you judge for yourselves what is right? (Luke 12:57)

Or suppose a king is about to go to war against another king. Will he not first sit down and consider whether he is able with ten thousand men to oppose the one coming against him with twenty thousand? (Luke 14:31)

Salt is good, but if it loses its saltiness, how can it be made salty again? (Luke 14:34)

Suppose one of you has a hundred sheep and loses one of them. Does he not leave the ninety-nine in the open country and go after the lost sheep until he finds it? (Luke 15:4)

Or suppose a woman has ten silver coins and loses one. Does she not light a lamp, sweep the house and search carefully until she finds it? (Luke 15:8)

So if you have not been trustworthy in handling worldly wealth, who will trust you with true riches? (Luke 16:11)

Were not all ten cleansed? Where are the other nine? (Luke 17:17)

And will not God bring about justice for his chosen ones, who cry out to him day and night? Will he keep putting them off? (Luke 18:7)

However, when the Son of Man comes, will he find faith on the earth? (Luke 18:8)

For who is greater, the one who is at the table or the one who serves? (Luke 22:27)

Why are you sleeping? (Luke 22:46)

For if men do these things when the tree is green, what will happen when it is dry? (Luke 23:31)

What are you discussing together as you walk along? (Luke 24:17)

What things? (Luke 24:19)

Did not the Christ have to suffer these things and then enter his glory? (Luke 24:26)

Why are you troubled, and why do doubts rise in your minds? (Luke 24:38)

Do you have anything here to eat? (Luke 24:41)

What do you want? (John 1:38)

Why do you involve me? (John 2:4)

You are Israel's teacher, and do you not understand these things? (John 3:10)

I have spoken to you of earthly things and you do not believe; how then will you believe if I speak of heavenly things? (John 3:12)

Will you give me a drink? (John 4:7)

Do you want to get well? (John 5:6)

How can you believe if you accept praise from one another, yet make no effort to obtain the praise

that comes from the only God?
(John 5:44)

If you do not believe Moses'
writings how will you believe me?
(John 5:47)

Where shall we buy bread for these
people to eat? (John 6:5)

Does this offend you? (John 6:61)

What if you see the Son of Man
ascend to where he was before!
(John 6:62)

You do not want to leave too, do
you? (John 6:67)

Have I not chosen you? (John 6:70)

Has not Moses given you the law?
(John 7:19)

Why are you trying to kill me?
(John 7:19)

Why are you angry with me for
healing the whole man on the
Sabbath? (John 7:23)

Where are they? Has no one
condemned you? (John 8:10)

Why is my language not clear to
you? (John 8:43)

Can any of you prove me guilty of
sin? (John 8:46)

If I am telling the truth, why don't
you believe me? (John 8:46)

Why then do you accuse me of
blasphemy because I said, 'I am
God's Son'? (John 10:36)

Are there not twelve hours of
daylight? (John 11:9)

Do you believe this? (John 11:26)

Where have you laid him?
(John 11:33)

Do you understand what I have
done for you? (John 13:12)

Don't you know me, even after I
have been among you such a long
time? (John 14:9)

Who is it you want? (John 18:4,7)

Shall I not drink the cup the Father
has given me? (John 18:11)

Is that your own idea, or did others
talk to you about me? (John 18:34)

Why question me? (John 18:21)

If I spoke the truth, why did you
strike me? (John 18:23)

Why are you crying? Who is it you
are looking for? (John 20:15)

Friends, haven't you any fish?
(John 21:5)

Do you love me? (John 21:17)

What is that to you? (John 21:22)

This is not a complete list of the questions that Jesus asked the various people he encountered. However, I hope that it helps you to realize that, in his way of communicating, Jesus is quite unlike our televangelists or our preachers. In reality, in order to accompany someone in discipleship we must learn how to communicate like he communicated. And hold on to this, the disciples who accompanied Jesus on the roads of Galilee remembered him as a master in the art of asking questions. According to their testimony, one can say that even after his resurrection from the dead, Jesus continued to communicate through the use of questions.

Our problem is that, like many others, certain believers like to teach, give counsel, and correct those around them. They realize that they are carriers of a message that is the response to the most important questions that can be asked concerning existence. Encouraged by the example of their pastors, and by a poor translation of the Greek word *kerusso*, they are convinced that they are to preach, and that others are to listen. Other believers, on the contrary, believe that they cannot accompany anyone in discipleship because they don't themselves sufficiently know the Bible, or feel incapable of teaching. These people know that they cannot respond to the questions that might be asked, or 'preach the gospel' to a neighbor. Both of these examples reveal a poor understanding concerning Jesus' way of communication, and of the type of communication that takes place in a discipling relationship.

A Description of Discipleship Accompaniment

Here is the way in which I describe the relationship of accompaniment in discipleship. It is the relationship of:

> *Two apprentices who, during a short or longer period of time, voluntarily and freely, decide to encourage, exhort, and build up each other with the goal of becoming more like their Master, under the direction of the Holy Spirit.*

Let's look at each of the components of that description.

"Two apprentices . . ."

I am referring to the relationship between two people who see themselves as 'apprentices', or novices, even though one of them may have begun following Jesus much earlier than the other. I want to stress again that this accompaniment is not the exclusive work of pastors, missionaries, evangelists or seminary students. It is the relationship between two 'ordinary' believers who want to grow in their relationship to Christ (Anderson & Reese 1999, 27).

It is therefore an exchange between two people that takes place within a specific context. The dominant aspect of this context is that it is relational. Ultimately, the accompaniment in discipleship is grounded in the conviction that two friends can help each other to understand and live more faithfully to the teaching of Jesus (Prov 27:17). And if this seems self-evident, it is simply because we are naturally relational beings. According to the traditional etymology, the word 'person' comes from the Latin word, *persona*, which is itself derived, according to Keith Anderson and Randy Reese, from the Greek *prosopon*, which can be translated by 'face-to-face' (1999, 21). Each human being is a person in so much as he or she is face-to-face', or turned toward, another human being in dialogue. In the accompaniment in the footsteps of Jesus, we experience a 'being-with' of a person and his neighbor that reflects and serves the 'being-with' of a person and God (Blocher 1988, 97).

Once again, that 'being-with' is specifically a face-to-face in which each is submitted to the other (Eph 5:21) in an attitude of mutual benevolence, humility and openness. It is a relationship composed of transparence and confidence in which the two partners help each other to be honest with themselves and with God. It is an exchange in which one speaks openly, and opens one's heart to the other without fear (2 Cor 6:11).

When you accompany someone in the footsteps of Jesus, your responsibility is to nurture the *process* of dialogue, more than it is to watch over its *contents* (Webb 2012, 32–33). When I speak of the 'contents' of the dialogue, I refer to its subject, or the facts, opinions and information that is exchanged. The 'process' of dialogue refers to the way in which the dialogue handles its contents. Look again at the example that I gave earlier in this chapter. Had I given priority to the contents of the dialogue, I would have given a lecture on the meaning of the biblical text (Luke 10:38–42). I would have insisted on the fact that it is important that the disciple determine a moment each day when, like Mary, she goes to the feet of Jesus to listen to him. I would ask the other person to commit herself to begin that practice. However, by accentuating the process, I do not allude to a personal quiet time, nor do I attempt to explain its importance. Instead, I accompany the other person in a way that allows her to discover for herself the joy one experiences when one goes to the feet of Jesus to listen to him. I do not say that God wants to speak to her through his Word. By accompanying the individual in this experience, through my presence and by the questions that I ask, she hears the voice of God. And she gains a conviction the she must spend time regularly listening to Jesus. Not because I have said so, but because she has experienced it. Moreover, without even being aware of what is happening, she is already learning how to have a quiet time. And she is growing in an understanding of how to apply what she discovers in the Word of God in her daily life (Clinton & Clinton, 1991; Hendricks, 1995).

I am a university lecturer and a pastor. The different schools, universities and seminaries that I have attended have shaped me to teach, to propose ideas, and to find solutions. All of that is the 'content'. This explains why, in spite of all that I have just written, when I am in a relationship of accompaniment, my first impulse is to create a curriculum, prepare a class, propose a meditation, or lead a Bible study. My training was focused above all on the 'content', and not on the 'process'. Yet what is it that gives a conversation the power to really transform lives? Is it the 'process' or the 'content'? (Kraft 1991, 37; Anderson & Reese 1999, 17). I am convinced of this truth. In the accompaniment of someone in discipleship, the 'content' alone does not bring transformation! Transformation is linked above all to the quality of the relationship, to the experience of being listened to and 'questioned', and to the motivation that comes from having someone who believes in you. One can go so far as to affirm that the acquisition of new knowledge only plays a secondary role in the process (Stoltzfus 2005, 290).

". . . under the direction of the Holy Spirit."

When we accompany a believer on the path of discipleship, we must remember that he is also the temple of the Holy Spirit. The Spirit of Jesus, the Spirit of Truth (John 14:16–17) who teaches and reminds us of what Jesus said and did lives in him (John 14:26). Neither you, nor I, can take the place of the Holy Spirit. In our desire to help, this is something that we can easily forget. Our knowledge, our experience, our discernment and our intuition can persuade us, wrongly, that we have what the other person needs (Webb 2012, 31).

What can we do to resist the temptation to respond before we have really listened (Prov 18:13)? We can ask God to give us wisdom and discernment by his Spirit (Jas 1:5). We can also try to not react too quickly to the questions or shady areas that we identify in the other person's life (Jas 1:19). When we see something in the life of the person that we are accompanying, we are not obligated to say it (at least not at once). Growth does not happen when we see a need in the life of the person whom we are accompanying, but only when the person whom we are accompanying is ready to acknowledge his need. Progress in the knowledge of Christ is progressive (2 Pet 1:2–11). Don't be in too big a hurry. That will allow you to be flexible. Personal accompaniment in discipleship is particular. What has helped one person that you have accompanied will not necessarily help another. What was useful for the person you are accompanied in the past may not be so useful today.

Fundamentally, the question that is raised is whether or not you really trust the work of the Holy Spirit in the life of the person you are accompanying. Are you convinced that *it is not your responsibility* to make the person you are accompanying into a disciple of Jesus? Even though the Holy Spirit can use you in that work, he alone has the power to transform a person. That is his responsibility. We have the privilege of working in synergy with him so that the conditions that foster transformation are optimal. Recognize also that it is not your responsibility to 'correct' everything that you find wrong in the lifestyle or doctrine of the person you are accompanying. It might be that the Holy Spirit will use you to help that individual to straighten up some part of his life (as was the case of Daniel in my own life in the example that I gave in chapter 5). However, it might be that he intends on using some other means, or perhaps some other time, to change that aspect of the life of the person you are accompanying.

You must realize that God was already at work in the life of the person you are accompanying before you ever entered the picture. After you are gone, he will continue his work. As the apostle Paul wrote: "Being confident of this, that he who began a good work in you will carry it on to completion until the day of Christ Jesus" (Phil 1:6). Our role is to discern what God is doing in the life of the person we are accompanying, and then join him in that transforming activity.

"... voluntarily and freely,"

The partners enter into the relationship voluntarily and freely. This is not a relationship that is imposed by a pastor or a shepherd. If in this type of discipleship relationship the partners do not truly esteem or care about each other they will not be able to truly trust each other. And while it is true that a relationship can be cultivated when two people feel secure and confident about each other, it is equally true that such a relationship cannot be forced or imposed.

The partners enter into this relationship voluntarily. Tony Stoltzfus tells how, when he was seventeen years old, he desired desperately to find a person who could accompany him in a relationship like that which I am describing in this chapter. "If only," he writes, "I had a person whom I respect and who could help me to understand and live the Christian life!" He shares that adolescence was a difficult period in his life, marked by spiritual solitude. He says that several years later he was sharing about that difficult period of his youth with a retired friend of his father who had been one of the members of the faith community of his adolescence. After listening to his testimony, this man responded: "Do you know what? At that same time I wanted to invite you to spend some time with me learning more about Jesus together but (. . .) I was afraid to take the initiative to talk to you" (2005, 282). What a tragic testimony! God had heard Tony's prayer for someone to accompany him in discipleship. But he never received the accompaniment for which he had prayed.

It is evident that this kind of relationship does not happen haphazardly. And I must add that there is not one good and one bad way of initiating such an accompaniment. You can do it simply by inviting someone to meet with you in order to learn together how to better follow Jesus Christ. You could also invite the person to do a Bible study with you on the notion of discipleship in order to see if he is interested in going deeper in his walk with Christ. If you already have a good relationship with the person, you might suggest re-centering the relationship around the person of Jesus.

I want to insist again on the voluntary character of this very unique relationship. It is a relationship in which each of the partners learn concretely how to not only look to their own interests, but also the interests of the other (Phil 2:4). The spiritual growth of the other is what is most important. And toward that end each partner offers the other the gift of relationship, the gift of listening, and the generosity of hospitality. This is especially true for the person who is the most advanced in the faith. When you accompany young believers, for instance, it is their needs that should guide you in deciding the content of your conversations, their goals, solutions and applications.

"... during a short or longer period of time ..."

There are accompaniments that last for several weeks, others for a few months, and in some cases they can even last for years. What is important is not the duration of the accompaniment, nor the frequency of the one-on-one encounters, but their usefulness. This accompaniment is really transformational because it is focused on what God is doing in the life of the person who is being accompanied. It is during the times when that person is receptive and ready to learn, or when life circumstances are squeezing and putting pressure on him, that accompaniment is especially transformational. When a personal accompaniment that aims toward spiritual growth is added to such a situation, the potential for deep transformation is magnified.

Because the accompaniment does not exist for itself, but is justified only to the extent that it fosters life transformation, when one or the other of the partners no longer feels that the relationship is playing that role, the accompaniment should be terminated (at least in this form). The end of a relationship of accompaniment does not mean that it failed! This you can be sure of. God will continue his work in the life of the person you have accompanied, moreover, through the process of accompanying the other person you have also been enriched and edified in your life with Christ. Remember that the person is not your disciple! He belongs to Christ, and it is he who allowed you to have this experience with him.

"...encourage, exhort, and build up each other..."

When you accompany someone in discipleship you are doing several things in that relationship that encourage that person, that push her to take responsibility for her life, and that propels her forward.

The first of these edifying elements is the fact that you listen to her. This is very rare in our cultures where we tend to finish the sentence that the other person has begun, or to speak more loudly than the other in order to make our opinion known. Second, you are asking questions. The art of asking the right question at the appropriate time is the most important tool that you will use in the accompaniment of a disciple of Jesus. Third, you will observe more than you will speak. There are many areas of life where we know that we all need to progress: to become a better parent, a more loving spouse, to make better use of our time, etc. However, before intervening in the life of the other person, one must take the time to discern the area where the Holy Spirit is actively at work. Fourth, you will act more like a coach and a mentor than like a supervisor.[2] As a coach you will seek to develop the competency of the

2. In popular use, the *counselor* orients, the *coach* develops a competency or capacities in a given domain, the *consultant* recommends and the *mentor* tends not only to develop the motivation and creativity of the person he is mentoring on a professional level, but also to

individual, whereas the mentor seeks, like an experienced guide, to develop the character. When you accompany someone in discipleship you are playing this double role. In the fifth place, you will suggest practical actions that can be done to stimulate spiritual growth (for example: to fast for a day, to read a book, to do a Bible study, to memorize a biblical text, to write a letter to someone, to give her testimony, to help a neighbor in need, etc.). But these tasks are always assigned while respecting the free will of the person you are accompanying. Sixth, you will be doing her the enormous favor of holding her responsible for choices that are made. To be responsible means to give an account for a specific aspect of one's life. Finally, you will demonstrate your friendship and commitment to that person by allowing her to question you about what she sees in your life that is not yet fully conformed to the image of Christ.

Although it is true that the 'process' is more important than the 'content', we do have 'content' to communicate in the act of accompanying someone in discipleship. The apostle Paul said to the believers living in Colossae: "So then, just as you received Christ Jesus as Lord, continue to live in him, rooted and built up in him, strengthened in the faith as you were taught, and overflowing with thankfulness" (Col 2:6–7). It is important to observe that, in this instruction, the New Testament does not give us an exact sequence to follow. It is also clear that everything cannot be learned immediately or at the same time (Hesselgrave 1982, 305–306). I think nevertheless that every new believer should grow in the orientations, competencies and practices mentioned below:

— Voluntary submission to the authority and lordship of Jesus Christ through the confession of sin, and daily offering of one's self to him as a living and holy sacrifice (Luke 6:40; 9:23; Rom 6:3–4; 12:1–2).

— Regular time spent feeding one's self spiritually through the reading, hearing, and study of the Word of God. Learning to take every thought captive to the obedience of Christ (through meditation), and seeking to change ways of acting so as to comply with the Scriptures (John 8:31–32; 14:21; Phil 4:8–9; 2 Cor 10:5).

— Grow in intimacy and communication with God in prayer. Learning to rely on God for one's own needs, as well as the needs of others, while

---

foster his personal development through a high quality human relationship.

asking that his will be done. This prayer should also be characterized by thankfulness, praise and worship (John 14:13–14; 15:7; 16:23–24; Phil 4:6–7).

— Grow in charity, in the image of Christ, by placing one's self at the service of others, believers or not, in humility and generosity (Gal 5:13; Phil 2:3–8; Jas 2:14–17; Isa 58:6–12).

— To care for the spiritual, social, mental and physical health and development of other believers (Heb 10:24–25; Phil 2:3–4; John 13:34–35).

— Allowing one's self to be led by the Holy Spirit (Rom 8:4–14; Gal 5:16, 25).

— Regularly profiting from the ordinances (or sacraments) that Jesus Christ has established for the spiritual health of his disciples (Matt 18:20; Mark 14:22–25; Luke 22:15–20; 1 Cor 11:23–25).

— Being neither a rebel nor independent. Actively seeking to discover how the abilities, talents, spiritual gifts and life experiences that shape one's identity can be placed at the service of others (Rom 13:1–12; 1 Pet 5:5–6; Heb 13:17; 1 Cor 13).

— Growing in the art of reconciliation. Becoming an artisan of peace. Pursuing actively the unity of the disciples of Jesus (John 17:20–21; Rom 12:8; 2 Cor 5:17–21).

— Remaining faithful to one's commitments. Being a person who keeps his or her word even when it is costly to do so (Prov 20:6; 1 Cor 4:2–5; 2 Tim 2:2; Rev 2:10, 13).

— Managing one's finances and other goods according to biblical principles (Matt 6:19–21, 25–34; Luke 6:38; Prov 11:24; Phil 4:19).

— Living one's sexuality in faithfulness to biblical teaching (Gen 2:24; Gal 5:19; 1 Thess 4:3; 1 Cor 6:13).

— To be a perpetual learner. To not be satisfied with progress already made, but to seek actively to grow in the quality of one's relationships with others, in one's intellectual life, and in divine wisdom (Rom 12:3, 16; Prov 10:17; 12:1; 25:2; 27:7).

— To grow in the art of listening to others and that of asking pertinent questions that help them to progress (Prov 18:2; 20:5; John 11:41–42; Jas 1:19).

— Regularly lead non-believers to Jesus Christ through one's personal testimony in act and in word. To accompany those people not only in their initial conversion experience, but also as disciples of the Master (Matt 4:19; 6:33; 28:19–20; 2 Tim 2:2).

This list is more suggestive that exhaustive. It can be enlarged to include other convictions or abilities such as: how to live like a disciple of Jesus in family relationships, how to give and receive counsel, how to develop a Christian worldview, how to resist demonic attack, how to set and maintain priorities, how to manage one's time, how to discover and act according to one's spiritual gifts, how to lead a small group Bible study, how to exercise spiritual discernment, how to be a spiritual director.

"... with the goal of becoming more like their Master."

"Those God foreknew he also predestined to be conformed to the likeness of his Son" (Rom 8:29). It is with these words that Paul declares that God wants us to grow and develop the characteristics of Jesus Christ. To be like Jesus means a transformation of our character and of our personality. Paul wrote: "... put off your old self, ... to be made new in the attitude of your minds; and put on the new self, created to be like God in true righteousness and holiness" (Eph 4:22–24).

Unfortunately we witness millions of Christians who get older, but don't ever seem to grow. They are stuck in a sort of perpetual spiritual infancy. One of the principle causes of this state of affairs is the fact that these people have never profited from a personal accompaniment that fosters that kind of growth. Spiritual growth is not something that automatically happens. It depends on a solid commitment to become more like Jesus, which motivates the individual to enter into a relationship of spiritual accompaniment. One must want to change, decide to grow, and enter actively into a relationship that liberates the action of the Holy Spirit. This process of life transformation into the likeness of Jesus always seems to begin by a decision that is made by two people.

Contrary to popular belief, God's priority is not our material well-being. He seeks rather to change our character. In this chapter I have argued that this transformation is tied to a *process* more than it is based on the acquisition of *knowledge*. Our practices strangely resemble the ways in which the Greeks trained people. Their model was academic, based on a monolog that took place in a small group setting or in a classroom. It was a method in which the apprentice was passive and the instruction was theoretical. This should not surprise us since the Greek philosophers gave more importance to ideas than they did to concrete reality. The model of accompaniment in the footsteps of Jesus that I have described is closer to a Hebrew understanding of training. Their model was relational and focused more on experience than on theoretical explanations. For the Hebrews, the trainer communicated with the apprentice in dialogue and through an active and practical exchange. The role of the trainer in this model was to stimulate the apprentice through the questions that he asked.

Conclusion

Accompanying someone in the footsteps of Jesus is like playing soccer. In reading a book about this sport you would undoubtedly develop a good theoretical understanding of the game. However, if the following day you were to go to the playing field, you would see for yourself that you would be no better at making a pass or scoring a goal that you would have been had you never read the book. The book can, certainly, give you the information that you need in order to succeed, but only through practice can you obtain a real competency. When one wishes to play a sport professionally, one must train one's self in order to develop the necessary muscles, the motor reflexes and necessary confidence. In the same way the reading of a book can offer you the conceptual understanding that is necessary in order to accompany someone in discipleship. However, that understanding will not be able to 'automatically' transform your relationships with others. Through your past experiences and training, you have acquired a certain way of acting which is not necessarily appropriate for the accompaniment of others. For this reason you must discover the process of accompanying someone else through your own experiences. And don't fool yourself – this will take work. To accompany others in a transformational relationship will undoubtedly require a change in your ways of thinking and of acting.

Questions to Think About:

1. In your opinion, why did Jesus ask so many questions? What are the strengths and weaknesses of teaching through the use of questions?

2. Think of someone whom you could accompany for a period of time in the footsteps of Jesus. How might you present that idea to him or to her? What is keeping you from doing it?

3. Among the areas that are touched by discipleship, and that are mentioned in this chapter, on which aspect of your own life do you feel that God is actually at work? Who among the people that you know, could accompany you in a one-on-one relationship with the goal of fostering deep life transformation in that area of your life?

9

The Disciple of Jesus, the Demon, and Deliverance

Nearly forty years ago, Robert Boyd Munger (1910–2001) wrote a brochure that has become a classic of Christian literature and that sold more than ten million copies. In that work entitled "My Heart – Christ's Home", the author imaginatively explores what it might mean to invite Jesus into the home of our heart (Munger, 2002). From one room to the next, we consider with our Lord what he wants from us. Are we ready to spend time with him each day in the living room? In the dining room, we examine the appetites that should or should not control us. Is there a cupboard in our life that he wants to help us to clean out? The goal of the pamphlet is to help us to examine what it means to make Jesus Christ the Lord of each aspect of our life.

Personally accompanying someone on the path of discipleship has this same objective. However, sometimes in the process we sometimes run up against roadblocks – moments when the person we are accompanying finds it difficult to advance for reasons that even he or she does not understand. These barriers are sometimes the work of demonic forces.[1] Recognizing and dealing with this kind of obstacle to spiritual transformation is the subject of this chapter.

---

1. There are more than one hundred references to demons in the New Testament. Four Greek words refer clearly to demons: *daimon* is found one time (Matt 8:31); *daimonion* is found 63 times, *pneumata* (spirits) forty-three times; and on several occasions the general word for angels, *angelos*, is used to designate demons (Matt 25:41; Rev 12:7, 9).

Can the Disciple of Jesus be Demonized?

For one year I had the privilege to serve as teaching assistant to Dr Charles Kraft, once a missionary in Nigeria, and at that time professor of anthropology and intercultural communication at Fuller Theological Seminary School of Intercultural Studies. During that period, Dr Kraft offered, once a week, a time when seminary students could meet with him for personal prayer. One evening, as I remember it, a man around thirty years of age, came, accompanied by his wife. This committed Christian complained that he no longer desired to spend time reading the Word of God. He also shared that he found it difficult to pray. Dr Kraft asked this man when this had started. After a short time of reflection the person was able to answer. Then Dr Kraft asked if there had been any unusual or significant things that had taken place in his life at that time.

Immediately the man's face lit up. "It was at that time that I was healed," he exclaimed joyfully. He then went on to explain that he had been born with one leg that was shorter than the other, and how all of his life he had to wear a corrective shoe on one foot to compensate for the shorter leg. He explained that he had suffered much from this physical condition and had often asked for divine healing. During the time period in question, he had attended a Christian gathering during which he had been healed. His short leg 'grew' several centimeters, and since then he could wear normal shoes without stumbling.

After listening to this testimony, Dr Kraft asked him, "Don't you find it curious that your lack of appetite for the Word of God and your difficulty in prayer began at the same time that your leg was healed?" The young man said that he had never made a connection between the two phenomena. Dr Kraft continued the conversation stating that there was, perhaps, no link between his physical healing and his spiritual difficulties, but he asked if the man would be willing to 'test' his healing to see whether or not it came from God. The man seemed troubled by the thought that his healing might not have come from God, since he was a Christian, a seminary student, committed to Christ, and the healing had happened during a Christian meeting. How could a healing under those conditions not have come from God? How could his healing not be a response to his many prayers?

Dr Kraft suggested that he pray something like this: "Heavenly Father, if the healing of my leg came from you, I accept it with joy. However, if it did not come from you, I reject it. I would rather limp in my flesh and walk upright with you."[2] The man followed Dr Kraft's suggestion and prayed that prayer. In the following instant, his leg shortened. He left our time together limping, but he had recovered his hunger for the Word of God and for prayer.

Here we have one example of a disciple of Jesus who experienced blockages in his walk with the Master, the origins of which were spiritual. This story illustrates the fact that the Evil One is very active in both the lives of the believers and the unbelievers. His demons must sometimes be confronted when the person seeks to submit specific areas of his or her life to Jesus Christ. Dr Kraft testifies:

> Since my occupation is teaching missionaries and international church leaders, I frequently get to cast demons out of these dear people. Many have inherited demons. Others have become demonized through cursing by the people they have worked among. On one mission station, I met at least four missionaries who had experimented with Satanism in their school days, and several who had been into communal experiments involving sexual promiscuity. Some were still struggling with pornography. What often happens to people with such backgrounds is that they get gloriously converted and give themselves for the Lord's work without getting cleaned up. The demons within them are smart enough to lie low until the people get involved in something really important to God's Kingdom, and then they sabotage them. I have met missionary after missionary who has had a crippling demonic experience at a crucial time in his or her ministry. (Kraft 1997, 250–251)

There has been a lot of discussion around the question of whether or not a Christian can be demonized. One of the problems is with our terminology. One often hears the expression 'demon possessed'.[3] This is unfortunate, since the word 'possession' implies ownership. In reality, the demons do not own

---

2. Dr Kraft has experienced several cases of legs that have lengthened, and other healings during his sessions (Kraft 1989, 127).

3. Pentecostals traditionally distinguish between 'demonic possession' and 'demonic influence'. And while affirming that a believer might be oppressed by the demon, Pentecostal commentators categorically refuse the possibility of 'demonic possession' among Christians (McClung 1990, 206). Evangelicals seem to agree to say that a Christian cannot be 'possessed' by the demon (Reddin 1990, 191). Dr Kraft maintains that we should avoid using the terms like 'possession' or even 'oppression' when speaking of demonization. He prefers to find degrees of demonization on a scale of one to ten, with the level 1 being the weakest 'attachment' of a demon to a person, and 10 the strongest (1989, 129).

anything – nothing belongs to them! The New Testament considers them to be squatters, or invaders who occupy places that do not belong to them. In reality, even the demons belong to God since he is their creator and their judge. Moreover, the notion of demonic 'possession' evokes all kinds of false ideas and fosters fear.

All of us wish that the believer were exempt of all demonic habitation, but experience tells us otherwise. Those who deal regularly in the area of spiritual deliverance frequently help Christians find spiritual freedom. Here is what C. Fred Dickason, whose book entitled *Demon Possession & the Christian* looks extensively at this question, writes:

> I have encountered from 1974 to 1987 at least 400 cases of those who were genuine Christians who were also demonized. (. . .) I would not claim infallible judgment, but I know the marks of a Christian and the marks of a demonized person. I might have been wrong in a case or so, but I cannot conceive that I would be wrong in more than 400 cases. (1987, 175)

Dr Kraft writes that he had encountered more that five hundred cases of demonization of people who were "undeniably committed to following Christ" (1997, 250). The testimonies of others concur on this point.[4] All these testimonies lead us to believe that Christians can be demonized. Dickason concludes his testimony with a challenge:

> The burden of proof lies with those who deny that Christians can be demonized. They must adduce clinical evidence that clearly eliminates any possibility in any case, past or present, that a believer can have a demon. (. . .) Further, we must note that those who deny that Christians can be demonized generally are those who have not had counseling experience with the demonized. Their stance is largely theoretical. (Dickason 1987, 175–176)

I would however like to underline an important fact that is not always mentioned by those who examine the subject of demonization:

> Demons cannot live in a Christian in the same way that he is indwelt by the Holy Spirit. The Spirit of God enters the believer at the moment of his salvation, and indwells him permanently (John 14:16). By contrast, a demon enters as an invader and as

---

4. See for example (Bubeck 1975; Koch & Lechler 1978; Murphy 1992; Unger 1977; White 1990).

a squatter who can legitimately be cast out at any moment. The demon never legitimately inhabits the life of a saint as the Holy Spirit does. (Unger 1977, 51–52)

Dr Kraft maintains that when a human being gives himself to God, the Holy Spirit attaches himself to the most intimate part of his being – the 'spirit' or 'heart'. However, even though after the new birth the demons cannot touch that area which is exclusively and eternally reserved for the Spirit of God, they can, in his opinion, influence other areas of the believer's life:

> I conclude, therefore, that demons cannot live in that innermost part of a Christian, the spirit, since it is filled with the Holy Spirit (see Rom 8:16). That part of us becomes alive with the life of Christ and is inviolable by the representatives of the enemy. *Demons can, however, live in a Christian's mind, emotions, body, and will.* We regularly have to evict them from those parts of Christians. I suspect that one reason a demon can have greater control of an unbeliever is because it can invade even the person's spirit. (1994, 91)

I have often heard Dr Kraft compare demons to detestable rats. Rats damage property and transmit dangerous diseases. They are rodents that prefer run down and humid places, sewers and garbage. They are attracted to unhealthy places where waste has accumulated. If we discover rats in our house, we must locate what it is that has attracted them. According to Dr Kraft, it is the same for demons:

> Inside a human being, emotional or spiritual garbage provides just such a congenial setting for demonic rats. Wherever such emotional or spiritual garbage exists, demonic rats seek and often find entrance. If, however, the garbage is disposed of, the rats cannot stay or, at least, cannot remain strong. With people as with homes, the solution to the rat problem is not to chase away the rats but to dispose of the garbage. *The biggest problem is not the demons, it is the garbage.* (Kraft 1994, 97)

I agree fully with Dr Kraft on this point. Demons are most often tied to wounded emotions or to sins (and often to the two at the same time). The demon looks for a place where it can attach itself to us in order to hinder our progress (Eph 4:27). The Evil One found no place of access into the life of Jesus (Matt 4; Luke 4; 22:53; John 14:30; Heb 2:8; 4:15; 5:7–8). But he did find access into the life of Peter (Luke 22:31–34). And his agents continue to successfully enter into the lives of many believers. Authentic believers, born-again and Spirit-filled, can (through exceptional conditions, created by their own sin, or the sins of others), experience complete or partial control of their life by a demon (Murphy 1990, 60).

The Power of the Demon is in Deception

I do not pretend to deal with all of the aspects of demonology in this chapter. I do not address either the activity of demons in the life of a non-believer, or his or her deliverance through the intervention of a saint. Neither do I examine the warfare against the demons that the apostle Paul labels 'rulers', 'authorities' and 'spiritual forces of evil in the heavenly realms' (Eph 6:12). I am limiting my discussion here to the evil spirits that can be at work in the life of a disciple of Jesus. And in the life of a disciple of Jesus, I claim that deception is the master strategy of the enemy of our soul. In Revelation 12:9 Satan is described as the one who 'deceives' or who 'leads the whole world astray'. He is the one who deceived Adam and Eve and led them into error (Gen 3) and demons do the same thing in their efforts to sidetrack the disciple of Jesus and stymie his progress.

When someone deceives another person, he leads him to make a mistake in judgment. The person is led to take something for something else. The theologian Krister Stendahl writes in this line: "What blocks our vision, is not so much what we don't know, as what we think we do know" (Stendahl 1976, 7). Many in the west, for example, think they know that demons don't exist. And even those who do acknowledge their existence fool themselves into thinking that they are not active today. There are some Bible schools and seminaries, for instance, who teach that even if the first disciples of Jesus cast out evil spirits, and healed the sick, their actions were exceptional and shouldn't be copied today (Acts 5:12–14). Some people say: "The Great Commission instructs us to teach and to baptize, but does not mention casting out demons or healing the sick." These individuals have been fooled by demons when they conclude that we should limit our ministry to teaching (Brown, 1979).

Africans and other peoples dwelling in the Southern hemisphere have no problem admitting the presence and activity of demons. Their traditional cosmologies are filled with the spirits of the ancestors, genies, fees, and capricious forces of all kinds that can disturb the balance of an individual.

When the members of these societies suffer, they tend to think that someone has cast a spell on them, or that there is an evil spirit at work against them. This perspective largely explains the proliferation of exorcists, healers, and tribal chiefs who 'know' the remedy and can apply it to the situation. No, the majority of people in the world are not fooled into thinking that demons do not exist or are inactive.

However, demons fool some disciples of Jesus who live in these parts of the world when they convince them that they cannot fight, themselves, against their power. It is easy to think that only pastors, apostles, or other 'men of God' can fight against demonic powers. One easily develops the thought that God responds favorably to the prayers of those who are obedient and victorious over sin. But when one has sinned, when love for God has become cold, when one doesn't feel particularly 'spiritual', or when one has abandoned the Word of God – then one thinks logically that God reacts by withholding his blessing. However, even if there is some truth in this logic, the demon fools us in exaggerating the importance of our piety, and in downplaying the generosity of God's grace in our understanding.

Demons wish to intimidate us. Sometimes the reality of sin and the presence of the demon seem much more real to us than the presence and activity of God. This is part of Satan's deception. But the demon's power is limited, and he has already been defeated by the death and resurrection of Jesus Christ. One of his tricks is to make us believe that we are helpless against him. But Jesus taught throughout his ministry that if he expulsed demons, that meant that the kingdom of God is already present among us (Luke 11:20). All during his lifetime Jesus showed that he acted with the authority of God. He came to defeat Satan both during his time in Galilee and by his death and resurrection. Jesus also showed clearly that he shared his authority with his disciples. He gave power and authority to the Twelve so that they could cast out evil spirits and heal the sick (Luke 9:1–2). The same is true for the seventy-two (Luke 10:9). Armed with that authority, they were to demonstrate that "the kingdom of God is near" (Luke 10:9). Later, he would say to his disciples: "As the Father has sent me, even so send I you" (John 20:21). And as we have seen in chapter 3, Jesus ordained his disciples to teach others to "put into practice" all that he had taught them (Matt 28:19). He had promised: "Anyone who has faith in me will do what I have been doing. He will do even greater things than these, because I am going to the Father" (John 14:12).

Sometimes demons fool disciples of Jesus into believing that if they are active in their life, it is certainly because they have a spiritual problem. Dr Kraft affirms that, in most cases, the presence or absence of a demon has nothing to do with the spiritual condition of the individual, except to degrade it. He writes that the people who show signs of demonic activity in their life are, "very often very mature spiritually in spite of the impeding spirits inside them." "They usually have become demonized," he continues, "through inheritance, through some kind of abuse, or through pre-Christian involvements, rather than through spiritual failure and rebellion. But the demons have pushed them to fear the worst" (1994, 93).

One of the methods that the demons use to trick us, is to accuse us. The word Satan, originally meant 'the one who accuses' (Unger 1977, 972). Many of the accusations brought against us by the demons are negative thoughts or phrases that we have heard others say about us, either imagined or real. One of the preferred tactics of demons is to push us to accuse ourselves, accuse others, and accuse God for the difficult circumstances in which we find ourselves:

> Demons encourage such things as rumors, disrupted relationships based on misunderstandings and anger at God, and blame of God for things he allows to come our way. Among their devices are pushing people to retain guilt even after they have received forgiveness from God, convincing people that there is something incurably wrong with them, enticing people into blaming themselves for abuse they have received from others, and strongly suggesting that the troubles they experience are from God and are deserved because of their failures. They also like to push people to blame others or God for their difficulties. (Kraft 1994, 95)

In the Sermon on the Mount (Matt 7:22–23) and in his Olivet Discourse (Matt 24:4, 23–25), Jesus took deception very seriously. The disciple of Jesus pays special attention to these warnings. The first stage of seduction is being fooled to believe that one cannot be seduced. If Paul feared that the Thessalonians or the Corinthians would be deceived, it is probably not because they were beyond deception (2 Thess 2:2; 2 Cor 11:2–4). The disciple of Jesus remembers that since Satan disguises himself as an angel of light (2 Cor 11:14), it is not strange that the demons do not act openly. Like him, their aim is to "steal and kill and destroy" (John 10:10). Dr Kraft points out that even though the demons cannot create problems out of nothing, they can, and do, use things that already exist. For that reason, he writes, "They push, prod, tempt, and entice people to make bad or at least unwise decisions. They work to make bad things worse and to get people to overdo good things so that they are no longer positive" (Kraft 1994, 91–92).

The Disciple of Jesus and Deliverance

If it is true that demons, like rats, are attracted to trash, the disciple of Jesus has every reason to guard against the deception that he has no elements in his life that need to be cleaned up (1 John 1:8). Many disciples of Jesus suffer from demonization because they hold onto bitterness, they don't forgive others, they seek revenge, they live in fear, etc. Others open the door to demons because they give in regularly to temptations (like drugs, pornography or sexual promiscuity, lying). There are also those who inherit demons through the sins of their forefathers, through curses, pledges, initiation into secret societies, and by the traumatic experiences of their ancestors, etc. Apparently the demon has no entry into those people who are spiritually clean (John 14:30; Prov 26:2). However, there are many people (even believers) who are carrying around enough garbage and dirt to allow the enemy access into their lives.

Based on the analogy of demons and rats, Dr Kraft draws the conclusion that demonic infestation always implies a problem on two different levels: a human problem, and a demonic problem. And he argues that there is never a problem that is *either* emotional *or* spiritual. In his understanding it is always a problem that is *both* emotional and spiritual. And he states: "If there is a demon, there is automatically an emotional or spiritual problem that must be resolved, either before, or after, expelling the demon" (Kraft 1997, 244).

Sometimes the expulsion of a demon is experienced as a violent and desperate fight between two powers. Neil Anderson maintains that we should understand it rather as a battle between truth and deception (Anderson, 1990). Jesus said, "If you hold to my teaching (. . .) then you will know the truth, and the truth will set you free" (John 8:31–32). It is because of deception that the entire world has come under the domination of evil powers (1 John 5:19). To come back to the image developed by Dr Kraft, we must begin by 'cleaning up' the trash through the application of the truth. He affirms that when we proceed in that fashion, demons lose their grip almost always without violence (Kraft 1997, 244). Anderson has grouped into seven different categories the domains where the demons invade the life of a believer: (1) occultist experiences and secret societies, (2) deception, (3) bitterness, (4) rebellion, (5) pride, (6) willful sin, and (7) the sin of ancestors, including curses (Anderson 1991).

What follows has been adapted from his article.

Steps to Deliverance in Christ

These steps can be taken by the person whom you are accompanying in discipleship. Individuals who find themselves blocked somewhere in their walk with Christ should pray the prayers and affirmations of faith that follow. If a demon manifests its presence during the session, you can simply affirm out loud that it must be quiet, and that it can do no harm to either of you during or following the session. The session should begin with prayer, confession of one's weakness, and the request that the Holy Spirit take charge of the session (Kraft 1989, 149–151).

Imitation vs. Authentic

The first step toward freedom in Christ consists in renouncing all past or present participation in the occult, cults and other religions inspired by Satan. You must cut off ties to any activity or group of people who deny Jesus Christ, offer spiritual guidance or counsel from sources other than the Word of God, or who require secret initiation. A disciple of Jesus has no reason to actively participate in a group where there is not total transparency in all of its actions (1 John 1:5–7).

It is necessary not only to choose the truth, but also to renounce Satan and his lies. There is no 'neutral' territory when it comes to the truth.

You can do a sort of written spiritual inventory where you mention all of the spiritual experiences of the individual whom you accompany in order to identify all of the occult practices in which he has been involved.

<u>Prayer</u> (to be read by the person you are accompanying):

> Heavenly Father, I ask you to reveal to me all occult practices or
> false religions in which I have been involved, along with any false
> prophet that I have listened to or followed, be it consciously or
> subconsciously (Ps 139:23–24).

Write down anything that God reveals to you. Once the list is complete, pray the following:

Confession:

> Lord, I confess that I have participated in _____.
> I ask you to forgive me for that involvement, and I renounce _____, which is not an example of what is best for me.

Deception vs. Truth

God desires truth in the inner parts of the human being (Ps 51:6). For this reason Paul exhorts us to put off falsehood and speak and act truthfully with those around us (Eph 4:25).

Prayer:

> Dear heavenly Father, I know that you desire truth in my inner being (Ps 51:6) and that facing this truth is the way to liberation (John 8:32). I acknowledge that I have been deceived by the father of lies (John 8:44) and that I have deceived myself (1 John 1:8). I pray in the name of the Lord Jesus Christ that you, heavenly Father, would rebuke all deceiving spirits by virtue of the shed blood of the Lord Jesus Christ and his resurrection, and that I, by faith, having received you into my life, and being seated with Christ in the heavenly realms (Eph 2:6), I command all deceiving spirits to depart from me during this time of prayer to be sent wherever the Lord Jesus Christ sends them. I now ask the Holy Spirit to guide me into all truth (John 16:13), and ask that you would "search me, O God, and know my heart; test me and know my anxious thoughts; and see if there be any offensive way in me, and lead me in the way everlasting" (Ps 139:23–24). In Jesus' name I pray. Amen.

Bitterness vs. Forgiveness

Probably no area of the life of a Christian is more often the entry point for satanic forces than that of bitterness (2 Cor 2:10–11). God asks us to whole-heartedly forgive our brothers and sisters, otherwise we will be turned over to our tormentors (Matt 18:34–35).

We should face up to the fact that God does not treat us according to what we deserve. Rather, he graciously comes to our help according to his mercy. In like fashion we should be merciful, as our heavenly Father is merciful (Luke 6:36). We should forgive as we wish to be forgiven (Eph 4:32).

However, forgiving is not forgetting. Those who attempt to forget the offense find that it is impossible. God declares that he "will remember no more" our sins and lawless acts (Heb 10:17); yet, he is all-knowing and cannot forget. What this text means is that he chooses not to use our past against us (Ps 103:12).

Not remembering the offense can sometimes result from forgiveness, but it is never the means of forgiveness. When we bring up past hurts and the situation wherein someone has made us suffer, we have not truly forgiven him. Forgiveness is a choice, a critical phase of our will. When God asks us to forgive, he knows that we are capable of forgiveness. At the same time we find it difficult to not remember an offense because it goes against our idea of justice. We would rather pursue revenge for the injustices that we have experienced. However, the Scriptures specifically tell us not to 'take revenge' (Rom 12:19).

So we protest: "Why should I wipe the slate clean?" It is true that you wipe the slate clean, but God never overlooks someone's wickedness. He will deal with it impartially – something that we are incapable of doing. Rather than retaliate when he was mistreated, Christ entrusted himself to him who judges justly (1 Pet 2:23).

When you fail to forgive those who mistreat you, or who sin against you, you remain tied to them. When you forgive the offense, you not only act in his favor, you are doing what is best for you – reclaiming your freedom. The need to forgive is an affair not so much between yourself and the person who has offended you, as it is between you and God (Matt 6:14–15).

So how does one go about forgiving wholeheartedly? Ask God to remind you of those people you should forgive while reading aloud the following prayer:

Prayer:

> Dear heavenly Father, I thank you for the riches of your kindness, forbearance and patience, knowing that your kindness has led me to repentance (Rom 2:4). I confess that I have not extended that same patience and kindness toward others who have offended me, but instead I have harbored bitterness and resentment. I pray that during this time of self-examination that you would bring to

mind only those people that I have not forgiven from my heart in order that I may do so (Matt 18:35). I also pray that if I have offended others that you would bring to my mind only those people from whom I need to seek forgiveness and to what extent I need to seek it (Matt 5:23–24). I ask for your guidance that I should not fall short of your will, and that in no way would I go beyond it. I ask this in the precious name of Jesus. Amen.

Place the list of those people who have offended you at the foot of the cross:

Heavenly Father, I forgive _____ (his or her name) for _____ (the wrong that he or she did to you)

Rebellion vs. Submission

We live in the midst of a rebellious generation. We are also tempted to rebel against authority. The Word of God shows how we are to respond to authorities: civil authorities (Rom 13:1–5; 1 Tim 2:1–4; 1 Pet 2:13–16), family authorities (Eph 6:1–3; 1 Pet 3:1–2), and professional authorities (1 Pet 2:18–21). Accepting to submit to human authorities is a proof of our faith.

Ask God to forgive you for the times when you have not been submissive. Having confessed all deliberate rebellion that you have displayed, pray the following prayer aloud:

Prayer:

Dear heavenly Father, you have said that rebellion is as the sin of witchcraft and insubordination is as iniquity and idolatry (1 Sam 15:23), and I know that in action and in attitude I have sinned against you with a rebellious heart. I ask for your forgiveness for my rebellion and pray that by the shed blood of the Lord Jesus Christ that all ground gained by evil spirits because of my rebelliousness would be cancelled. I pray that you would shed light on all my ways that I may know the full extent of my rebelliousness so that I will choose to adopt a submissive spirit and a servant's heart. I pray that you would guide my examination in this area – that it would not be of self but of you. In Jesus' name I pray. Amen.

Pride vs. Humility

Pride is deadly. It says, "I can do it alone, I don't need God." According to James 4:6–10 and 1 Peter 5:1–10 many spiritual conflicts happen because of pride. Express your commitment to live humbly before God through the following prayer:

Prayer:

> Dear heavenly Father, you have said that pride goes before destruction and an arrogant spirit before stumbling (Prov 16:18). I confess that I have not denied myself, picked up my cross, and followed you (Matt 16:24). In so doing I have given the enemy ground in my life. I have believed that I could be successful and live victoriously by my own strength and resources. I now confess that I have sinned against you by placing my will before you and by centering my life around self instead of you. I now renounce the self-life and by so doing cancel all the ground that the enemies of the Lord Jesus Christ have gained in my members. I ask you to fill me with your Holy Spirit and teach me to walk in faith by the Holy Spirit in order that I may glorify you in my body (1 Cor 6:19–20). I crucify the flesh with its passions and desires (Gal 5:24) and no longer place any confidence in the flesh (Phil 3:3). I pray that you will guide me so I will do nothing from selfishness and empty conceit, but with humility of mind regard others as more important than myself (Phil 2:3). I ask this in the name of Christ Jesus my Lord. Amen.

Bondage vs. Freedom

The disciple of Jesus learns how to escape the spiral of sinning, confessing that sin, then sinning again, by giving an account of his life to the person who is accompanying him in the footsteps of Jesus (Jas 5:16). This is what David did when he wrote Psalm 51. The goal of this process is not gossip, or self-abasement, or relief from feelings of guilt. It is an act by which one allows a person of confidence to know one's weaknesses and failures so as to obtain prayer support. In this action, the disciple of Jesus relies on the promise of God that when we confess our sins, he is faithful and just and will forgive us our sins and purify us from all unrighteousness (1 John 1:9).

Pray the following prayer,

Dear heavenly Father, you have told us to put on the Lord Jesus Christ, and to make no provision for the flesh in regard to lusts (Rom 13:14). I acknowledge that I have given in to fleshly lusts which wage war against my soul (1 Pet 2:11). I thank you that in Christ my sins are forgiven, but I have transgressed your holy law and given the enemy an opportunity to wage war in my members (Eph 4:27; Jas 4:1; 1 Pet 5:8). I come before your presence to acknowledge these sins and to seek your cleansing (1 John 1:9) that I may be freed from the bondage of sin (Gal 5:1). I now ask you to reveal to my mind the ways that I have sinned and grieved the Holy Spirit.

List all the sins of the flesh, then pray:

Prayer:

I now confess these sins, and ask for your forgiveness and cleansing. I cancel all ground that evil spirits have gained through deception or by my willful involvement in sin. I now put on the whole armor of God and ask that you, heavenly Father, will fill me with your Holy Spirit that I may be able to stand against the schemes of the devil (Eph 6:10–18). I ask this all in the name of my Lord and Savior, Jesus Christ. Amen.

Acquiescence vs. Renunciation

The last step toward freedom in Christ involves breaking all ties with the sins of your ancestors, and with all curses that may have been made against you (Exod 20:4–5).

If you have been involved in satanic rituals, there is a good chance that you have a spiritual 'guardian' or 'parent'. You must specifically renounce those spiritual relationships along with any blood pacts that tie you to anyone other than Jesus Christ.

Prayer:

As a child of God purchased by the blood of the Lord Jesus Christ, I here and now reject and disown all the sins of my ancestors. As one who has been delivered from the power of darkness and translated into the kingdom of God's dear Son, I cancel all demonic working that has been passed on to me from my ancestors. As one who has been crucified with Jesus Christ and raised to walk in newness of life, I cancel every curse or spell that has been put on me or on any objects of my possession or dwelling. I announce to Satan and all his forces that Christ became a curse for me when he hung on the cross. As one who has been crucified and raised with Christ and now sits with him in the heavenly places, I reject any and every way in which Satan may claim ownership of me. I declare myself to be internally and completely signed over and committed to the Lord Jesus Christ. I now command every familiar spirit and every enemy of the Lord Jesus Christ in or around me to go to the pit and to remain there until the Day of Judgment. I now ask you, heavenly Father, to fill me with your Holy Spirit and I submit my body as an instrument of righteousness, a living sacrifice that I may glorify you in my body. All this I do in the name and authority of the Lord Jesus Christ. Amen.

Deliverance

To win a battle does not mean that the war has been won. Nevertheless, as far as demonic infestation is concerned, the Word of God teaches us that deliverance and freedom in Christ is the inheritance of every disciple of Jesus (John 8:36; 2 Cor 2:14; Gal 5:1, 13; 1 John 5:4–5).

Deliverance from the power of demons comes by the truth, and the strength of the disciple springs from truth, while the strength of the Evil One is grounded in deception and lies. One of the reasons why the disciple of Jesus must seek after truth is because it is the key to his or her victory in the fight against demonic beings.

Questions to Think About:

1. What is your opinion of the affirmation that the confrontation with the demon is more a question of truth than that of power?

2. Among the "Seven Steps to Freedom" described by Anderson, which ones seem the most important in your own life? Which ones seem most important in the lives of the people you are accompanying in Christian discipleship?

3. In your opinion, should these "Steps to Freedom" be gone through by all of Jesus' disciples, or only by those who are experiencing a problem in their spiritual walk? Why?

10

The Disciple of Jesus and *Ecclesia*

I will begin this chapter with a quick examination of the life and work of two men who lived during the same time period. There are many similarities between these two people, between the communities that they founded, and the renewal movements that they initiated. However, there are also some striking and important differences. If I have chosen to open our reflection on the disciple of Jesus and *ecclesia* with the study of these two men, it is because their context strangely resembles our own (Holl, 1980). First, these individuals lived during a period of important cultural transition (between the Middle Ages and the Renaissance). In Africa, we are also in the midst of a period of cultural transition marked, among other things, by the birth of States, rapid urbanization, and the westernization of traditional cultures.

Another similarity between the time period of these men and our own involves religious experience. The religion of that day had commercialized Jesus. Many people became religious leaders out of a desire to earn a living. The teaching that was given to the faithful was either so academic that the ordinary person had difficulty understanding, or so standardized that it was irrelevant. Laymen and laywomen felt used and abused by the religious 'professionals'. And religion was dangerously mixed with power, politics, and warfare. For these reasons and others, people didn't hesitate to practice their religion while all the while following occult spiritualities and returning to traditional beliefs and practices.

Moreover, this was a time period that witnessed the birth of an economic system based on mercantilism and fed by aggressive capitalism. The pursuit of material gain, the greedy desire to possess and the quest for pleasure were the motors of the society. Added to all this, the Christians of that day were at war with Muslims.

I will let you make the comparison between the times of those men and your own context.

Peter Waldo (1140 – 1217)

Peter, a merchant and citizen of the French city of Lyon, profoundly troubled by the sudden death of one of his friends during wild orgiastic revelry, sought out a theologian and asked the way to heaven. In response, he received the instruction of Jesus to the young rich man: "If you want to be perfect, go, sell your possessions and give to the poor, and you will have treasure in heaven. Then come, follow me" (Matt 19:21). Waldo resolved to forsake the world and to put into practice the teaching of Christ. He reimbursed his creditors, distributed all his wealth to the poor, and began begging for his daily bread (Tourn, 1980). Peter gave all his attention to the reading and study of the Bible. It is even said that he translated several of the books of the Bible from Latin into the common language. Inspired by this translated text, he set out to imitate Christ (Jalla, 2003). Antoine Monastier gives us some other details about Peter Waldo:

> He preached the gospel and other things that he had learned by memory in the streets and in other public places. He encouraged men and women to follow his example, drawing them around himself, and teaching them the Gospels. He sent men of every profession, even the most lowly, out into the countryside. These ignorant and illiterate men and women spread all over the land, penetrating into homes and preaching in public places in the towns and villages. (Monastier, 1847)

Peter quickly drew other people who wanted to live according to the teaching of Jesus. His disciples called themselves the 'spiritually poor', or 'the poor of Lyon'. They came from all layers of society, but were for the most part simple people. Most of them were laymen and laywomen. Right from the beginning, in imitating Christ and the apostles, they taught personal piety and good works (Audisio, 1990; Santini, 1999). Detachment from the world and zeal to advance the kingdom of Jesus Christ according to the gospel, were the distinguishing characteristics of this movement. Following what they understood to be the example of Jesus and the apostles, they went out two by two, simply clad, barefooted, living only from what those who listened to them were willing to give them to eat. Even their enemies described them as non-pretentious, skilled, working with their hands, virtuous, not given over to food or drink, sober and honest in their words, forgiving, and considering that it is wrong to accumulate wealth (Le Goff, 1968).

I am using Peter Waldo and his followers as the first example of what I will call '*ecclesia*-movement'. We will come back to examine what precisely I mean by this expression, but first, let's look at the second example, that of a man that the historian, Latourette, describes as "One of the most captivating men of all of Christian history" (1975, 429).

Francis of Assisi (1182 – 1226)

Born in Assisi (in Italy) in 1182, which explains his title, "Francis of Assisi", Francis belonged to a rich family. He lived many of the experiences of the other youth of his day: festivals, adventures, and even warfare during which he was captured, imprisoned and became sick. During his convalescence he felt profoundly dissatisfied with life.

In his pursuit of a better life, Francis began visiting chapels that were in disrepair. One day, while he was in prayer before a crucifix in the chapel Saint-Damien, he heard Christ speak to his heart: "Francis, go, repair my house which, as you can see, is falling into ruins!" Taking that message literally, he sold the merchandise from his father's business in order to undertake the restoration of the old dilapidated chapel (Longpré 1966, 21).

Infuriated by the eccentric behavior of his son, Peter Bernardonne ordered that he reimburse the monies that had been spent and brought him to justice. Francis, who claimed the status of a 'penitent' which placed him outside the jurisdiction of civil authorities, would be called to justice before the bishop. At his audition in the public square of Assisi, during the Spring of 1206, Francis gave back all of the money that he had left, along with his clothes, and finding himself naked said to his father and to the crowd that had gathered: "Until now I have called you 'father' on earth; from this point on I can say 'Our Father who art in heaven' since it is to him that I have given my treasure and in him placed my faith" (Schneider 1953, 32). At that point the Bishop of Assisi decided to take Francis into his protection, and Francis left for Gubbio. On his return to Assisi toward the summer of 1206, he went about begging to obtain from the population the necessary stones for the construction and restoration of several chapels (Arnold & Fry, 1988).

At the start of 1208, while in the chapel of Portioncule, Francis finally understands the gospel message: "Do not take along any gold or silver or copper in your belts; take no bag for the journey, or extra tunic, or sandals or a staff" (Matt 10:9–10). As a result he withdrew into utter poverty, consecrating himself to preaching and winning his daily bread either through manual labor or begging. He exchanged the clothing of a hermit that he had been wearing for a simple tunic. He replaced the belt with a simple cord (Green 1983, 83).

After his 'conversion', Francis went about preaching publicly, and quickly drew others to join him. He taught them to sell all that they possessed, and to give the money to the poor. They were to go out having neither a tunic, nor money, nor food, preaching the kingdom of God and healing the sick. Latourette says that the preaching of Francis and his disciples was 'simple and direct', focusing on the worship of God, repentance, generosity, and the forgiveness of offenses. "It advocated the love of neighbor and enemy, humility, and renouncing of vice, including the vices of the flesh" (Latourette 1975, 431). But what is even more remarkable is the fact that Francis and his companions lived their message. Francis gave away all that he possessed because he wanted to show that it is really possible to trust Jesus in all things. He traveled about barefooted, kissed the wounds of lepers and embracing them because he wanted them to know the love of God. In the middle of winter, he gave to others the clothes off his back to keep them from freezing to death, and he thanked them for the opportunity that they gave him to act in this way. He said: "Preach the gospel all the time, and when necessary, use words."

Francis and his companions are my second example of an 'ecclesia-movement'. However they are not unique. We could, for example, look at Benedict and the monastic movement, Philipp Spener and the *collegia pietatis*, Nicolas von Zinzendorg and the *Unitas Fratrum*, and John Wesley and the early Methodists, as 'ecclesia-movements'. In each of these cases, and in many others that I have not named, we have movements that were born of a desire to live a more radical[1] attachment to Jesus Christ. That deeper and more essential attachment to Christ, seen first in the life of one person, becomes a model for others. It is both a reorganization of habits, of physical discipline, of a commitment to honesty, integrity, purity, a desire to follow the example of Jesus fed by Bible study and prayer, and a commitment to give an account to others, to live responsibly for one's actions.

---

1. The word 'radical' means that which belongs to the essence of a thing, its deep nature. In this sense these historic examples show the *ecclesia* that springs up when men and women apply themselves to learn in community how to live according to the example and teaching of Jesus (Clark 1972, 70).

Jesus says in Matthew 18:20: "Where two or three come together in my name, there am I with them." This is undoubtedly one of the most surprising affirmations of the Holy Scriptures. However, these words come at the end of a teaching that Jesus was giving about sin, conflicts, the need to hold one another responsible for our actions, and repentance. We can therefore understand that Jesus is going far beyond giving the simple promise that he would be present when people gather in a faith community. He is speaking specifically of his presence in the midst of two or three persons who have come together for mutual accompaniment in learning how to live as his disciples.

The *Ecclesia*-institution

Despite the fact that the *ecclesia* was in its origins an informal, relatively unorganized, network of people having a very rudimentary understanding of the faith, but attached to the person of Jesus Christ, Avery Dulles explains that it was slowly institutionalized up to the thirteenth century when that process was accelerated (Dulles, 1987). During the time of Waldo and Francis, Zinzendorf, Wesley and his brother Charles, the *ecclesia* had largely evolved into an institution. One can say that from a historical perspective, the *ecclesia*-institution considered the mass of believers very much like a society that needed to be managed. It was clerical, for it considered the pastors as the center of all power and initiative. It was also judiciary, for it saw itself as mandated to pursue justice and to settle civil disputes. It was triumphalist, for it saw itself as an army that was set against Satan and the forces of evil.

So we find ourselves in front of two historical expressions of the *ecclesia*: the *ecclesia*-movement (based upon laypeople who seek to live according to the teaching of Christ) and *ecclesia*-institution (based upon the pastors who seek to preserve the orthodoxy and orthopraxy of the faith).[2] We will examine the ways in which the members of these two forms of the *ecclesia* see each other, but first we must look at the meaning of '*ecclesia*'.

---

2. These two forms of *ecclesia* remind me of the thesis of Ralph Winter. In his opinion, in the New Testament and throughout the centuries that have followed, these two expressions of *ecclesia* have always coexisted. On the one hand, the ecclesias of the New Testament gathered young and old, men and women. Winter calls these assemblies 'Modalities'. On the other hand, the missionary team of Paul – a 'Sodality' according to Winter, is considered to be a prototype of latter missionary teams. These Sodalities gathered committed workers who were engaged in ministry responsibility that went beyond that of the first structure. Both of these forms are both legitimate and necessary according to Winter (Winter 1995).

What is the *Ecclesia*?

Our word 'church' is a translation of the Greek word *ecclesia* which signifies 'called out of' (from the Greek *ek*, meaning 'out of', and the verb *kaleo*, meaning to 'call'). E. W. Bullinger informs us that this word was used in reference to an "assembly, but more particularly an assembly of citizens, or of a group of them, the 'bourgeois'" (Bullinger 1995, 72). In the New Testament it is used 115 times – on three occasions translated by the word 'assembly', and 112 times where the translators have opted for the word 'church'. A look at the three occasions where this word is translated 'assembly' should suffice to demonstrate the fact that it was not used exclusively to designate Christian assemblies. In effect, Acts 19, in reference to a manifestation against the apostle Paul that took place in Ephesus, states:

> [32] The assembly (*ecclesia*) was in confusion: some were shouting one thing, some another. Most of the people did not even know why they were there (. . .). [35] The city clerk quieted the crowd and said (. . .) [39] "If there is anything further you want to bring up, it must be settled in a legal assembly (*ecclesia*)." (. . .) [41] After he had said this, he dismissed the assembly (*ecclesia*).

We can conclude from this passage that the word *ecclesia* was used to designate non-Christians, and, in this exact case, even to signify an antichristian assembly!

The general meaning of the word *ecclesia* which is 'assembly' is also apparent in the way it is used in the Septuagint.[3] In that version of the Old Testament in Greek, the word is used 71 times, always to translate the Hebrew '*qahal*' which signifies "assembly, company, congregation; and in a larger sense any assembly or multitude of men, of troops, of nations, of the wicked, of the righteous, etc." (Wilson 1987, 92). J. P. Lewis specifies that even if that assembly is often for religious purposes, it may also be for evil counsel or deeds (Gen 49:6; Ps 26:5), civil affairs (1 Kgs 2:3; Prov 5:14; 26:26; Job 30:28), or war (Num 22:4; Judg 20:2) (Lewis, 1980). The assembled (*ecclesia*) armies of the Philistines and the Jews witness the fight between David and Goliath (1 Sam 17:47). In the book of Genesis, (23:8; 48:4) the assembled multitude of nations is labeled (*ecclesia*) and even the dead (Prov 21:16).

---

3. In the third century BC, the Jews of Egypt translated the Bible into their habitual language, Greek. The Septuagint groups the books into four categories (Law, History, Poetry, Prophecy) and adds books that were written in a more recent period in either Greek or Hebrew.

To conclude, let's admit that the general meaning of the word that our Bibles translate by 'church', is 'assembly' (Grudem 1994, 854, note 3). In fact, the biblical text does not give the word *ecclesia* the meaning that it has today. The word was not used as a label for uniquely Christian assemblies, nor to designated the buildings that house such assemblies. Instead, at the time of the writing of the New Testament, and even 300 years before the birth of Jesus of Nazareth, it was a general term that was used to describe any kind of assembly whatsoever. Wayne Grudem reminds us that the Septuagint was the Bible that the authors of the New Testament used. They could hardly have been ignorant of the varied nature of the assemblies that the word *eccesia* designates in that text (Grudem 1994, 854, note 2).

The problem is that we tend to identify *ecclesia* with the Sunday morning worship service, the faithful who attend our weekly activities, the construction of special buildings for religious use, finances, committees, the choir or 'praise team', the sound system, preaching, ordinances (or sacraments), prayer meetings, and pastors or evangelists, etc. However, the word *ecclesia* only really means an assembly or gathering. We must also admit that there is not a uniquely distinct form or nature of that 'gathering' (Dulles, 1987; Brunner, 1952). For this reason I suggest that the most fundamental expression of the *ecclesia* happens when two or three people gather in the name of Jesus Christ with the goal of learning how to be his disciples (cf. Matt 18:20).

It is Jesus himself who builds the 'assembly' (*ecclesia*) of "two or three" in his name (Matt 16:16–19). This gathering is based upon the revelation that he is the Messiah, the Son of the living God (Matt 16:16–17; 1 Cor 3:11). It takes place on the foundation of the apostles and the prophets (Eph 2:20), or in other words, based upon all of the inspired Scriptures, for they testify to Christ (John 5:39). The apostle Paul, who used the word *ecclesia* more often than any of the other New Testament authors, argues that this 'gathering' in the name of Jesus is the work of the Spirit of God, and not of men (1 Cor 2:1–16).

I will say once again, the *ecclesia* is neither a building, nor a denomination, nor a ministry, nor a method, nor a doctrinal position, nor an organization, nor a dispensation, nor an institution. The *ecclesia* is the gathering in the name of Jesus (be it only two or three individuals) in whom the Spirit of Christ lives by faith (cf. Rom 8:9 – "If anyone does not have the Spirit of Christ, he does not belong to Christ"). In its beginnings, the *ecclesia* was an illegal movement, more or less clandestine, whose members had the threat of the sword hanging over their heads. The members of this movement were recruited among the lower middle class, among artisans and workers, liberated slaves, and in the large class of domestic and 'industrial' servants. The spreading of the *ecclesia* was the enormous work of thousands of anonymous believers, of workers who spontaneously began to win others to Christ in their random trips and haphazard meetings. Its style, or habitual way of expressing itself as a relational and informal network, that I have labeled '*ecclesia*-movement' was largely the product of its illegal status. The Roman government, which sought to control the inhabitants of the empire, felt threatened by this movement.[4]

But in the fourth century, the situation was reversed. Constantine, the Roman Emperor, by the Edict of Milan in AD 313, granted Christianity an official character, and the *ecclesia*-movement was transformed. Rapidly, there was permanently put into place an ecclesiastic organization that mirrored that of the State. At the Council of Nicea in AD 325, foundational principles were laid for the hierarchy. Next, from council to council, one worked to make things function smoothly; old procedures were confirmed, and rules were adopted to respond to immediate needs. Like today's clergy, that of the fourth century was clearly distinguished from the faithful and constituted a distinct social category.

The institutional church was a great success – its growing identification with all of contemporary society meant that overall one had Christianity without necessarily being a Christian, and one didn't need to be a follower of Jesus even though one was called a Christian. With the Edict of Thessalonica issued in AD 380 by the Emperor Theodosius, every citizen was to abandon the ancient gods and embrace Christianity, or experience the wrath of the Roman State. This provoked a massive entry of 'converts' into the *ecclesia*-movement that also largely contributed to its mutation into *ecclesia*-institution. The 'committed soul' was being replaced by, in the words of Péguy, 'the accustomed soul' (Rakotoarison, 2014). "Going to church," lamented John Chrysostom, "is often a question of habit. (. . .) It used to be

---

4. As an example, toward the year 110, to formulate the opposition between the kingdom of God and the Roman Empire, the author of the Letter to Diogenes used the following expression: "The Christians live on earth, but only as though they are passing through. There is not a foreign country that isn't theirs, and not a country that they find foreign" (Département de Théologie Spirituelle de la Sainte Croix, 2014). Sometime later, Tertullian would write: "For us Christians, nothing is more foreign that the Republic! We recognize only one republic, that of all men!" (Tertullian, 1914). Origen (*Contre Celse* III.29–30) explains that the church of Jesus Christ has one *politeia*, or conception of citizenship, different than that of those who worship demons. And he argues that though the Christians were foreigners, and from humble origins, they were much wiser than the pagans. He concludes by affirming that because of their moral conduct, even the least perfect among their leaders was superior to the existing civil authorities.

that houses were churches, now it is the churches that appear to be no more than ordinary houses!" (Pargoire, 1900).

I am not saying that the *ecclesia*-institution is bad, or that it should be abandoned! I believe that the Holy Spirit has been at work guiding the people of God throughout this process of transformation. However, I want to question our understanding of what the *ecclesia* is. My argument is that the *ecclesia*-movement is just as much a legitimate expression of the *ecclesia* as is the *ecclesia*-institution.[5] If I am right, then we are mistaken when we say, for instance: "We are a movement, we are not a church." For in reality what we are saying is: "We are a movement, we are not a gathering of disciples of Jesus Christ." What the words, "we are not a church" are really intended to communicate is the notion that the group that one belongs to is an expression of *ecclesia*-movement rather than an expression of *ecclesia*-institution.

Why, you might ask, is all this important? It is because the dynamics and structures of the *ecclesia*-movement and the *ecclesia*-institution are not the same. According to Richard Niebhur, the essential differences between the *ecclesia*-movement and the *ecclesia*-institution are that one is conservative, while the other is progressive. In his opinion, the *ecclesia*-institution is more or less passive and submitted to external influences, while the *ecclesia*-movement exercises a greater influence than it endures. Finally, Niebhur says that the *ecclesia*-institution is turned more toward the past, while the *ecclesia*-movement is looking more to the future (Niebhur 1959, 11). David Bosch adds that the *ecclesia*-institution is fearful and seeks to protect its frontiers, while the *ecclesia*-movement is ready to take risks in crossing its frontiers (Bosch 1995, 69). We will see a little further on the kinds of tensions that are born naturally between these two expressions of the *ecclesia*. However, before going there, I want to look in more detail at some of the specific characteristics of the *ecclesia*-movement, for history teaches us that the multiplication of the disciples of Jesus takes place primarily through that expression of the *ecclesia*.

---

5. The Catholic Church recognizes, for instance, the new ecclesiastic movements that sprang up in its midst during the 1970s and that signaled the return of a lay spirituality. These movements center on the importance of personal faith and involvement in a community that is the visible sign and concrete realization of that individual spirituality. These elements clearly distinguish these movements from the different groups of believers that existed already in the ecclesiastical structure.

Factors That Have Accompanied the Multiplication of the Disciples of Jesus

The examples of Peter Waldo and of Francis of Assisi, and many others, indicate that the multiplication of disciples of Jesus very often happens during times of social, economic, cultural, political, or religious tension. That tension creates an environment of discontent due to the current conditions, and a deep desire for change.

History also teaches us that God frequently uses an individual to promote a new understanding. The level of commitment of baptized believers varies enormously. As far as renewal[6] and the multiplication of the disciples of Jesus in the *ecclesia*-institution are concerned, they are always the result of the radical obedience of a few. In other words, the personal accompaniment in discipleship precedes the spiritual renewal of the *ecclesia*-institution. The primary motivation of Waldo, and of Francis and their companions was not to renew the *ecclesia*-institution. They were seeking, above all, complete obedience to Christ. Those people who wish to renew the *ecclesia*-institution must begin with their own spiritual deepening. This is true whether the person seeking the spiritual renewal of the *ecclesia*-institution is a pastor, a priest, a bishop, an apostle or an ordinary lay believer. Historic examples indicate that the spiritual renewal of the *ecclesia*-institution happens when there is the deepening of the spirituality of a handful of people who are growing in their knowledge of Christ and in the conformity of their lifestyle to his teaching.

These people, who are totally committed to Christ and who because of their level of commitment find themselves outnumbered within the *ecclesia*-institution, are most effective in evangelism and the forming of new disciples of Jesus outside of the *ecclesia*-institution when they are banded together in communities of people who share the same vision, the same values, the same passion, the same identity and the same goals (*ecclesia*-movement). The *ecclesia*-movement can be described as a heterogeneous and diffused community of people who are actively and intentionally following the same goal – that of conforming their life to the teaching of Jesus Christ. I say that the *ecclesia*-movement is heterogeneous because it holds together people who come from different backgrounds and diverse *ecclesia*-institutions. I also

---

6. I use the word 'renewal' and not 'reformation' in speaking of the *ecclesia*-institution. The 'reform' of the *ecclesia* means to improve the *ecclesia* in either eliminating or abandoning its imperfections and errors. The 'renewal' of the *ecclesia*-institution signifies rather the restoration of the spiritual vitality of the people who are gathered around Jesus in the *ecclesia*-institution.

suggest that *ecclesia*-movement is diffuse because it tends to be disseminated and decentralized in its organizational functions. The profound and total commitment to follow Jesus Christ is the glue that holds the members of the *ecclesia*-movement together. The *ecclesia*-movement finds expression in a common lifestyle.

The simplicity and specificity of the message of the *ecclesia*-movement are tied to what I have just said about its missionary orientation. In the historic examples that we have discussed, we find uncomplicated communication of the gospel message concerning reconciliation with God through the gift of Jesus Christ on the cross, and a clear call to repentance and conversion to Christ. Waldo, Francis and the others, had a specific message to communicate. They proclaimed personal salvation through faith in Jesus Christ, and they did not separate that call to spiritual conversion from the call to life transformation. This explains why, in connection with the communication of the gospel, they underscored the importance of feeding the hungry, clothing the poor, helping the stranger, and visiting the sick and the imprisoned.

Let's return now to the experience of Waldo and of Francis to see how the *ecclesia*-institution views the *ecclesia*-movement, and the trap that this represents for those of us who wish to make disciples of Jesus who reproduce what they have received in the lives of others.

The Reaction of the *Ecclesia*-Institution to Waldo and to Francis

The Transformation of the *Ecclesia*-Movement of Waldo

The movement initiated by Waldo was not set out to change the dogmas of the *ecclesia*-institution of its time. Nor did it want to become another *ecclesia*-institution. In fact, the leaders of the *ecclesia*-institution would have found no reason to fight the members of this movement had they not taken the liberty to preach in public. It was the unauthorized preaching of laymen and laywomen in public that brought suspicion and led the archbishop of Lyon to oppose the movement.

Faced by the opposition of the archbishop, Waldo appealed to the pope. The pope was favorable to the lifestyle adopted by the members of the movement in their imitation of Christ. He therefore granted them permission to preach in the dioceses where the bishops were in agreement. Soon, however, the members of the *ecclesia*-movement found that the pope's decision restricted their apostolic ambitions. To submit to the decision of the pope would have meant the end of their preaching in some dioceses. For that reason they chose to disobey the pope. As a result, opposition to their activities increased. They then requested the authorization that they desired from the Third Lateran Council (1179) so as to be able to preach wherever they felt that the Holy Spirit was leading them, even if the bishop of that area was disagreed. The council refused their request. In spite of that refusal, they persevered in their practice.

Up to this point the members of the movement taught no doctrines that could have been considered heretical. They only rejected practices within the *ecclesia*-institution that clearly contradicted the Word of God. They continued to attend the worship services of the *ecclesia*-institution, and worked to keep their own meeting private. Although Waldo and his disciples (known as the Vaudois or Waldensians) had no problems with the doctrines of Rome, their disobedience to the pope concerning public preaching led, in 1184, to their condemnation by a synod of bishops. To their great dismay, Waldo and his friends found themselves excluded from the *ecclesia*-institution and declared heretics (Le Goff, 1968).

Despite persecution, the Vaudois continued to expand in France, in Italy, in Germany, and all the way to Poland. But their exclusion from the *ecclesia*-institution pushed them to reexamine their dogmas and to embrace teachings that were considered schismatic by the medieval *ecclesia*-institution. Henceforth, they listened to neither pope nor bishop, and they taught that laypeople, men and women, could preach in public. They criticized the prayers that were said in Latin because they were not understood by most people, and they made fun of the liturgy of the *ecclesia*-institution. They taught that a person need obey only those priests or bishops who adopted their form of discipleship. And they instructed those who listened to them that any lie is a mortal sin, that oaths, even those made in a court of law, are contrary to the teaching of Jesus. They celebrated their own Eucharist (Holy Communion), and in the case of necessity, any layperson could administer it. Their only forms of prayer were the Lord's Prayer, and the blessing of meals. They had their own clergy with bishops, priests and deacons, and a person placed at the head of their movement.

The Vaudois became the most widespread non-conformist *ecclesia*-institution of the Middle Age. Its members were excommunicated and massacred. During 682 years they were hunted down and killed. They hid in caves, and were hunted and exterminated like vermin. With the Reformation, many of those who survived became Protestants. The Vaudois *ecclesia*-

institution numbers around 20,000 faithful today in Italy, and perhaps as many as 5,000 in diaspora (Thouzellier, 2010).

The Preservation of the *Ecclesia*-Movement of Francis of Assisi

Francis was anything but a heretic. A simple layman, he willfully submitted to the leaders of the *ecclesia*-institution. In 1209 he traveled to Rome accompanied by several of his disciples to obtain permission from the pope to continue the lifestyle that they had chosen. He sought, with his companions, to follow the example of Jesus as faithfully as he could. He and the members of his movement had no earthly possessions, to the extent that they clothed themselves in the rags that the poorest of the poor had thrown out. They lived in huts built of branches in the winter, and the wandered the roads of Europe, looking for ways to earn their daily bread. They were not submitted to a rigid schedule, did not follow complicated rules, had no hierarchy, and did not practice any austerity other than that imposed by their lifestyle. There was no period of novitiate, and the members could freely leave the movement whenever they felt that they could not live according to the ideals imposed by the community. They not only took care of the poor, the hungry, the sick and the persecuted, they joined them.

Pope Innocent III (1196 – 1215) was touched by their idealism, but he doubted that they could live up to their ambitions. Nonetheless, he gave them permission to follow the life they proposed, and he promised to give them protection. It is truly amazing that he acted in this way, since without a rule to live by, and without a hierarchy, each Franciscan would be free to act as he wished. It is true that the Franciscans met together once a year, but that time was devoted to sharing their vision and experiences, rather than to set rules or settle disagreements. Francis thought that each person is responsible for his or her own choices and actions. Here we have evidence of a primitive Franciscan conviction that each person has the right to refuse an order that he or she finds immoral or unjust (Thompson, 2012).

However, the conviction that everyone is responsible for their own actions was not used by Francis and his disciples as a pretext to not submit themselves to the *ecclesia*-institution. For instance, public preaching by laypeople was one of the ideals of the Franciscans as it was for the Vaudois. Hesitantly, and after an extensive investigation by the Roman Curia, the pope gave Francis and his lay disciples permission to continue. But he imposed the normal condition (the same imposed on the Vaudois) that they first obtain the permission of the bishop of the diocese, and that they elect a superior who would be accountable for their actions. The Franciscans voluntarily submitted to that decision. They left with the decision to preach only in the dioceses where the bishop would give them that freedom.

Having received the benediction of the pope, Francis and his friends went back to Assisi where they continued to lead the lifestyle they had proposed. They demonstrated the power of the gospel. And they gave hope to the poor, to the excluded, to the despised, by their love of others and their passion for Christ. Consequently, the movement grew beyond what either Francis or the pope had imagined. Thousands of laypeople joined the movement, and as a result some of the leaders of the *ecclesia*-institution began to fear the popular movement which was independent, raised up and trained its own leaders, lived off of its own resources, and propagated itself without outside intervention. For this reason some people began trying to control the movement. Francis left to join the Fifth Crusade with the hope to evangelize the Muslims (1219–1220), and during his absence, a powerful group began to transform the movement into a religious order like the Benedictines, the Cistercians, etc. Francis hurriedly returned to try to stop those changes, but he could do nothing but accept the installation of a representative of the pope, the beginning of a novitiate, and the new rule that those who joined the movement could no longer leave it at will. It seems that considerable pressure was put on him to change some of his initial beliefs as well. It is perhaps out of discouragement, or because he found himself unable to direct such a large movement, that Francis left his function at the head of the movement, and died in isolation in 1226.

In summary, we can say that the relationship between Francis and his movement to the *ecclesia*-institution was one of dialogue, but also one of conviction and of creativity. Very demanding with himself and with his brothers, Francis created a dynamic that gave a new face to the sluggish *ecclesia*-institution of his time. However, Francis and his community walked a very difficult road. They stayed in the *ecclesia*-institution, running the risk of seeing their movement confiscated by others and directed away from its initial intuitions. The period that followed the death of Francis witnessed the birth of three groups in the movement, each one claiming that their approach was that of the founder. The 'spiritual Franciscans' sought to maintain the ideal of poverty and opposed all attempts to transform the movement into a religious order. They also resisted the brothers who began to teach in the universities, who studied law, or who became administrators of the *ecclesia*-institution. They called for the movement to return to the ideals of its beginnings. The group of 'softening' pleaded for the abandonment of the principles of poverty and simplicity that had been at the origin of the movement. The most important group was the 'moderates'. They thought that the members of the movement could live a lifestyle of poverty and of simplicity while at the same time playing a role in education or influencing the *ecclesia*-institution (Dennis, Nagle, Lobeda & Taylor, 2003).

One last remark about Francis: Latourette says that he was "a resolute and joyous missionary in his projects and in his practice" (Latourette 1975, 432). In other words, he was not content to only make disciples of Jesus within the *ecclesia*-institution. He traveled all over Italy communicating the gospel and calling for conversion to Christ. He desired to go to the Muslims. He left for Palestine, but was stopped when his boat sank. He traveled to Spain in order to reach the Muslims who had taken refuge there. But he had to turn back when he became ill. Finally, in 1219, he traveled with the Fifth Crusade all the way to Egypt. He was troubled by the lack of discipline and the sordid lifestyle of many of the soldiers who carried on their blazon the sign of the cross. Among them he won some who would participate in the spreading of the movement into the North of Europe. He presented the gospel to the Sultan and won, it seems, some esteem. He returned to Italy, going through Palestine and Syria. And he sent his brothers on mission in Europe and Morocco.

How Do the Members of the *Ecclesia*-Institution View the *Ecclesia*-Movement?

The leaders of the *ecclesia*-institution are convinced that it is the primary tool that God uses in his project of redemption in our world. For this reason the legitimacy of the structures and activities of the *ecclesia*-institution is never fundamentally questioned. The periods of decline or of unfaithfulness in the history of the *ecclesia*-institution are seen to be the result of the character of its leaders, or of negative cultural forces. One finds it difficult to imagine that the periods of stagnation or decadence could come from the *ecclesia*-institution itself. In fact, the stability and the survival of the *ecclesia*-institution, in spite of the periods of decline, of opposition, or of fragility, are considered to be its glory. They reveal the wisdom of Divine Providence wherein the *ecclesia*-institution was established as the means to carry the good news to the world.

Seen from this angle, there is never a fundamental problem with the *ecclesia*-institution. The question of the propagation of the message of Christ and the renewal of the *ecclesia* is therefore, almost exclusively, that of spiritual renewal and the mobilization of the members of the congregation. The problem is simply that the faithful neither believe, nor behave, as they should. They should attend meetings that are organized (especially the Sunday morning worship service), cover the financial needs, and accompany their non-believing friends to the activities that are organized so that they can hear the good news. We understand why, according to this scheme, the leaders of the *ecclesia*-institution are viewed as the point of origin of any new spiritual or evangelistic impetus.

For these reasons the initiatives that the laity takes outside of the *ecclesia*-institution quickly draws suspicion, or even hostility. The people who are the keepers of the *ecclesia*-institution suspect that those initiatives aim to steal their members. They find it difficult to see how it could be otherwise. It is unthinkable, for them, that a movement could be born outside of their *ecclesia*-institution that would not result in the creation of another *ecclesia*-institution. The presence of an *ecclesia*-movement is also seen as an implicit questioning of the validity of the *ecclesia*-institution in its current forms. These tensions are inevitable, and their results are predictable. They mean that the *ecclesia*-movement will go in one of three directions:

1. The *ecclesia*-movement will become increasingly extremist and find itself, eventually, obligated to leave the *ecclesia*-institution, as was the case for the Vaudois. This is the tendency that comes to the forefront especially when there are forces within the two expressions of the *ecclesia* that push for separation or schism. When that happens, three possibilities appear. According to the extremism of the members of the *ecclesia*-movement, and the violence of their criticism of the *ecclesia*-institution, and according to the reaction of the *ecclesia*-institution to the movement: (a) the *ecclesia*-movement will form a new *ecclesia*-institution or sect; (b) the *ecclesia*-movement will disappear, or (c) the *ecclesia*-movement will find a compromise with the *ecclesia*-institution that gives it a measure of autonomy in exchange for a recognition of the institution's legitimacy. It is the attitude of the members of the *ecclesia*-movement, the socioeconomic factors of the situation, and the virulence of the reaction of the *ecclesia*-institution that, in large part, determine the evolution of the situation.

2. Another possibility is that the *ecclesia*-movement will lose its vitality to the point where it no longer represents a threat to the *ecclesia*-institution.

3. But the *ecclesia*-movement can also accommodate itself to the *ecclesia*-institution in accepting a limited place within the institution, as was the case for the Franciscans. In the case of the Franciscans, in adapting to the *ecclesia*-institution, their dynamism and missionary zeal largely contributed to the renewal of the *ecclesia*-institution. On the other hand, the process of accommodation gave birth to sharp conflicts within the movement, and as Latourette points out: "In fact, no other large order in the Catholic Church has had such an explosive history, or has been as split by so many schisms" (Latourette 1975, 434).

Conclusions

In this chapter I have maintained that the *ecclesia* is essentially an assembly or a gathering of people around Jesus Christ. This gathering can be structured around programs, with a pastor or other 'religious professional' at their head. In some cases this assembly is structured around a small community and its activities are led by a trained layperson. Within the framework of our reflection on personal accompaniment of one layperson by another, learning together how to better follow Jesus, I suggest that this model is yet another form of *ecclesia*. But in each of these cases, I argue that the structures exist to foster the formation of disciples of Jesus. The *ecclesia*-institution tends to see the accompaniment in discipleship as a means to promote the spiritual and numeric growth of the members of the congregation. I insist, however, that this is an erroneous understanding. The New Testament nowhere tells us explicitly to implant the *ecclesia*. The biblical text does, however, command us explicitly to make disciples of Jesus (Matt 28:18–20). I conclude that the goal is not the *ecclesia*. In other words, the Christian assembly is not the goal of our mission. The goal of our mission is the forming of disciples of Jesus Christ – and when we gather two or three people around Jesus, with the goal of learning how to be more like him, to live according to his teaching, then we have "planted the *ecclesia*." The assembly exists for the good of the disciples of Jesus, and not the opposite!

I repeat, we implant an *ecclesia* when we accompany someone in Christian discipleship (Matt 18:20). But we do not necessarily make disciples of Jesus when we multiply ecclesiastic structures, meetings or programs. I will even go so far as to say that there are many elements in our ecclesiastic assemblies that are detrimental to the formation of disciples of Jesus. There are too many sermons and too many meetings. There are also things that are lacking: too few occasions for laypeople to exercise their ministries, too little teaching, too little personal accompaniment and account giving for one's life, too little time spent together outside the 'official' meetings, too little intentional pursuit of discipleship.

What I am suggesting in this book is a return to *ecclesia*-movement based upon the multiplication of laypeople who learn and teach others how to become disciples of Jesus. A movement of men and women who intentionally, and voluntarily, place themselves in a position where a deep transformation of their way of thinking and living is fostered. The examples of Peter Waldo and Francis of Assisi show that such a movement can spring from a single person who lives and shares that vision. Their stories illustrate as well the tensions that come between this 'apostolic' expression of the *ecclesia* and the *ecclesia*-institution. If you begin to accompany some people in an apprenticeship in the footsteps of Jesus, and they are outside of the *ecclesia*-institution that you attend, and if you train them and allow them to reproduce the same thing without seeking to incorporate them into your *ecclesia*-institution, you will be misunderstood, and criticized by your friends who will oppose you. But Jesus commands us to make disciples of the nations – he does not command us to grow the *ecclesia*-institution that we attend. Having said this, I am convinced that a movement of disciples of Jesus who make disciples of Jesus, without being programmed, controlled, or even financed by an *ecclesia*-institution, will end up renewing and making that *ecclesia*-institution grow.

In the midst of the madness that reigned in Nazi Germany, the theologian Dietrich Bonhoeffer, in a letter addressed to his brother, wrote these words:

> The restoration of the church will surely come from a new monasticism that shares with primitive monasticism a non-compromising attitude of a life lived according to the Sermon on the Mount in the footsteps of Christ. (quoted in Wilson-Hartgrove 2010, 15)

Questions to Think About:

1. What do you think of the distinction that the author makes between the *ecclesia*-movement and the *ecclesia*-institution? What examples can you think of that illustrate those two ecclesiastic expressions?

2. What are two lessons that you want to remember from the example of Waldo and Francis of Assisi? What relationship could there be between what you have just thought of and the act of accompanying others in Christian apprenticeship in the footsteps of Jesus?

3. What in your estimation causes the most problems for a movement of disciples who make disciples outside of the *ecclesia*-institution? Is it the fact that the movement is or might become bigger than the *ecclesia*-institution? Is it the fact that the movement escapes the immediate control of the *ecclesia*-institution? Is it a question of finances? What other problems come to mind?

11

How to Help the Members of an *Ecclesia*-Institution Make Disciples of Jesus

W e have just looked at two movements that were situated outside of the *ecclesia*-institution that God used to renew his people and to reach people who had never heard about Christ. Like the Vaudois, the Franciscans wanted to join the people of their day as witnesses and communicators of the gospel, while at the same time seeking – through their radical poverty – to live utterly detached from the world. These two movements were not the fruit of the missionary projects of the *ecclesia*-institution. They did not come from the strategies that had been formulated by the pastors or other official leaders of the *ecclesia*. On the contrary, they were born spontaneously when Peter Waldo and Francis of Assisi, two laymen, began living according to the example and teaching of Jesus Christ.

We should not be surprised by the fact that God used two laypeople in this way. In his book, *A History of Christian Missions*, Stephen Neill points out that the main work of the early church was done by laypeople. Underlining the fact that it was the entire body of believers that was active in the mission of the *ecclesia*, he adds:

> Where there were Christians, there would be a living, burning faith, and before long an expanding Christian community. In later times great churches were much set on claiming apostolic origin – to have an apostle as founder was a recognized certificate of respectability. But, in fact few, if any, of the great churches

were really founded by apostles. Nothing is more notable than
the anonymity of these early missionaries. (Neill 1990, 22)

Robert Tuttle observes along this line that the message of Christ had a
greater impact on non-believers when it came from poor and simple folk,
rather than from people of power or prestige[1] (Tuttle Jr. 2006, 122). And
he adds:

In the midst of persecution, Christianity was predominantly a
lay movement. Until the end of the empire-wide persecutions,
ministry was – for the most part – lay led and rural. Not that
there were no great urban bishops and priests, there were, and
they died under the sword – in droves. It's just that for the first
150 years of Christendom every Christian was a priest. Then for
the next 150 years, most lay Christians continued to take the
Great Commission as a personal mandate to spread the word.
(Tuttle Jr. 2006, 132)

In his study of the propagation of the gospel by the primitive ecclesia,
Michael Green says that one of the most amazing things is the diversity of
people who participated in that work. He writes that the spreading of the
gospel was not reserved for the most zealous, or for the religious professionals.
On the contrary, it was the prerogative and the responsibility of each member
of the community: "The ordinary church member saw it as his responsibility:
Christianity was supremely a lay movement, spread by informal missionaries"
(Green 2001, 332).

The problem with movements is that, sooner or later, they quit moving
(Neill 1990, 440). It seems to be in the nature of things that finally, with the
passing of time, sooner or later inertia imposes itself. And in the case of the
ecclesia, there were powerful forces that accelerated that process in separating
the clergy from the laity, and in transferring the bulk of the ministry to
specially ordained people. As a result, some theologians today are even saying
that laypeople should not take the initiative in communicating the gospel and
in accompanying others in the faith (Lloyd-Jones 1972, 101). In their opinion
preaching, exhortation and edification, along with evangelization and the

---

1. Tuttle also points out that the majority of the first Christians were 'people of color'. In
the year AD 70, the world population would be 0.1% Christian, and 85% of those would be
people of color. By AD 150 nearly 2% would be Christian, and 75% of those would be people
of color. This situation would remain unchanged until the ninth-century scholastics made
Christianity a white religion (Tuttle Jr. 2006, 82).

training of disciples of Jesus, is to be done solely by those who are "called by a special act of God" to a vocation that is greater than the call to follow Jesus which the majority of the faithful have received.

The Historical Meaning of the Laity

Today, that marked distinction between the pastor and the other members of the faith community is increasingly questioned. And it seems to me that those people who criticize that notion have solid grounds to do so.

The word 'lay' comes to us from the Greek word *laikos*, that meant 'of the people'. In primitive Christianity, this word came to denote "the elected people of God", a meaning stemming from the Greek word *laos* ("people of an unknown origin"). In the New Testament, a distinction is made between the Jewish people (*laos*) and its priests and leaders (cf. Matt 26:23; Acts 5:26; Heb 7:5, 27).

Before the end of the first century AD, the term *laos* had taken on an ecclesiastic connotation. The word *laikos* is used by Clement of Alexandria (AD 200) to distinguish a layperson from a deacon or a presbyter. In the *Apostolic Canons*, the laity (*laikoi*) is distinguished from the clergy. Stanley Lusby informs us that the distinction between the laity and the clergy was modeled after the Greek political distinction between the *kleros* (from which we have the word 'clergy'), and the people (*laos*), or in other words, the two groups of people who formed the administration of a city (Lusby, 1987).

As we said previously, it was Constantine who, on 13 June 313, in the city of Milan, gave the faithful who belonged to the *ecclesia*-movement the freedom to practice their religion. He restored to them the goods that had been taken from them and put an end to their persecution. Before the end of the fourth century, conversion to Christ had become compulsory for all the inhabitants of the Roman Empire. At that time, nine generations after Jesus Christ, 7.3 percent of the world population was Christian. In the two following centuries, that number grew to nearly 20 percent. It was therefore necessary for the *ecclesia*-movement to get organized. And it is precisely during that period of institutionalization, marked by challenges and controversies surrounding the affirmations of the Christian faith, that the divide deepened between the laity and the clergy.

Later, in the Protestant tradition, Luther and Calvin would attempt to diminish the divide that had grown between the laity and the clergy. They insisted upon the universal priesthood of all believers, and saw no ontological difference between pastors and the faithful. However, they recognized that particular ministries were necessary for the healthy functioning of the congregation. In their opinion, there needed to be people who are specially given to preaching and to the sacraments in order to assure the organization of the congregation and its continued faithfulness to Jesus Christ (Willaime 2002, 436).

I am convinced that the current tendency to center the life of the *ecclesia* around the Sunday morning worship service, with its professionalization of the witness of the people of God, has largely weakened the participation of the laity. It is undeniable that despite the rediscovery of the priesthood of all believers by Luther and Calvin, the dominant understanding remains that of Christian ministry monopolized by specially consecrated individuals. This is true even though Jesus of Nazareth broke with Jewish tradition when he chose his disciples from among fishermen, tax collectors, and the like, rather than among the members of the priestly class. This is also contrary to the *ecclesia* established by Paul that were not called 'synagogues', but simply 'gatherings' (cf. 1 Cor 11:17, 18, 20, 33, 34; 14:23, 26), and that happened in private dwellings – for three hundred years (Bosch 1995, 626).

Moreover, the notion of the pastor placed at the center of the *ecclesia*, and armed with considerable authority,[2] produces the understanding of the *ecclesia* as a sacred society directed by 'in house authorities', with the pastor or minister installed in a privileged and central position (Burrows 1981, 61 & 74).

The Biblical Role of the Laity

The biblical text which, for me, explains most clearly the articulation between the laity and the clergy in the mission of God is found in Ephesians 4:

> [1] As a prisoner for the Lord, then, I urge you to live a life worthy of the calling you have received. [2] Be completely humble and gentle; be patient, bearing with one another in love. [3] Make every effort to keep the unity of the Spirit through the bond of peace. [4]There is one body and one Spirit – just as you were called to one hope when you were called – [5] one Lord, one faith, one baptism; [6] one God and Father of all, who is over all and through all and in all. [7]

---

2. From a Protestant perspective, that notion was largely reflected in the three ministers of pastor, elder and deacon.

But to each one of us grace has been given as Christ apportioned it. (. . .) [11] It was he who gave some to be apostles, some to be prophets, some to be evangelists, and some to be pastors and teachers, [12] to prepare God's people for works of service, so that the body of Christ may be built up [13]until we all reach unity in the faith and in the knowledge of the Son of God and become mature, attaining to the whole measure of the fullness of Christ.

[14] Then we will no longer be infants, tossed back and forth by the waves, and blown here and there by every wind of teaching and by the cunning and craftiness of men in their deceitful scheming. [15] Instead, speaking the truth in love, we will in all things grow up into him who is the Head, that is, Christ.

We can enter into this text by first identifying those to whom it is addressed. Who are the people that Paul calls 'you' in verses 1 to 6? In the beginning of the epistle, the apostle says that he is writing to "the saints who are in Ephesus, the faithful in Christ Jesus" (1:1). Who were these people that Paul labels 'saints'? In a well-known text, the apostle specifies that he was dealing with people who were weak, lowly, and despised by the world (1 Cor 1:27). We know that a good number of them were either poor or enslaved (Col 3:22). The cynical philosopher Celsus, quoted by Origen, wrote with disdain about those who followed Christ: "We find those who work with wool and leather, and the most ignorant and ordinary people who do not even dare speak a word in the presence of their elder and wiser masters."[3] A contemporary of Celsus, the apologist Athenagoris, offers a different perspective: "Among us, you will find the illiterate, artisans and old women who, in spite of the fact that they cannot express by their words the advantages of our instruction, demonstrate by their actions the value of their principles" (Chadwick 1984, 54). And Pliny, speaking of the faith community of Bithynia, affirms that people coming from all of the levels of society were part of that assembly.[4]

The people Paul identifies as 'saints' were, therefore ordinary people. In fact, the label 'saint' is the title most often used in the New Testament to speak of the believers who would later be called the laity (Beckwith 1988, 609). The title 'saint', when applied to those who follow Jesus Christ, does not mean that they are sinless, or that they have reached moral perfection. It signifies

---

3. *Contra Celsum*, 3, 55.

4. Pliny the Younger, *Correspondence with Trajan from Bithynia (Epistles X)*, (Warminster, Wiltshire: Aris & Phillips, 1990).

above all else that the person is neither secular nor profane! In the words of Kenneth Wuest:

> That person is called a *hagios*, a set apart for God person, a consecrated person. He is, as such, looked upon as a non-secular person, a distinctively religious person, in that he has been set apart for God, his worship and service. (Wuest 1966, 18)

This text from the letter to the Ephesians is addressed, therefore, to people we could call 'consecrated laypersons'.[5] Every layperson who is born from on high, and in whom dwells the Spirit of Jesus, is a saint. He is consecrated because he has been set apart for God's service. This has nothing to do with his function in the faith community. It depends neither on his capacities, background, education, sex, or social status. All don't share the same profession (work or occupation), but all have the same vocation (calling, mission). Laypeople are not only the *goal* (souls to be saved), they are also the *means* by which the mission of God is accomplished in our world. Without exception or exclusion, they are set apart for that mission – to make disciples of Jesus.

Sometimes in evangelical circles one encounters the idea that pastors, evangelists and missionaries are 'saints' because they exercise sacred activities, while laypersons are profane because the exercise secular activities. This is an error. God did not place us in a world where certain activities and certain objects are sacred, while all the rest is secular. The entire world belongs to him with all that it contains. Each one of us is a creature of God – without exception – and all of the parts of our being belong to him. All of creation is sacred when we realize that it belongs to God and exists under the lordship of Christ.

This being the case, all legitimate human activities are sanctified. It is noteworthy that the Bible uses the same Hebrew word, *havoda*, to signify both manual labor and the acts of worship done by the Jewish people (Brown, Driver, & Briggs 1906, 715). As William Tyndale, known as the first translator

---

5. This is not to be confused with the 'consecrated laity' of the Roman Catholic world which is intended to reflect what is lived in the religious congregations. The Catholic consecrated laity chooses to radically offer their lives to Christ while living in the world by living the evangelical recommendations of poverty, chastity and obedience. They do not live the shared life of the religious orders, and normally ply a secular trade. My argument is that every layperson that follows Jesus is consecrated, or if you prefer, set apart for service.

of the New Testament from the Greek text into a modern language[6] said: "No action is preferable to another, none pleases God more: to pour water, do the dishes, be a shoemaker or an apostle, all is one. To do the dishes or to preach, as actions, both please God equally." In other words, laypeople are not less consecrated because they work at secular jobs, than are pastors and those who have religious employment.

I will not comment on what the apostle wrote in the first six verses of chapter 4 of his letter to the 'saints' in Ephesus. Note simply that there is a contrast between verses 6 and 7, for Paul moves from 'you' to 'to each one of us': "But to each one of us grace has been given as Christ apportioned it." When Paul speaks of "each one of us," he is not saying: "But (contrary to what is true for you) to each one of us (apostles, prophets, evangelists, shepherds, teachers) grace has been given as Christ apportioned it." That reading of this verse would betray Paul's thought. Paul is not saying that there is a class of people in the faith community who have received an exceptional gift of grace! In fact, he is saying the exact opposite. He has already written that saving grace, grace that saves sinners, is accorded to all who believe (Eph 2:5–8). Now he is arguing that grace 'for service' has also been accorded to all the 'saints' (Stott 1995, 150).

Paul had already spoken of that grace for service when in the beginning of chapter 3 of his epistle he wrote: "Surely you have heard about the administration of God's grace that was given me for you" (v. 2). In this text Paul speaks of the 'administration' of divine grace. The expression signifies the organizing of a work or of a labor (Col 1:25). Paul is referring to the 'equipping' that he had received that enabled him to carry out his mission (Eph 3:7–8) (Wood 1978, 45). It is in this line of thought that he writes: "But to each one of us grace has been given as Christ apportioned it." The notion of grace implies a 'gift', and Paul underlines the thought that all 'saints' (every layperson) have received from Christ the equipping that they need to complete their mission. This being the case, we can ask what is the specific role of pastors and other leaders of the faith community.

Paul writes that the Lord has given "some to be apostles, some to be prophets, some to be evangelists, and some to be pastors and teachers, to prepare God's people for works of service, so that the body of Christ may be

---

6. William Tyndale (or Tindale), born in Gloucestershire in 1494, was executed by strangulation on 6 October in Vilvorde. He was a brilliant and learned Protestant who spoke Hebrew, Greek, Latin, Spanish and French "so well that each of these languages could have been his maternal tongue".

built up" (Eph 4:11–12). The goal of these ministers is clearly spelled out in these verses. It is the 'perfecting' or 'preparing' of the 'saints' for the works of service. The Greek word translated 'perfecting' or 'preparation' is *katartizo*, which means to 'rectify'. In medicine one used this word to indicate that one had put a broken bone back into place (Wood 1978, 58). In the New Testament this word was used for the 'preparing' of fishing nets (Matt 4:21; Mark 1:19) and the 'restoration' of someone who is caught in a sin (Gal 6:1; 2 Cor 13:11). It can also refer to the realization of a project (1 Cor 1:10; 1 Thess 3:10) or the training in character (Luke 6:40; Heb 13:21; 1 Pet 5:10). All of the people that Paul mentions, in their special functions, have only one reason for being – the equipping, perfecting, or preparing of the 'saints', or in other words, the laity.

And why does the Lord desire the perfecting of the laity? So that they will do "the works of service". The grace of God for service is given to each of us. Each 'saint' receives the divine favor that is necessary to accompany others in discipleship in the footsteps of Jesus. The reason leaders of the Christian community exist, is in order to prepare laypeople for that task (Julien 1976, 141). Paul writes to Timothy that he should "be strong in the grace that is in Christ Jesus," just before he exhorts him to pass on to others what he had himself received from the apostle (2 Tim 2:1). The leaders of the Christian community have this role. They must repair, restore, exhort and encourage the 'saints' to live fully the grace that they have received which allows them to make disciples of Jesus.

Christian ministry belongs to the laity! In the biblical perspective, the laity does not have the role of supporting the leaders of the Christian community in their ministries. The leaders of the community exist because the laypeople have been set apart for the work of God in our world. The problem is that our faith communities have reversed the roles. One compares our faith communities to a soccer match. During a soccer game, there are twenty-two players on the field who need some rest, being watched, encouraged, and cheered by a multitude of people in the stands who need a bit of physical exercise. It seems to be like this in our faith communities. We often find a handful of specialized individuals who are counted upon to 'do the ministry', and who are watched, encouraged, and supported by a crowd of people who are otherwise largely inactive.

How Can We Change Our Way of Doing Things?

Now things are getting uncomfortable. There is nothing easier than reading what others have lived concerning accompanying someone, face-to-face, in the footsteps of Jesus. In the same way, it is not too difficult to understand how Christian ministry has been transferred from the laity to the religious professionals. But how are we to go back to a more biblical model? How can we spark a movement of spiritual reproduction among the laity within a context ecclesial that has lost that perspective? There are no easy answers to these questions. However, I want to underline some of the important elements that must be present in that process.

Be a Facilitator

You can hardly initiate a movement of disciples, makers of disciples, if you have not embraced personally, deeply, and permanently the Great Commission mandate. That kind of engagement is birthed only in the personal encounter with God in prayer, in his Word, and in obedience to his Spirit. It is deepened in the experience of personally accompanying a few people in Christian discipleship, and then freeing them to repeat that process in the lives of others.

As a facilitator, your responsibility is to be a catalyst so that others reproduce themselves spiritually. You do that by creating an environment in which they are encouraged and helped in the process of personal evangelism and follow-up resulting in spiritual multiplication. This means, for instance, that you must renounce, right from the start, the temptation to attempt to control everything. You must also allow that these people accompany others without you being present. You will need to put into place only those structures and activities which are absolutely necessary for spiritual growth, and avoid structures and activities that aim to control or govern. In short, you must be willing to take risks.

To 'initiate' or 'launch' means to put into action, to engage something in a specific direction and with a determined goal. It means provoking a reaction or effect, liberating what is blocked, putting something into action. This is what you do when you personally accompany your first apprenticeship partners on the path of following Jesus. And you strengthen that process by fighting the sterility of conformity, of calculated results, and of micromanagement.

Do not fall into the trap of attempting to delegate to someone else the initiative of launching a disciple-making movement. If you delegate this role to someone else, you will not have the passion (from past participle stem of Latin *pati* 'to suffer, endure'), which is necessary if are you to make the necessary sacrifices that a disciple-making movement requires.

Develop a Biblical Vision

Movements of accompaniment in discipleship spring up where there is a clear vision, a sort of philosophy or creed that expresses clearly what it is that one is seeking to accomplish, and the values and principles upon which actions are based. I have argued in this book that the mission that Jesus Christ gave to his disciples should be the measure of all Christian ministry. Are the laity in our faith communities in the process of accomplishing the ministry that Christ gave to his disciples and to each one of us? Are they making disciples of Jesus who are making disciples of Jesus? Are we in the process of reproducing life in Christ, or in our religious activities and structures? Have we allowed our mission to be defined by our material means, by our religious activities and by our official actions?

Randy Pope states that if we are to reintroduce the practice of Christian discipleship into our assemblies, we must first begin by reflecting on questions like these with 'brutal honesty':

> Ask yourself these questions. Then listen to your responses. Are we effective in making disciples of Christ? Are our small groups really helping in the spiritual formation of our faithful? Is the number of leaders in our faith community stagnant? (Pope 2013, 193)

Pastor Sam Rainer also offers a list of questions that have proved helpful in the development of a biblical vision (Rainer, 2009):

— How does the New Testament define a disciple of Jesus?

— How is the process that trains a disciple of Jesus described in the New Testament?

— What specific phases of discipleship are apparent in the biblical model?

— How could all of the faithful in our assembly experience this process?

— What values must be present in order that disciples of Jesus be made in our assembly?

— How could our assembly aim at the forming of disciples of Jesus on all levels?

— In what ways do the practices of our assembly maintain the vision of making disciples of Jesus?

— How will our assembly foster, recognize and liberate the leaders who make disciples of Jesus?

— How will our assembly mobilize the laity to make disciples of Jesus within the greater community?

It is most important that you develop a precise vision of the calling that you have received. You will need to come back to this incessantly. It is the only way to come to harmony, unity and balance between your aims and your mission, between your roles and your objectives, and between your priorities and your projects. And it is in this way that you will avoid having your programs corrupted by the pursuit of profit, or by the egotism of your leaders (Putman, Harrington, & Coleman 2013, 218).

Pastors and other Christian leaders know that we should be making disciples of Jesus Christ. But when they are asked if they are personally accompanying others in discipleship, they often respond with: "I would like to be doing that, but with all my responsibilities, I don't have the time," or with "I have not yet found the person with whom I would feel comfortable in that role" (Johnston 2014, 1). And you, how would you respond to these questions? Are you motivated by the important and irresistible task of making disciples of Jesus? Is your life, your activities, and your preoccupations organized around this vision?

Alvin Reid and Mark Liederbach claim that when a Christian assembly loses from sight, forgets, or does not intentionally aim at the accomplishment of a missionary vision, it loses its dynamic as a movement and enters into the dynamic of institutionalization (Liederbach & Reid 2009, 145). We must see ourselves as we are, and not shut our eyes to the truth. It is of utmost importance that we answer the questions that are being raised with complete honesty. In the United States of America, and in Europe, faith communities are experiencing significant difficulties, and in Africa, the lives of the faithful are not always transformed by their participation in the worship services.

Many evangelicals feel that we need to be more active in evangelism. There are those who argue that we should win more souls for Jesus. I claim that we can incorrectly save souls without making disciples of Jesus, but we cannot make disciples of Jesus without the salvation of souls. We must learn how to better resemble Jesus, and how to accompany others in the process of becoming like him.

Robert Coleman explains the heart of that vision in these words:

> The Great Commission does not consist in simply going to the ends of the earth and preaching the gospel (Mark 16:15), or in baptizing many converts in the Trinitarian name of God, or even in teaching them the precepts of Christ, but in making "disciples" – in other words, in forming people to be like themselves. They were so gripped by this mission, this mandate from Christ, that they not only set out to follow him, but they also accompanied others on that same path. (Coleman 1972, 101)

The goal of our assemblies is not to gather a crowd in order to pass on information. Nor should it be to create an emotional experience that will motivate the faithful for a few hours, and give them the desire to come back. The goal is not to pray for the sick and cast out evil spirits. The goal of our Christian assemblies is to stimulate and train laypeople, disciples of Jesus, and disperse them in the world so that they can evangelize, follow-up and train other disciples of Jesus.

If we want to see a transformation in our Christian assemblies, there must be a new vision of what we are all about. Every change necessitates the abandonment of existing priorities and values. The faithful must see that the new vision is more significant than the present situation and direction. Without that understanding, they will not make the necessary sacrifices so that the new vision can be realized.

The Importance of Small Groups

Bill Hull believes that the accompaniment in discipleship must take place in the context of a small group (Hull 2010, 219). Jim Putman and Bobby Harrington agree with him, but insist that in order for the group to play that role, it must focus on the Word of God and intentionally aim at discipleship:

> We are not advocating small groups that aim only at better knowledge and sharing with each other. We define a small group

> as an intentional gathering, led by a spiritually mature person who understands that his role is to help the participants grow as disciples of Jesus. (Putman, Harrington, & Coleman 2013, 135)

According to these authors, "the group exists to develop relationships with others that foster discipleship". Randy Pope distinguishes between the kinds of small groups that already exist in some *ecclesia*, and those that seek really to make disciples of Jesus. In his opinion, the first kind works intentionally to *transfer* knowledge, while the second kind works for life *transformation*. In the first case, it is the *leader* who prepares the contents of the time together; in the second, it is the *participants* who prepare its contents. Existing small groups require *little commitment* on the part of the laypeople who participate in them, according to Pope, while small groups that aim intentionally at making disciples of Jesus require a *deep* personal *commitment*. He also observes that it is normally the *participants who choose* their small group, while in the model that he advocates, it is the *leaders of the ecclesia* who form the groups. Current small groups include eight to twenty-five members. In the model that aims at discipleship, these groups should only include four to ten people. According to Pope, traditional small groups are centered on instruction, prayer, sharing, and caring for one another in order to *strengthen the community ties within the ecclesia*. Small discipleship groups, on the other hand, seek transparence, training, personal responsibility, mobilization and openness to others with the goal of producing *trained laypeople* who are faithful to their calling. In many cases today, small groups bring together lay believers and non-believers, men and women. However, in the small group that is more favorable to the training of disciples, Pope suggests that this kind of mix should be eliminated. In traditional small groups, leaders see themselves as *teachers*, while in the model that Pope is pleading for, the leader is a disciple of Jesus who plays the role of *mentor* and *coach*. Finally, Pope affirms that most small groups reinforce *fellowship*, while the groups he wishes to see recognize, train and send out *new leaders* (Pope 2013, 211).

What should be your attitude if you find yourself in an *ecclesia* in which there are small groups that don't intend to make disciples of Jesus? Should they be dissolved and then replaced with groups that are intentionally structured to foster discipleship? That is probably not the best solution. Why kill a friend? You could also give the leaders of the current small groups a series of Bible studies to do on discipleship. Even though, in itself, that would not be a bad thing to do, it would not as effectively transform the entire *ecclesia* as might a third way of proceeding.

I would counsel you to keep the existing small groups, publicly affirming their contribution to the overall work of the *ecclesia*. Then discreetly and in a non-programmed way, begin one or two small groups that function according to the model described by Pope. Bill Hull says that these new groups function as prototypes that allow their members the possibility of learning the aptitudes that are essential to disciple-making groups:

> In this group you will be a model in several areas: the way to lead a Bible discussion, the way to lead a time of prayer, the way to discern the real needs of the participants, and the way to strengthen community ties. The members of this pilot group will also learn, as they, in turn, lead the meetings. (. . .) As a group you will hold each other accountable, and you will assist each other in trials. (Hull 2006, 230)

Your role in such a small group will be to help the participants seek actively and intentionally to resemble Jesus Christ. You will help those who are more adult in the faith to accompany those who are younger in Christ or who are experiencing difficulty in their relationship with God. You will seek to discern where each member of the group is in their walk with Christ, and in which domain he or she should grow. At the same time, you will be attentive to the signs that God is in the process of raising someone up who could be your apprentice, and then become a leader.

The members of this small group must authorize you to share with them personally whatever you see in their lives. It is something that they should actively seek, since they will have a biblical view of growth and maturity. For it is the spiritually mature who desire that others help them to see what should change in their lives so that they become more like Christ. This is a key to the vision that you will want to establish in the *ecclesia*. The faithful must understand that when someone shares an honest word of encouragement or questions an action or attitude, it is an act of courageous brotherly charity. Rather than being offensive, the mature Christian will respond with humility and thankfulness. The members of the *ecclesia* must understand that the small group is not a club. It is a group that meets for a specific purpose – to grow to be more and more like Christ (Putman, Harrington, & Coleman 2013, 148).

Personal Accompaniment

As far as I am concerned, I prefer to begin with the personal accompaniment of one or two people who are outside of the ecclesiastic groups or activities. Ideally, it starts with accompanying these people in their conversion to Christ. The accompaniment in discipleship follows naturally from that experience. And I prefer waiting awhile before introducing that new believer to a small group. I want the personal accompaniment that he or she receives from me to become the fundamental experience that will influence his or her way of living all of the other aspects of life as a follower of Jesus. In fact, I counsel you to accompany your new converts, personally and regularly, one-on-one, for two or three months before gathering them together into a small group. In that way the laypeople you accompany will learn how to accompany others in places where there is no small group, and the action of accompanying others in Christian discipleship will become engraved in their spiritual DNA.

My experiences have convinced me that if your new believers enter too quickly into a small group (even a small group that aims at discipleship), that will slow down the multiplication of disciples. For, once comfortably installed in a group, the majority of them will find it most difficult to invest themselves personally in the lives of those who are not in the group.

If you are a leader of a community of faith, you can also introduce this model of personally accompanying others within the *ecclesia* by doing so with one of the other leaders:

— Praying for the person daily by name.

— Offering the person your ear, your support and a personal spiritual and emotional accompaniment.

— Meeting regularly with the person, one-on-one, for an accompaniment that is adapted to his or her needs.

— Giving the person things to do (Bible studies, memorization, books to read, concrete assignments) to help him or her grow in the areas of life where there is need.

— Counseling the person as they begin the accompaniment of their first disciples of Jesus.

If you find yourself regularly in a small group, with elders or other leaders of the *ecclesia*, you can profit from those occasions by transmitting the vision of disciple making. These are also times when it could prove beneficial to share some of the ups and downs that you are experiencing as you accompany someone.

I have already addressed the importance of regularly giving account to others for our lives. The absence of this kind of relationship between believers is one of the most blaring weaknesses of the contemporary *ecclesia*. And since these relationships do not come about spontaneously, one must enter intentionally into them. Let's admit that there are many of us who do not want to grant to anyone else the right to look into all of the areas of our life. One of the reasons for that reticence is the fact that we find it difficult to understand the goal that is pursued in such a relationship. The goal is not only to help others not to fall into sin. It is also useful in aiding them to keep their commitments to God. This kind of accompaniment helps them to live fully their vocation as lay followers of Christ in the world. Every member of the Christian assembly is supposed to live in a way that supports others toward that goal. The magnificent words of Paul to the 'saints' living in Thessalonica come to mind: "We urge you, brothers, warn those who are idle, encourage the timid, help the weak, be patient with everyone" (1 Thess 5:14).

Remember what we saw at the beginning of this chapter. The leaders of the Christian community exist because the laity has been set apart for the work of God in the world. You should help your elders and other leaders of the *ecclesia* to repeat with some laypeople the same type of accompaniment that they are receiving from you. If they are unwilling to personally accompany laypeople in Christian discipleship, I have a difficult time understanding how they might justify their title as 'elder'.

Every 'saint' born of the Holy Spirit has been set apart for the work of God. However, without the multiplication of trained, motivated and liberated laypeople, the decentralization of the ministry will not happen.

To begin this process within the *ecclesia*-institution, I suggest that you follow the simple plan proposed by the evangelical philosopher, Dallas Willard:

> I recommend that you do not announce that you are going to change anything. Begin simply by doing things differently, including of course, teaching others to do what Jesus taught. Begin with teaching what discipleship is, giving its theological and biblical foundations. Continue by fostering relationships that make disciples within all of the programs of the church. Teach in depth the essential elements of the doctrines of the New Testament: the existence and nature of God, his kingdom, the

person of Christ in that scheme, the discipleship as a lifestyle, and how to become someone who, through the transformation of his thoughts, his will, his body, his soul, and his social relationships, does what Jesus expects of him. This is the method which, throughout all ages, has permitted the growth of the church: Christians more and more mature. And it is precisely that which Jesus told us to do. (Willard, 2009)

Questions to Think About:

1. In what ways did the study at the head of this chapter question or confirm your understandings of the role of the laity and its relationship to the clergy?

2. In your experience, which ways of thinking and practices keep the laity from assuming fully their calling?

3. How would you describe the current vision of the *ecclesia* that you attend? In what ways does that vision contradict the vision of training laypeople to reproduce their life with Jesus in the life of others?

12

The Disciple of Jesus and Unity

"Master," said John, "we saw a man driving out demons in your name and we tried to stop him, because he is not one of us." "Do not stop him," Jesus said, "for whoever is not against you is for you." (Luke 9:49–50)

As is the case for many of us, the apostle John liked to distinguish himself from others. In his eyes, there were those who, like himself, were clearly with Jesus, and others whom he considered to be different. In this incident, John meets a man who was doing exorcisms. He was chasing out evil spirits using the name of Jesus. But John did not know this man!

There were many exorcists at the time. These exorcists appealed to all kinds of names: from that of Beelzebub all the way to that of Solomon. However John met a man who was using the name of Jesus. This exorcist appealed to a name that was very important to John. John had spent a couple of years with Jesus, and he didn't recognize this other fellow. By what authority could he be using the name of Jesus, for by all evidence, he was assuredly not one of the disciples? John thought that he had to keep him from using the name of his Lord in this way. He most certainly told that individual he did not recognize that he had no right to use the name of Jesus.

"Master," he said, "we saw a man driving out demons in your name and we tried to stop him . . ." Why would John try to stop this unknown person from driving out demons in Jesus' name? He did so because that man was "not one of us", because he was not a member of John's group.

It is exactly this that bothered John! "If you don't follow Jesus with us," he seems to be saying, "then you have no reason to call on the name of Jesus."

However, Jesus did not agree with John. "Do not stop him!" is Jesus' order. Leave him alone! You have obviously not understood that whoever is not against you, is for you.

We still find it difficult to recognize the legitimacy of others. We find it hard to imagine how someone who is not with us can be for us. And this creates scandalous divisions between the disciples of Jesus who belong to differing ecclesiastic traditions. More than thirty years ago, Paul Billheimer wrote (1981, 7):

> The most important, momentous, crucial, but the most ignored, neglected, and unsolved problem that has faced the church from its infancy to the present throbbing moment, is the problem of disunity. The continuous and widespread fragmentation of the church has been the scandal of the ages. It has been Satan's master strategy. The sin of disunity probably has caused more souls to be lost than all other sins combined. Possibly more than anything else, it is the one thing that binds the hands of the Holy Spirit and thwarts his work of convincing of sin, righteousness and judgment.

Contrary to our actual practice of basing fellowship with others primarily on conceptual, theological and organizational persuasions and practices, Donald Bloesch has pointed out that one of our fundamental beliefs as evangelical Christians is that we must work to promote the unity for which Jesus prayed in John 17:

> Christian disunity is a contradiction of Christ's prayer that his people be one (John 17:20–23). It also conflicts with Paul's declarations that there is only "one body and one Spirit . . . one Lord, one faith, one baptism" (Eph 4:4–5). Disunity on theological and even sociological grounds betrays an appalling ignorance of the nature of the church. Indeed, the classical marks of the church of Jesus Christ are oneness, holiness, apostolicity and catholicity. The last term denotes universal outreach and continuity with the tradition of the whole church. . . . In my view, there will never be real evangelical unity, let alone Christian unity, until there is an awakening to the oneness and catholicity of the church. (1983, 64–65)

I think of the negative example of the experience of my mother who grew up in a small town located in the northern region of the state of Minnesota, in the USA. In that small town Catholics and Protestants had very little to do with each other. They would walk on opposite sides of the street, shop in different stores, go to different schools, vote for different political candidates, and avoid each other at community events. The relationships between the members of those two Christian traditions in that rural community were characterized by distrust, animosity, and from time to time, open hostility.

And this kind of hostility did not begin yesterday. Quarrels between people, quarrels over questions of knowledge and doctrine, over questions of sympathy and antipathy, of bitterness, of jealousy and the pursuit of honor – all that has done its destructive work ever since the beginning of the first Christian assembly. And for centuries, instead of working and praying to reestablish and maintain unity, everyone has become so accustomed to these divisions that they are seen as normal. They have become a sort of permanent structure of the *ecclesia*. There are sometimes meetings that bring together the faithful who come from differing ecclesial horizons, but once those meetings are over, everyone goes back to his or her assembly.

Most Christians have sadly accepted this state of affairs. Most do not believe that we can ever come to an end of these discords, divisions, and splits between the true disciples of Jesus on earth. However, the cause of every discord is, in reality, sin in all its ugly forms. Whether it be sympathy, or antipathy, jealousy, pride or intolerance (Staal, 2014).

In this last chapter, I suggest that a new appreciation of the biblical notion of discipleship can help us to transcend some of the questions that have provoked so many of our divisions in the past. My argument is as follows: our common mission demands that we take seriously the prayer of Jesus for the unity of those who follow in his footsteps:

> "*Father . . . My prayer is not for them* (those whom you gave me out of the world) *alone. I pray also for those who will believe in me through their message, that all of them may be one, Father, just as you are in me and I am in you. May they also be in us so that the world may believe that you have sent me.*" (John 17:20–21)

What is Our Common Mission?

All throughout these pages, I have insisted that Jesus has called us to one task. In Matthew 4:19, Jesus says to Peter and his brother Andrew: "Follow me, and I will make you fishers of men." We are called to follow Jesus, and to accompany others as they learn to follow him. We call this discipleship. Jesus confirmed this call in Matthew 28:19: "Go into all the world and make disciples of the nations." This is the mandate that we have received from the Master. We are to be followers of Jesus who, with God's power, make other people followers of Jesus too. Paul clarifies this calling in 2 Timothy 2:2, "And the things you have heard me say in the presence of many witnesses entrust to reliable men who will also be qualified to teach others." This is what Jesus has called his people to do – *to make disciples who can make disciples*. Dr Howard Hendricks puts it like this: "Make disciples is the mandate of the Master. We may ignore it, but we cannot evade it" (Hendrichsen 1974, 5).

Whether we are Evangelical Protestants, Roman Catholics, Orthodox, Presbyterians, Methodists, Lutherans, Pentecostals, Apostolic, Mennonites, or any other tradition which identifies itself with Christ, we are called to make disciples of Jesus. This is our common mission.

So now we find ourselves faced with an important question. If we make disciples of Jesus through a relationship of personal accompaniment in which both partners give an account of their lives and seek to help each other to become more like Christ, can we legitimately assume that there are members of our faith communities who are not really disciples of Jesus? The fact that someone is a member of one or the other of the faith traditions that I have named, does it guarantee that person is voluntarily submitting, each day, to the lordship of Jesus? Does the fact that a person faithfully attends the meetings of a religious tradition indicate that he or she is actively seeking to renew intelligence in conformity to the teaching of Christ? In short, can a person be Baptist, or Evangelical, or Catholic, or Methodist, or Pentecostal, or Presbyterian, or Orthodox, etc., without ever becoming a disciple of Jesus? The answer to this question is clearly, "Yes." It seems that there does not exist any Christian assembly that is exclusively made up of true disciples of Jesus Christ.

At the same time, if it is true that all of the members of an assembly are not real disciples of Jesus Christ, it seems equally true that there are some real disciples of Jesus inside each or these faith communities. You can be a disciple of Jesus and an Evangelical Protestant, or a Pentecostal, or a Roman Catholic, or a Presbyterian, or a Lutheran, etc. Discipleship is not a question of ecclesiastic affiliation. Belonging to a specific Christian tradition does not automatically make a person a disciple of Jesus Christ. Neither does it exclude a person from discipleship!

It is therefore not the Christian tradition with which a person is associated that is of primary importance, but discipleship. Jesus calls us to attach ourselves to him and to his teaching. The various Christian traditions offer precious resources that encourage and sustain that relationship, but they cannot replace it (Bjork & March, 2006). In like manner, our mission consists in promoting Jesus Christ, and not our faith tradition. Jesus is the good news that we have to share with our world. This is what the apostle Paul said in 1 Corinthians 2:2 – "For I resolved to know nothing while I was with you except Jesus Christ and him crucified." Jesus Christ is the message that we have to communicate to all of creation. He is the gospel, the heart of the Christian message and experience.

We sometimes fall into the trap of thinking that our tradition 'owns' Jesus; that those who belong to a different tradition cannot follow him as we do. This is a very widespread error. For example, Evangelical Protestants often think that everybody must place their faith in Jesus and begin to follow him in exactly the same way. Because many Catholics, Presbyterians, Lutherans, etc. do not follow that model, evangelicals find it difficult to understand how the members of those faith communities can enjoy the same relationship with Jesus that they think they know.[1]

I want to say here that what is most important is not the way in which a person began following Jesus, or the Christian tradition with which he or she identifies, but the fact that he continues to progress by faith and submission to Jesus Christ. He is the same Lord of all, yet there are no two lives that are exactly alike. And God did not want there to be. What he wants above all else is that each one of us remain in contact with Jesus in our own way, according to our personality and our particular history, and with our heritage and distinct Christian experiences. What counts, is our conscious, intentional and ongoing attachment to Jesus. This is our common call. It is the foundation of our common mission.

---

1. Scott McKnight affirms that there are three basic orientations to conversion: socialization, liturgical acts, and personal decision. In other words McKnight recognizes that many people 'become Christians' by growing up in the faith and often do the same with their children, these he labels 'socialized converts'. The 'liturgical' Christians are those who 'became Christians' through the rites performed by the church on their behalf. And the third basic orientation to conversion emphasizes the importance of personal faith on the part of a converting individual. Some call this 'born again Christianity'" Each of these three basic orientations to conversion "is aligned with a major component of the church," writes McKnight, "and each appears allergic to the others" (McKnight 2002, 1).

My Own Experience[2]

I first began to appreciate this truth in 1981. Two years earlier, the Missionary Church (the Christian denomination that we had grown up in) had asked my wife and me to open a new missionary work for them in Europe. So, after a time of prayerful consideration, we moved with our four-year-old daughter and two-year-old son to the Normandy region of northwest France to begin a 'church-planting ministry'.

After settling in an apartment in a city of about 100,000 people, I began a small Bible discussion group with some students at the local university. What an interesting group of young men that was! If you were to have asked them to identify themselves, the majority of them would have said something like this: "I am French. I am Catholic. I believe in reincarnation. I am an atheist. I am a scientist. I go to a healer when I am sick. I am a rationalist."

As you can no doubt imagine, we had some very engaging discussions as we looked at the life and words of Jesus as recorded in the gospel of John. Only one or two of these young men claimed to have ever opened a Bible before in their life. Only one of them was a regular attendee in his local Catholic parish church. None of them had ever before investigated the gospel account in this kind of environment.

Over a period of several months we met and slowly progressed through the gospel. It was exciting to watch each week as these men grappled with the fantastic claims of Jesus of Nazareth. One evening, after our study, Marc and Henri approached me with the request that I accompany them to church the following Sunday.

So here I was faced with a dilemma. These university students were just beginning to come to grips with the person and teachings of Jesus. Their new discoveries had apparently sparked in them a desire to worship. Consequently, they wanted to go to church for the first time since they were children. The only problem was that I had not yet begun the church that I had been sent to France to 'start'. Besides, Marc and Henri didn't want just to go to a church; they wanted to go to their church. These guys had been faithfully attending my study and now they were looking to me for reassurance and guidance. Hesitantly, reluctantly, (even fearfully perhaps), I gave in to their urgings.

---

2. This testimony was also shared in the author's two previous books: David E. Bjork, *Unfamiliar Paths: the Challenge of Recognizing the Work of Christ in Strange Clothing* (Pasadena, William Carey Library, 1997), and David E. Bjork and Stephen J. March, *As Pilgrims Progress: Learning How Christians Can Walk Hand in Hand When They Don't See Eye to Eye* (San Diego: Aventine Press, 2006).

A painful discovery

I will never forget the mixed emotions that I felt when I first entered *l'église Saint-Pierre*. Although I had previously visited several cathedrals and church buildings in France, I had never attended Mass and didn't really know what to expect.

The first thing that struck me was the large number of people present at the Mass. The church was packed with between 600 and 650 people. This was unheard of in our area! In fact, I was later informed that just three years earlier only around fifty people regularly attended Mass in this same parish. Here, to my amazement, was a full church service.

I also felt very uncomfortable in the liturgical setting. It was a completely foreign environment to me, and I never knew when I was to sit or stand (it seemed that the Catholics were continually changing their position) or when to speak or be silent. I had a difficult time following along in the Missal, and couldn't even join in reciting the Lord's Prayer (this was not something that I had memorized in French). I felt like a fish out of water.

As real as this discomfort was, it was insignificant compared to the devastating experience that took place in the middle of Mass. What occurred hit me so powerfully that I began to tremble. We were standing in prayer when suddenly, unexpectedly, I began to sense the presence of God's Spirit. What I was sensing couldn't be true! God was not supposed to be there! Everything that I had been taught, everything that I had taught others said that God would not be present at a Roman Catholic Mass! In other words, I believed that God could go to Mass to convict people of their sinfulness and need of the Savior, but he wouldn't hang around afterwards! My theological convictions were that God's Spirit should not be at a Roman Catholic Mass.

When we left Mass I told my wife, "I am never going to go to Mass again! I don't like what I felt in there!"

Checking it out

A couple of weeks later another member of our Bible study group "took me by the hand" and led me back to Mass at St. Peter's. Once again I was overwhelmed during the Mass by a sense of God's presence. I imagine that what I felt must have been similar to the emotions Peter experienced when the Holy Spirit fell on Cornelius and his household before he had a chance to finish his sermon (Acts 10:44). Peter must have wondered how God could be so quick to give his Spirit to this Roman soldier. Peter hadn't had the time to 'straighten him out'. The Scriptures don't even indicate that Cornelius had time to 'repent' and be 'converted' (although I am sure that this actually took place). As had happened with Peter in his relationship to Cornelius, God sneaked up on me and surprised me by his grace to an 'outsider'.

Now, I should remind you that I come from a conservative evangelical Protestant background. I have been taught not to put my trust in what I feel or sense. So when the conflict came between what I was 'sensing' and what I 'knew to be true', I automatically favored the discernment of my mind. At the same time, in my spirit I was deeply troubled. At the end of the second experience of the Mass I felt led to get together with the parish priest to see if I couldn't sort some of these things out.

We met in Father Norbert's office the following afternoon. During the three or four hours together I shared with him the story that you have just finished reading. He graciously listened, and then shared his own testimony with me. After I had asked him some specific questions concerning doctrines over which our churches are in disagreement, we spent some time in prayer.

This meeting with Father Norbert only deepened my confusion. I continued to sense that I was in the presence of a man in whom dwelt the Spirit of the living God. As I listened to his testimony I could identify specific moments of conversion in his life, and his devotion to our Lord Jesus Christ came through loud and clear. At the same time, he held beliefs that I couldn't accept. How could this be? Was I reading him correctly? At times I felt that we were saying the same things, and at others I sensed that we were in completely different worlds.

In order to try to discern more clearly what was going on, I asked if Father Norbert would meet with me for prayer once a week. As a result we met and prayed together nearly every Wednesday morning for three and a half years. Sometimes we prayed together for 15 or 20 minutes; sometimes this time of sharing and prayer took the entire morning.

I am sad to have to admit that it took three and a half years for God to overcome my religious prejudices. The first hurdle was recognizing Father Norbert as my brother in Christ. That hurdle was overcome rather quickly. As I got to know Father Norbert, as I witnessed the vitality of his faith and the consistency of his obedient submission to the Spirit and the Scriptures, I was not only convinced of his relationship with the Savior, but also challenged in my own walk with Christ. The second hurdle was more difficult to overcome. I was still plagued by the question: How can Father Norbert be an obedient disciple of Jesus Christ and remain a practicing Roman Catholic priest? The words of Paul Billheimer, a former radio pastor and Bible college president, helped me to understand that this is a question between Father Norbert and God, and not a question between Father Norbert and me:

> If you are scripturally born again you are a member of the Body of Christ and a son of my very own Father. As a member of the same family, you are my own brother, whether you realize it or acknowledge it or not. As far as I am concerned, this is true whether you are a Charismatic or anti-Charismatic; whether you believe that everyone should speak in tongues or whether you believe that speaking in tongues is of the devil; whether you believe that the gifts of the Spirit are in operation in the church today or whether you believe they ceased at the close of the Apostolic age; whether you are an Arminian and believe in eternal security or in falling from grace; whether you accept only the 'King James' or prefer a modern version; whether you believe in baptismal regeneration or no ordinances at all; whether you believe in immersion or sprinkling, infant or adult baptism; whether you wash feet or don't; whether you are a Methodist, Baptist, Presbyterian, Disciples of Christ, Church of Christ, Mennonite, Amish, Seventh Day Adventist, Episcopalian, Catholic or no denomination at all; whether you believe in female or only male ordination; whether you think that Saturday is the true Sabbath and should be kept holy or whether you think that the day is indifferent; whether you eat meat or are a vegetarian; whether you drink coffee, tea and soft drinks or only water, fruit juices and milk; whether you wear a toupee or sport a bald head; whether you color your hair or not; whether you are a pre-, a post-, or an amillennialist; whether you are a Republican, a Democrat or a Socialist; whether your skin is white, black, red, brown or yellow; and if there be any other doubtful matters over which we differ. If you are born again, we are still members of the same family and organic parts of the same spiritual Body. I may think some of your beliefs are as crazy as a loon, but if I have sufficient love for God, agape love, I will not reject you as a person. (Billheimer 1981:114)

As I got to know Father Norbert I began to realize that God's family extends beyond the limits of my own church denomination and reaches even into unexpected places. Perhaps Jesus was alluding to this reality when he said: "I have other sheep that are not of this sheep pen. I must bring them also. They too will listen to my voice, and there shall be one flock and one shepherd" (John 10:16). I learned through a slow, painful, and drawn-out process that my ability to fellowship with Father Norbert could not be based on shared theological understandings, liturgical practices, or on concepts and opinions concerning 'non-essentials'. If we were to come together it would have to be on agreement over evangelical truths which are basic to salvation and on our common life in Christ.

This experience raised a number of unavoidable questions: What value should I accord to the faith and Christian witness of Catholics? Since Father Norbert, and undoubtedly others, had come into an intimate, personal and saving relationship with Christ within that church, could I treat it as deficient or unfaithful to the gospel?[3] What relationship should I keep with the brothers and sisters who come from a different Christian tradition than my own? And with their church? Since in a desire to maintain the biblical orthodoxy and orthopraxy of the faith, most evangelical Protestants avoid relationships of mutual discovery and dialogue with Catholics and Catholicism, is it worth the risk? Won't that kind of openness be misunderstood by the members of my church. And since I militate for conversions, and personal adherence to Christ, even among those who have already received baptism, isn't there also the risk that my actions will be misunderstood by the Catholics as an attempt to infiltrate a parish community or movement of the church with the goal of 'stealing sheep'? Moreover, I knew that I would not change the stance of my own church, or more largely, evangelical Protestantism, or the pretention of the Catholic Church to be the only faithful church founded on the apostles. So why enter into a relationship of dialogue and discovery with Catholics and their church if the majority of my fellow evangelicals act differently?

---

3. I must point out that today many Catholics continue to believe that Catholicism is Christianity and that the Catholic Church is the *ecclesia*. Groups that have separated from the Catholic Church are therefore 'sects'. Through ecumenical endeavors, Lutheran and Reformed Churches are no longer as quickly classified as sects as they once were. But Evangelical Protestants continue too often to carry this handicap. See "L'Eglise et les sects" by Monsignor Jean Vernette in *l'Eglise Catholique en France*, 1997, edited by the Conférence des Evêques de France, Paris, Cerf/Centurion, where worries are expressed about the 'evangelical groups'.

Some Principles Drawn from This Testimony

In this chapter I cannot explain how my wife Diane and I have answered these questions. Allow me to say simply that we were led to live our faith in Christ, in association with Catholics, while at the same time clearly communicating our identity and convictions as evangelical Protestants. We were led to act like evangelical Protestant disciples of Jesus Christ, who live their faith in the midst of a Catholic community, and we chose deliberately to serve that community. This decision was founded on the conviction that the evangelization of the world depends in some way on the visible unity of the disciples of Jesus Christ (cf. John 17:20–21), and on the choice of Christ who being in very nature God, humbled himself taking the very nature of a servant, so that we might be saved (cf. Phil 2:5–8). This means, concretely, that we continued to evangelize our neighbors and friends, but that we never founded an evangelical Protestant church. Instead, we accompanied our converts on the path of discipleship and reinsertion into their church of origin, the Catholic Church. For thirty years we helped 'Catholic atheists', who were far from their church, to become 'Catholic disciples of Jesus Christ', who rediscovered their church and who helped other 'good Catholics' to deepen their obedience to Christ and accompany others on the path of discipleship.

Neither does space allow me to share all of the ups and downs of such a missionary enterprise. I have just enough room to draw a few lessons from our experience and propose a last theological reflexion that gives legitimacy to this kind of synergistic relationship between disciples who belong to differing traditions.

From this testimony, I will make three rapid observations:

1) First, I recognize our human tendency to reject all other Christian experiences than our own. We consider our own experience to be uniquely faithful to the Word of God. This was my case at the beginning of this pilgrimage. At that time, I thought that only the believers and churches who reflected my religious sensitivities and expressed them as I did my tradition, to be truly Christian. These were the only ones that I thought were faithful to divine revelation. This was largely through ignorance. I had received, at that time in my life, only an understanding of Catholicism based upon centuries of accusations of infidelity and reciprocal excommunications. I had no personal experience of Catholicism, no personal relationship

with a practicing Catholic whom I admired for his devotion to Christ. This leads me to my second observation.

2) This experience underlines the importance of personally encountering the members of the other Christian traditions.

3) Third, some Christians reject all collaboration with others out of a fear of compromising or of losing one's identity. That was one of our fears when we began hanging around Catholics. In fact, we have experienced quite the contrary. It is when we found ourselves in dialogue and common action with Catholics that we began to really understand our particularities. The experience of living our faith, as evangelical Protestants in a Catholic setting, pushed us continually to deepen our consecration to Christ and to examine under new light the acts of piety that we have received from our own tradition.

At this point a meditation on the way in which the Holy Spirit accompanies us will be extremely valuable, for it will reveal how God lives and acts in synergy with us.

The Holy Spirit as the Model of Personal Accompaniment

In what follows I will draw lessons from the actions of God, the Holy Spirit, as they might be applied to the way we accompany someone in Christian discipleship who does not belong to our faith family. I am fully aware that in some ways the work of God's Spirit cannot be mirrored in our accompaniment of others. He is uniquely capable of guiding Jesus' followers along the way of the truth (John 16:12–15), and empowering them to testify to Jesus (John 15:26–27; 20:21–23). There are, however, several ways in which we might find it appropriate to model our mission after the example of the Holy Spirit. I believe that the most foundational of these is found in what Jesus Christ said the Spirit would do with and for us when he described him as the *Paraclete*.[4]

'*Parakletos*', often printed in English as '*Paraclete*', challenges the translator of John's gospel. Major translations render it as 'Comforter' (KJV), 'Helper' (NASB), 'Advocate' (NRSV) and 'Counselor' (NIV). The Greek word itself contains all those meanings, describing one called or sent for to assist

---

4. The term *Paracletos* (paravklhtoß) as a designation of the Holy Spirit occurs only in John's gospel (14:16, 26; 15:26; 16:7).

another (Mounce 1993, 353). *Paraclete* is the Greek term sometimes used of an attorney who 'comes alongside' a client in the courtroom. In like fashion I propose that we who seek to make disciples of Jesus can work synergistically with Christians holding different doctrines, traditions, methods, goals, and orientations than our own by intentionally coming alongside them for the explicit task of stimulating faith, supporting them in their obedience to Jesus' teaching, and encouraging them to accompany others in discipleship. In the face of ever increasing diversity within global Christianity I hold that it is appropriate for us to act '*paracleticly*' by coming alongside the followers of Jesus from different ecclesial traditions for a period of time, brief or extended, in partnership with the Holy Spirit, so as to help them to produce "fruit that remains" (John 15:8).

I will not attempt to formulate a 'how-to-do-it' approach. Instead, I will offer three general principles that I believe must govern a *paracletic* approach.[5] (1) A *paracletic* model of mission will be *respectful* – it will take seriously the story that is being written in the lives of the other followers of Christ. (2) A *paracletic* model of mission will be *participative* – it will be primarily the ministry of involving ones' self in what God is already doing in the life of that person. (3) A *paracletic* model of mission will be *intentional* – it will have a trajectory, an aim, a target and a purpose.

To begin with, . . .

A *paracletic* model of accompaniment will be *respectful*

When the Holy Spirit teaches us (John 14:26; 15:13), brings things to our mind and helps us to understand them, he does so in a way that does not violate the particularities of our personhood. He does not impose himself on us in an approach that eradicates the story of our existence. Instead, he comes alongside us in a manner that emboldens us to look deeply *into* and *through* the events of our lives to discover the past and present action of God. He does not overlook or ignore the sinful twists and turns of our being. But even as he leads us into all truth (John 16:13), he does so as a 'Comforter', 'Helper' and 'Counselor' who enables us to face with respect and critical honesty both our shortcomings as well as the experience of God that is rooted in the events of our lives.

---

5. For what follows, I am relying heavily on the reflection about spiritual mentoring developed by Keith R. Anderson and Randy D. Reese (1999).

In the same way, a *paracletic* approach to accompaniment will be built upon the conviction that God's activity precedes our involvement in the life of that person. If you operate within this paradigm you will learn to see that there is a story that is being written in the lives of the followers of Christ that you encounter who are not members of your own faith tradition. You will pay close attention to that story and recognize there the already present action of God. You will not attempt to invent, or rewrite that story. Rather, you will understand that one aspect of your role is to assist those whom you have been led to serve to see ever more clearly the development of the narrative of God's action in their own experience. In fact, the success or effectiveness of such a relationship may be directly related to your ability to move beneath the most immediate, visible Christian rituals and creeds; to 'read between the lines', as it were, so as to discover the story that is being written in the lives of those you are called to accompany.

Learning to appreciate the truth that is embodied in the sacred story of other followers of Christ is not something that comes naturally to evangelicals. Our own experience of God is rooted in a history shaped by fundamentalist separatism and a biblical hermeneutic that has, more often than not, legitimized our experience of distancing ourselves from those followers of Christ with whom we disagree.[6] That was my own theological inheritance, which explains perhaps why one of the most significant shifts that has occurred in my thinking in the past 30 years has to do with my understanding of the legitimacy and importance of God's work through other Christian narratives.

When I arrived in France I was ignorant of what God had already been doing in that country through the Reformed, Lutheran and Roman Catholic faith communities. I was even unaware of the long history and impact of the witness of the Baptists, Brethren, Mennonites, Methodists, Pentecostals, and other Free churches in that country. In other words, I went to France with the naïve and somewhat arrogant feeling that I was carrying the most genuine communication of Spirit-filled Christianity that the French could encounter. I was sure of the validity of my own walk with Christ and certain that the people whom I encountered, who did not express their relationship with God through Christ in the same way, did not enjoy the same depth of communion with the Father. Moreover, the fact that so many of the baptized have yet

---

6. Some of the Scriptures used to justify this position are: 2 Cor 6:14–18; Rom 16:17; Gal 1:8–9; Eph 5:11; 2 Tim 3:1–5; Tit 3:10.

to be evangelized convinced me that their faith traditions were ineffective in communicating the Christian faith and forming true disciples of Christ. In sum, when I arrived in France I didn't think that I needed to be in any significant relationship with the other Christian families in that country. There was one French pastor who, early on in my ministry in France, said to me: "Most missionaries are ineffective in France because they do not come to serve the existing churches, but only to do their own thing." It took years, however, for me to learn the importance of sharing the Christian faith in a way that both honors one's own Christian narrative while hallowing that of the other.

Today, I believe that our accompaniment of others must take account of God's previous and current work and be marked by what I will call 'cruciformity'. In other words, since God is always actively at work in our world by his Spirit, and especially so within the different Christian families, an appropriate accompaniment of others must take seriously the work that God is already doing through the different communities of Christian tradition.[7] This can hardly be done while ignoring our common history, or denying our common calling and destiny under the common confession of Jesus as Lord. Additionally, our encounter with other Christians can never rest on an arrogant or triumphalist sense of superiority and possession. Rather, there must be 'cruciformity' or, if you prefer, a *kenosis*, a 'self-emptying', that leaves each of us open to the possibility of change and correction, as with the apostle Peter, who was instrumental in the conversion of the Gentile Cornelius (Acts 10) but who was himself also 'converted' through the realization that "God shows no partiality" (Acts 10:34–35). This was no 'easy' conversion for Peter because it overthrew his long-held opinions.[8] It pressed him to change his

---

7. Tilden Edwards offers one of the best definitions of Christian tradition that I have ever heard: "Christian tradition is the lived and tested experience and reflection of a diverse body of people over time united by a commitment to approach the purpose and way of life through the lineage of Jesus Christ" (1980, 35).

8. Kenneth Bailey (2008, 45) notes that the word used in Acts 10:19, where Peter received a vision commanding him to visit a Gentile family, is a variation of the Greek verb *thymos*, which occurs once in the Gospels where it is used to describe the 'wrath' of the congregation in the synagogue when it rose up to stone Jesus (Luke 4:28). He adds that the only verbal use of this same term in the entire New Testament is found in the story of the wise men, where Herod is in a 'rage' on discovering that the wise men left Bethlehem without reporting back to him regarding the whereabouts of the young child (Matt 2:16). So while English translations of Acts 10:19 commonly say the Peter 'was thinking about' or 'pondering' the vision, Bailey suggests that this was more than a peaceful contemplation or passive reflection. He affirms that this term might be better understood to be saying that Peter was 'very upset' or 'fuming' over the vision.

entire perspective on how God works in the world (Bailey 2008, 45). For this reason some theologians have suggested that Peter and company underwent a change that was more wrenching by far than the change experienced by Cornelius (Park 2005, 151).

Second, . . .

A *paracletic* model of accompaniment will be *participative*

When the Holy Spirit was given at Pentecost he enabled the waiting community to communicate the gospel with power and conviction. In this way he participated with the community that Jesus had called, prepared and commissioned as his witnesses. In fact, God's mission of salvation in the world is totally participative in that it is "the mission of the Son and the Spirit through the Father that includes the church" (Moltmann 1977, 64). In like manner when in disciple making we act *paracleticly* we will ask questions like: What is God up to in this situation? Where is his hand at work in the life of the person that he has led me to accompany at this time? What role would he have me play, to help this person better integrate and foster the faith community to which he or she belongs?

Acting *paracleticly* neither denies nor belittles the importance of the various Christian traditions (Congar 1963). It does not involve the rejection of the constraints of tradition and community. On the contrary, it recognizes that tradition or *paradosis* is a New Testament concept. The apostle Paul speaks of what he 'delivered' to the Corinthians (1 Cor 15:3–5) concerning Jesus. He also exhorts the church at Thessalonica to "stand firm and hold fast to the traditions that you were taught by us, either by word of mouth or by our letter" (2 Thess 2:15). Even the particulars of Christian life must be "according to the tradition": "Now we command you . . . to keep away from believers who are living in idleness and not according to the tradition that they received from us" (2 Thess 3:6). Instead of rejecting tradition, a *paracletic* approach recognizes that the Scriptures are always read from within, and the followers of Christ act out of specific traditions that are to be honored.

Accompanying others in the respect of their tradition does not mean that we become 'one of them'. However, involving ones' self *paracleticly* does entail drawing close enough to the person whom you are accompanying that a 'safe place' for mutual discovery, learning and growth is created. It means operating out of the conviction that each of our Christian traditions contributes a witness that corrects, expands, and challenges all other forms of witness in the worldwide church. And it entails continually overcoming the unsettling discoveries that faithfulness to Christ can, in cultures and traditions unlike our own, look different from the patterns we have evolved (Guder 2002, 90). It also implies confronting the realities, limitations and ambiguities of our traditions, and allowing God's Spirit to teach us how to better name the name of Christ.

None of our spiritual stories are static. As we come alongside other Christians to learn together how to better resemble Christ in the power of the Holy Spirit, we discover over time the fullness and depth of our common missionary mandate. As we make that discovery we encounter Christ in ways that broaden and deepen our understanding of the gospel and the story of our own experience. Rather than relating to other Christian traditions out of a hermeneutics of suspicion, a *paracletic* model of mission creates a 'place' where we can listen to God, to the Scriptures, and to our shared and particular stories in a manner that opens new spaces of meaning and action.

Finally, . . .

A *paracletic* model of accompaniment will be *intentional*

If we aren't seeking through that accompaniment of a person who already belongs to a faith community to plant or start a church, then what might be the trajectory, aim, target or purpose that we are pursuing? Throughout this book I have insisted that our only legitimate goal is to accompany others on the path of discipleship in the footsteps of Jesus. We seek deliberately and unashamedly to stimulate the person whom we accompany, by our actions and by our words, toward new levels of obedience to Christ. It is a relationship of mutual help in the process of spiritual growth and maturation. This process lasts the entire lifetime. It is a very personal course of ongoing *metanoia* and surrender to Christ. While it maintains that all of Christ's followers are called to grow in love for God and others, it acknowledges that each of us is unique and follows a particular path of surrender and commitment which is not a simple 'carbon copy' of the experience of others.

Because a *paracletic* model of accompaniment in discipleship brings our story into dialogue with the stories God is writing in other communities of Christian faith it can be used to awaken each of us to our uniqueness and to authentic acts of witness to Christ. This kind of unity in diversity is, in fact, essential to our witness. For this reason I persevere in affirming that personal accompaniment in discipleship must be at the heart of our pursuit of unity, and unity between the disciples of Jesus Christ must be a priority in our discipleship.

Questions to Think About:

1. Have you ever encountered a disciple of Jesus in a context that you were not expecting? How did you react to that discovery?

2. How do you respond to the idea of accompanying someone in discipleship without trying to integrate him or her into your faith community? How might your friends react to that kind of approach?

3. In your opinion, why did Jesus link our mission to our unity as his disciples?

Bibliography

Aldrich, Joseph C. 1981. *Life-Style Evangelism: Crossing Traditional Boundaries to Reach the Unbelieving World*. Portland: Multnomah Press.

Anderson, Keith R. and Randy D. Reese. 1999. *Spiritual Mentoring: A Guide for Seeking and Giving Direction*. Downers Grove: InterVarsity Press.

Anderson, Neil T. 1990. "Finding Freedom in Christ." In *Wrestling With Dark Angels*, edited by C. Peter Wagner and Douglas Pennoyer, 125–159. Ventura: Regal Books.

Arnold, Duane W. and C. George Fry. 1988. *Francis: A Call to Conversion*. Grand Rapids: Cantilever Books.

Audisio, Gabriel, ed. 1990. *Les Vaudois des origines à leur fin (XIIe–XVIe siècles)*. Turin: A. Meynier.

Bailey, Kenneth E. 2008. *Jesus Through Middle Eastern Eyes: Cultural Studies in the Gospels*. Downers Grove: InterVarsityPress.

Baker, Ian Martin. 1974 (March). "Forum Discipleship." *New Wine*.

Barclay, William. 1975. *The Gospel of John* (Vol. 1). Philadelphia: Westminster Press.

Barna, George. 2001. *Growing True Disciples*. Colorado Springs: Waterbrook Press.

Barna. n.d. *www.barna.org*. Accessed on 17 December 2011 on http://www.barna.org/transformation-articles/252-barna-survey-examines-changes-in-worldview-among-christians-over-the-past-13-years.

Barth, Karl. 1956. *Church Dogmatics* Vol. IV (1). London: T. & T. Clark.

Basham, Don. 1974 (March). "Forum: Discipleship." *New Wine*, 27.

Beasley-Murray, George R. 1954. *Baptism in the New Testament*. Londres: Macmillan.

Beasley-Murray, J. H. 1987. *John*. Dallas, TX: Word.

Beckwith, R. T. 1988. "Saint." In *New Dictionary of Theology*, edited by Sinclair B. Ferguson, David F. Wright and J. I. Packer, 609–610. Downers Grove: InterVarsity Press.

Benetreau, Samuel. 1997 (March/April). "Paul et l'enseignement de Jésus." *Fac-Réflexion* 40–41, 4–19.

Besse, George. 2014. *La Revue réformée*. (P. Wells, ed.) Accessed May 2014, on http://larevuereformee.net/

Bevere, John. 2002. *Under Cover: The Promise of Protection Under his Authority*. Nashville: Thomas Nelson.

Billheimer, Paul. 1981. *Love Covers: A Viable Platform for Christian Unity.* Fort Washington: Christian Literature Crusade.

Bjork, David E. 1997. *Unfamiliar Paths: the Challenge of Recognizing the Work of Christ in Strange Clothing.* Pasadena: William Carey Library.

Bjork, David E. and Stephen John March. 2006. *As Pilgrims Progress: Learning How Christians Can Walk Hand in Hand When They Don't See Eye to Eye.* San Diego: Aventine Press.

Blocher, Henri. 1988. *Révélation des origines.* Lausanne: Presses Bibliques Universitaires.

Blum, E. A. 1981. "2 Peter." In *The Expositor's Bible Commentary,* edited by F. E. Gaebelein, 255–289. Grand Rapids: Zondervan.

Borthwick, Paul. 2012. *Western Christians in Global Mission: What's the Role of the North American Church?* Downers Grove: InterVarsity Press.

Bosch, David. 1995. *Dynamique de la mission chrétienne: Histoire et avenir des modèles missionnaires.* Lomé/Paris/Genève: Haho/Karthala/Labor et Fides.

Brown, Colin. 1979. "Redemption." In *Dictionary of New Testament Theology* (vol. 3), edited by Colin Brown, 212–213. Grand Rapids: Zondervan.

Brown, Raymond E. 1966. *The Gospel According to John* (Vol. 2). New York: Doubleday.

———. 1997. *An Introduction to the New Testament.* Londres: Yale University Press.

Brunner, Emil. 1952. *The Misunderstanding of the Church.* London: Lutterworth.

Bubeck, Mark. 1975. *The Adversary.* Chicago: Moody Press.

Buckingham, Jamie. 1990 (January/February). "The End of the Discipleship Era." *Ministries Today,* 46–48.

Bullinger, E. W. 1995. *Figures of Speech Used in the Bible.* Grand Rapids: Baker Book House.

Burge, G. M. 1992. "Glory." In *Dictionary of Jesus and the Gospels,* edited by Joel B. Green, Scot McKnight and I. Howard Marshall, 268–270. Downers Grove: InterVarsity Press.

Burgess, Stanley M. and Eduard M. Van Der Maas. 2002. "The Shepherding Movement." In *The New International Dictionary of Pentecostal and Charismatic Movements,* edited by Stanley M. Burgess and Eduard M. Van Der Maas. Grand Rapids: Zondervan.

Burrows, William R. 1981 (1980). *New Ministries: The Global Context.* Maryknoll: Orbis Books.

Carson, D. A. 1984. "Matthew." In *The Expositor's Bible Commentary* (Vol. 8), edited by Frank E. Gaebelein, 1–599. Grand Rapids: Zondervan Publishing House.

Catéchisme ou abrégé de toutes les vérités de la religion chrétienne. 1815. Londres: G. Auld.

Chadwick, Henry. 1984. *Early Christian Thought and the Classical Tradition.* New York: Oxford University Press.

Clark, Stephen. 1972. *Building Christian Communities.* Notre Dame: Ave Maria Press.

Clinton, J. Robert. 1989. *Leadership Emergence Theory.* Altadena: Barnabas Resources.

———. 1993. *Leadership Perspectives: How to Study the Bible For Leadership Insights.* Altadena: Barnabas Publishers.

Clinton, J. Robert and Richard W. Clinton. 1991. *The Mentor Handbook: Detailed Guidelines and Helps for Christian Mentors and Mentorees.* Altadena: Barnabas Publishers.

Coleman, Robert. 1972. *The Master Plan of Evangelism.* Grand Rapids: Fleming H. Revell.

Congar, Yves. 1963. *La Tradition et les traditions: Essai théologique.* Paris: Fayard.

———. 1984. *La Parole et le Souffle.* Paris: Desclée.

Congrégation pour la doctrine de la foi. 2014 (June 14). Disponible sur: http://www.vatican.va/roman_curia/congregations/cfaith/documents/rc_con_cfaith_doc_20071203_nota-evangelizzazione_fr.html.

Coppes, L. J. 1980. "Adar." In *Theological Wordbook of the Old Testament,* edited by R. Laird Harris, L. A. Gleason and Bruce K. Waltke, 13. Chicago: Moody Press.

Cory, Lloyd, ed. 1977. *Quote Unquote.* Wheaton: Victor Books.

Cross, F. R. 1961. "The Priestly Tabernacle." In *The Biblical Archeologist Reader,* edited by David Noel Freedman and George Ernest Wright, 225–227. Garden City: Anchor Books.

Danby, Herbert. 1933. *The Mishna.* Oxford: Oxford University Press.

Daniélou, Jean. 1957. *Les manuscrits de la mer Morte et les origines du christianisme.* Paris: Editions du Cerf.

Daniel-Rops. 1965. *L'histoire de l'Eglise du Christ* (Vol. II). Paris : Librairie Fayard.

Département de Théologie Spirituelle de la Sainte Croix. 2014. (September 11). *Les chrétiens dans le monde.* Available on http://www.vatican.va/spirit/documents/spirit_20010522_diogneto_fr.html

Dempsey, Ron D. 1997. *Faith Outside the Walls: Why People Don't Come and Why the Church Must Listen.* Macon: Smyth & Helwys.

Dennis, Marie, Joseph Nagle, Cynthia Moe-Lobeda and Stuart Taylor. 2003. *St Francis and the Foolishness of God.* Maryknoll: Orbis Books.

Dickason, C. Fred. 1987. *Demon Possession & the Christian.* Wheaton: Crossway Books.

Dockery, D. S. 1992. "Baptism." In *Dictionary of Jesus and the Gospels,* edited by Joel B. Green, Scot McKnight and I. Howard Marshall, 55–58. Downers Grove: InterVarsity Press.

Dulles, Avery. 1987. *Models of the Church.* New York: Image Books.

Dunn, J. D. 1962. "Baptism." In *New Bible Dictionary,* edited by J. D. Douglas, 121–123. Downers Grove: InterVarsity Press.

Edwards, Tilden. 1980. *Spiritual Friend: Reclaiming the Gift of Spiritual Direction.* New York: Paulist Press.

Eims, Leroy. 1980. *The Lost Art of Disciple-Making.* Grand Rapids: Zondervan Publishing House.

Engle, James F. and Wilbert Norton. 1982. *What's Gone Wrong With the Harvest?* Grand Rapids: Zondervan.

Flinn, Frank K. 1999. "Conversion: The Pentecostal and Charismatic Experience." In *Religious Conversion: Contemporary Practices and Controversies*, edited by Christopher Lamb and Darrol Bryant, 51–74. New York: Cassell.

Foster, Richard J. 1899. *Celebration of Discipline.* New York: Harper & Row.

Furnish, Victor P. 1989. "The Jesus-Paul Debate: From Baur to Bultmann." In *Paul and Jesus, Collected Essays,* edited by A. J. Wedderburn, 47–48. London: Sheffeld Academic Press.

Gilliland, Dean S. 1983. *Pauline Theology & Mission Practice.* Lagos: Tryfam Printers Ltd.

Goma, David. 2014. *Centre du Réveil Chrétien.* Accessed 27 June 2014, on http://www.crcfrance.com/pages/index.php?action=fiche&id=68

Geiger, Eric, Michael Kelley and Philip Nation. 2012. *Transformational Discipleship: How People Really Grow.* Nashville: B & H Publishing Group.

Gesenius, Wilhelm. 1952. *Hebrew and English Lexicon of the Old Testament.* Ed. Francis Brown. New York: Oxford University .

Grebe, K. 1997. *www.cabtal.org.* Found on www.cabtal.org/pdf/RTApaper.pdf. and www.mission-amf.org/include/upload/doc/francophonie.pdf

Green, Michael. 1968. *The Second Epistle General of Peter and the General Epistle of Jude.* London: Tyndale.

———. 2001 [1970]. *Evangelism in the Early Church.* Eugene: Wipf and Stock Publishers.

Green, Julien. 1983. *Frère François.* Paris: Editions du Seuil.

Grossouw, W. 1958. "La glorification du Christ dans le quatrième Evangile." In *L'Evangile de Jean: Etudes et problèmes,* edited by M. E. Boismard, 135–140. Bruges: Desclée.

Grudem, Wayne. 1994. *Systematic Theology: An Introduction to Biblical Doctrine.* Grand Rapids: Zondervan Publishing House.

Guder, Darrell L. 2000. *The Continuing Conversion of the Church.* Grand Rapids: Wm. B. Eerdmans.

Hadas-Lebel, Mireille. 1986. *Histoire de la langue hébraïque.* Paris: P.O.F.

Harris, R. Laird, Gleason L. Archer and Bruce K. Waltke, eds. 1980. *Theological Wordbook of the Old Testament* (Vol. 1). Chicago: Moody Press.

Harrison, V. 1991. "Perichoresis in the Greek Fathers." *St Vladimir's Theological Quarterly* 35 (1), 53–56.

Hawkins, Greg L. and Cally Parkinson. 2007. *Reveal: Where Are You?* Chicago: Willow Creek Association.

Hawthorne, G. F. 1992. "Amen." In *Dictionary of Jesus and the Gospels,* edited by Joel B. Green, Scot McKnight and I. Howard Marshall. Downers Grove: InterVarsity Press.

Heideman, Eugene. P. 1996. "Proselytism, Mission, and the Bible." *International Bulletin of Missionary Research,* 20 (1), 10–12.

Hendricks, Howard G. 1995. *As Iron Sharpens Iron: Building Character in a Mentoring Relationship.* Chicago: Moody Press.

Henrichsen, Walter A. 1974. *Disciples are Made-Not-Born.* Wheaton: Victor Books.

Hesselgrave, David J. 1982. *Communicating Christ Cross-Culturally.* Grand Rapids: Baker.

Hoekendijk, Johannes C. 1967. *The Church Inside Out.* Londres: SCM Press.

Holl, Adolf. 1980. *The Last Christian.* Garden City: Doubleday.

Hull, Bill. 2006. *The Complete Book of Discipleship: On Being and Making Followers of Christ.* Colorado Springs: NavPress.

———. 2010. *The Disciple-making Church: Leading a Body of Belivers on the Journey of Faith.* Grand Rapids: BakerBooks.

Hunsberger, George R. 2008. "Is There a Biblical Warrant for Evangelism?" In *The Study of Evangelism: Exploring a Missional Practice of the Church,* edited by Paul W. Chilcote and Laceye Warner, 59–72. Grand Rapids: Wm B. Eerdmans.

Hunter, George. G. 1992. *How to Reach Secular People.* Nashville: Abingdon Press.

Jalla. 2003. *Pierre Valdo* (Vol. 1). Chailly-Montreux: Editions Vida.

Johnson, Luke Timothy. 1999. *Living Jesus: Learning the Heart of the Gospel.* San Francisco: HarperSanFrancisco.

Johnston, J. G. 2014. (September 19). *Discipleship: Stepping Stones to Developing Your Church's Strategy.* Nashville: LifeWay Christian Resources. Found on www. lifeway.com

Josèphe, F. 2013. *Guerre des Juifs* (Vol. 5). Edited by T. Reinach, translation Harmand. Paris: Hachette.

———. 2014. *Histoire ancienne.* Paris: Editions Paléo.

Julien, Tom. 1976. *Études sur l'Épitre aux Éphésiens.* Lugny: Editions CLE.

Kaiser, Walter C. 1978. *Toward an Old Testament Theology.* Grand Rapids: Zondervan.

Kapitao, D. n.d. "Accomplir la grande mission à travers l'implantation d'église", http://eatt-rhema.over-blog.org/article-accomplir-la-grande-mission-a-travers-l-implantation-d-eglise-47188076.html Accessed 23 August 2013.

Kittel, G. 1976. "kerusso." In *Theological Dictionary of the New Testament,* edited by G. Kittel (translation G. W. Bromiley, Vol. 3). Grand Rapids: Eerdmans.

Koch, Kurt. 1978. *Occult Bondage and Deliverance.* Grand Rapids: Kregel.

Kraft, Charles H. 1989. *Christianity With Power.* Ann Arbor: Servant Books.

———. 1991. *Communicate With Power.* Manila: OMF Literature Inc.

———. 1994. "Dealing With Demonization." In *Behind Enemy Lines: An Advanced Guide to Spiritual Warfare,* edited by Charles H. Kraft and Mark White, 79–120. Ann Arbor: Servant Books.

———. 1997. *I Give You Authority.* Grand Rapids: Baker Book House.

Kuyper, A. 1931. *Stone Lectures.* Grand Rapids: Wm. B. Eerdmans.

Lausanne Committee for World Evangelization. 2005. *Making Disciples of Oral Learners.* Lima: International Orality Network.

Lambert, Steven. 2003. *Charismatic Captivation: Authoritarian Abuse and Psychological Enslavement in Neo-Pentecostal Churches.* Chapel Hill: Real Truth Publications.

Latourette, Kenneth S. 1975. *A History of Christianity: Beginnings to 1500* (Vol. 1). San Francisco: HarperOne.

Leighton, T. 2008. (November 7). *coveringandauthority.com.* Available on Covering And Authority: http://coveringandauthority.com/covering-and-apostolic-authority/scriptures-used-in-covering-theology/heb-1317-obey-your-leaders-and-submit-to-them/

Le Goff, Jacques, ed. 1968. *Hérésies et sociétés dans l'Europe préindustrielle, XIème - XVIIIème siècle.* Paris-La Haye: Mouton.

Lenoir, Frédéric. 2008. *Petit traité d'histoire des religions.* Paris: Plon.

Léon-Dufour, Xavier. 1963. *Les Évangiles et l'histoire de Jésus.* Paris: Editions du Seuil.

L'Eplattenier, Charles. 1993. *L'Evangile de Jean*. Genève: Labor et Fides.

Lewis, J. P. 1980. "qahal." In *Theological Wordbook of the Old Testament* (Vol. 2), edited by R. Laird Harris, Gleason L. Archer and Bruce K. Waltke, 790. Chicago: Moody Press.

Liederbach, Mark and Alvin Reid. 2009. *The Convergent Church: Missional Worship in an Emerging Culture*. Grand Rapids: Kregel.

Lloyd-Jones, D. Martyn. 1972. *Preaching and Preachers*. Grand Rapids: Zondervan Publishing House.

Longpré, Ephrem. 1966. *François d'Assise et son expérience spirituelle*. Paris: Beauchesne.

Louw, Johannes P. and Eugene A. Nida. 1989. *Greek-English Lexicon of the New Testament: Based on Semantic Domains* (2nd ed., Vol. 1). New York: United Bible Societies.

Lusby, F. S. 1987. "Laity." In *The Encyclopedia of Religion* (Vol. 8), edited by Mircea Eliade, 425–429. New York: Macmillan Publishing Company.

MacArthur, John. 1990. *Back to Basics*. Chicago: Moody Press.

Mandryk, Jason. 2010. *Operation World*. Colorado Springs: Biblica Publishing.

McClung, J. L. 1990. "Pentecostal/Charismatic Understanding of Exorcism." In *Wrestling With Dark Angels*, edited by C. Peter Wagner and Douglas Pennoyer, 195–214. Ventura: Regal Books.

McDowell, Josh and David Bellis. 2006. *The Last Christian Generation*. Holiday: Green Key Books.

McKnight, Scot. 2002. *Turning to Jesus: The Sociology of Conversion in the Gospels*. Louisville: Westminster John Knox Press.

Mermet, Gérard. 2001. *Pour comprendre les Français : Francoscopie*. Paris: Larousse.

Merton, Thomas. 1999. *Thoughts in Solitude*. New York: Farrar, Straus & Giroux.

Meyer, I. 1988. "Vérité/Certitude." In *Dictionnaire de théologie*, edited by P. Eicher, 815–818. Paris: Editions du Cerf.

Milne, Bruce. 1993. *The Message of John: Here is your King!* Downers Grove: InterVarsity Press.

Molinier, Nicolas. 2007 (June). « A propos de l'histoire du signe de la croix ». Article published on http://orthodoxie.com and available at http://pistevo.free.fr/files/signedelacroix.pdf

Moltmann, Jürgen. 1977. *The Church in the Power of the Spirit: A Contribution to Messianic Ecclesiology*. London: SCM.

Moore, S. David. 2003. *The Shepherding Movement: Controversy and Charismatic Ecclesiology*. London: T. & T. Clark International.

Moore, T. M. 2010 (June 30). "Are You Jesus?", *breakpoint.org*. Accessed 28 June 2014, on www.breakpoint.org/the-center/columns/viewpoint/15463-are-you-jesus

Monastier, Antoine. 1847. « Pierre Valdo – origine du nom "vaudois" ». In *Histoire de l'Église vaudoise depuis son origine et des Vaudois du Piémont jusqu'à nos jours*, éd. Antoine Monastier. Paris: Delay. Found on http://www.info-bible.org/livres/Histoire.Eglise.Vaudoise.1/08.htm. Accessed on 8 September 2014.

Mounce, William D. 1993. *The Analytical Lexicon to the Greek New Testament.* Grand Rapids: Zondervan.

Munger, Robert Boyd. 2002. *Mon coeur, la demeure de Christ*. Québec: Editions Berekia.

Murphy, Ed. 1990. "We Are at War." In *Wrestling With Dark Angels*, edited by C. Peter Wagner and Douglas Pennoyer, 49–72. Ventura: Regal Books.

———. 1992. *Handbook of Spiritual Warfare*. Nashville: Nelson.

Neill, Stephen. 1990 [1964]. *A History of Christian Missions*. New York: Penguin Books.

Nelson, Alan E. 1994. *Broken in the Right Place: How God Tames the Soul*. Nashville: Thomas Nelson Publishers.

Niebuhr, H. Richard. 1959. *The Kingdom of God in America*. New York: Harper Brothers.

Nixon, R. E. 1994. "Glory." In *New Bible Dictionary* (2nd edition), edited by J. D. Douglas, 423–424. Downers Grove: InterVarsity Press.

Nunn, Philip. 2007 [1990]. *Working Abroad: Today's Tentmaking Challenge*. Found on www.philipnunn.com.

Oswalt, J. N. 1980. "kabed." In *Theological Wordbook of the Old Testament* (Vol. 1), edited by R. Laird Harris, Gleason L. Archer and Bruce K. Waltke, 426–428. Chicago: Moody Press.

Para-Mallam, G. 2013 (July). "Living out the Message." *SPAN* (1), 1–2.

Pargoire, J. 1900. "Les homélies de saint Jean Chrysostome en juillet 399." *Echos d'Orient* (1146–9447), 151–162.

Park, Joon-Sik. 2005. "Evangelism and the Practice of Hospitality." In *Considering the Great Commission: Evangelism and Mission in the Weslean Spirit*, edited by W. Stephen Gunter and Elaine Robinson, 147–158. Nashville: Abingdon Press.

Pew Foundation. 2011. *www.pewforum.org*. Accessed January 2012, on www.pewforum.org/...and.../sub-saharan-africa-executive-summary-fr.pdf

Phalippou, René. 2005. "Le traitement de l'actualité dans La Onzième Heure, "organe d'action évangélique" des Assemblées de Dieu en France." In

L'évangélisation: Des protestants évangéliques en quête de conversions, edited by
Jean-Yves Carluer, 87–115. Charols : Editions Excelsis.

Phillips, Keith. 1981. *The Making of a Disciple.* Old Tappan: Fleming H.
Revell Company.

Pippert, Rebecca Manley. 1979. *Out of the Saltshaker and Into the World.* Downers
Grove: InterVarsity Press.

Pliny the Younger. *Correspondence with Trajan from Bithynia (Epistles X).*
Warminster, Wiltshire: Aris & Phillips, 1990. Pope, Randy. 2013. *Insourcing:
Bringing Discipleship Back to the Local Church.* Grand Rapids: Zondervan.

Posterski, Donald C. 1989. *Reinventing Evangelism: New Strategies for Presenting
Christ in Today's World.* Downers Groves: InterVarsity Press.

Putman, Jim, Bobby William Harrington and Robert E. Coleman. 2013.
*Discipleshift: Five Steps That Help Your Church to Make Disciples Who Make
Disciples.* Grand Rapids: Zondervan.

Rakotoarison, Sylvain. 2014 (September 8). "Charles Péguy, la rigueur intellectuelle
et l'audace dans l'action" (2). Available on Agoravox: http://mobile.agoravox.fr/
culture-loisirs/culture/article/charles-peguy-la-rigueur-155470

Rainer, Sam. 2009 (January 18). "Ten Questions for Formulating a Discipleship
Process." Accessed on 19 September 2014, on Sam Rainer: Leading the
Established Church: http://samrainer.com/2009/01/ten-questions-for-
formulating-a-discipleship-process/

Ramm, Bernard. 1963. *Them He Glorified: A Systematic Study of the Doctrine of
Glorification.* Grand Rapids: Eerdmans.

Reddin, Opal. L. 1990. "The Holy Spirit and Power: A Wesleyan Understanding,
Response." In *Wrestling With Dark Angels,* edited by C. Peter Wagner and F.
Douglas Pennoyer, 184–193. Ventura: Regal Books.

Santini, Luigi. 1999. *De Pierre Valdo à l'Eglise vaudoise* (Vol. 1). Genève: Labor
et Fides.

Schneider, Reinhold. 1953. *François d'Assise.* Paris: Editions Beauchesne.

Siemens, R. E. 1999 [1981]. "Tentmakers Needed for World Evangelization." In
Perspectives on the World Christian Movement, edited by Ralph D. Winter and
Steven C. Hawthorne, 733–741. Pasadena: William Carey Library.

Simpson, C. 1974 (March). "Making Disciples." *New Wine,* 4–8.

Singlehurst, Laurence. 1995. *Sowing, Reaping, Keeping.* Leicester: Crossway Books.

Smeeton, Donald. D. 1980. "Evangelical trends in Europe, 1970–1980." *Evangelical
Missions Quarterly* 16 (4), 211–216.

Smith, D. K. 1999 (January). "Reviewing the Place of Western Missionaries for the
Third Millennium." *Evangelical Missions Quarterly* 35 (1), 56–61.

Spindler, M. 2001. "Baptême et mission." In *Dictionnaire oecuménique de missiologie: Cent mots pour la mission,* sous dir. Ion Bria, Philippe Chanson, Jacques Gadille, Marc Spindler, 34–37. Paris/ Genève/ Yaoundé: Cerf/ Labor et Fides/ Clé.

Staal, Jan-Hein. 2014. (March 19). *L'unité entre les chrétiens est-elle possible?* Accessed 21 September 2014, on Brunstag.org: http://www.brunstad.org/fr/ edification-chretienne/lunite-entre-les-chretiens-est-elle-possible

Stedman, Ray. C. 1992. *The IVP New Testament Commentary Series: Hebrews.* Downers Grove: InterVarsity Press.

Stein, Robert H. 1978. *The Method and Message of Jesus' Teachings.* Philadelphia: The Westminster Press.

Stendahl, Krister. 1976. *Paul Among Jews and Gentiles and Other Essays.* Philadelphia: Fortress Press.

Stoltzfus, Tony. 2005. *Leadership Coaching: The Disciplines, Skills and Heart of a Christian Coach.* Virginia Beach: Transformational Leadership Coaching. Found on www.Coach22.com

Stone, Bryan. 2007. *Evangelism after Christendom: The Theology and Practice of Christian Witness.* Grand Rapids: BrazosPress.

Stott, John R. W. 1995. *La lettre aux Ephésiens.* Mulhouse: Editions Grâce et Vérité.

———. 1999. "Make Disciples, Not Just Converts: Evangelism Without Discipleship Dispenses Cheap Grace." *Christianity Today* 43 (12).

Terry, J. O. 2008. *Basic Bible Storying: Preparing and Presenting Bible Stories for Evangelism, Discipleship, Training, and Ministry.* Fort Worth: Church Stating Network.

Tertullien. 1914. *Apologétique.* (translation J.-P. Waltzing) Paris: Librairie Bloud et Gay. Accessed 11 September 2014, on http://www.tertullian.org/french/ apologeticum.htm

Thompson, Augustine O. P. 2012. *Francis of Assisi: A New Biography.* Ithaca: Cornell University Press.

Thouzellier, C. 2010. *Hérésie et hérétiques.* Rome: Storia E. Letteratura.

Tourn, Giorgio. 1980. *The Waldensians: The First 800 Years.* (Translation C. P. Merlino). Torino, Italy: Claudiana Editrice.

Tuttle Jr., Robert G. 2006. *The Story of Evangelism: A History of the Witness to the Gospel.* Nashville: Abingdon Press.

Unger, Merrill F. 1977. *Unger's Bible Dictionary* (27th edition). Chicago: Moody Press.

———. 1977. *What Demons Can Do to Saints.* Chicago: Moody Press.

Vaus, Will. 2004. *Mere Theology: A Guide to the Thought of C. S. Lewis.* Downers Grove: InterVarsity Press.

Viguier, Philippe. 2014. *À Demain – L'homme face à la gloire de Dieu.* Found on http://unpoissondansle.net

Walls, Andrew F. 1996. *The Missionary Movement in Christian History: Studies in the Transmission of Faith.* Maryknoll: Orbis Books.

Webb, Keith E. 2012. *The Coach Model for Christian Leaders.* Active Results LLC. Found on www.activeresults.com

Webber, Robert E. 2001. *Journey to Jesus.* Nashville: Abingdon Press.

———. 2003. *Ancient-Future Evangelism.* Grand Rapids: Baker Books.

White, Tom. 1990. *The Believer's Guide to Spiritual Warfare.* Ann Arbor: Servant.

Wilkins, J. M. 1992. "Discipleship." In *Dictionary of Jesus and the Gospels,* edited by Joel B. Green, Scot McKnight and I. Howard Marshall, 182–189. Downers Grove: InterVarsity Press.

Wilkins, Michael. 1988. *The Concept of Disciple in Matthew's Gospel as Reflected in the Use of the Term "Mathetes."* Boston: E. J. Brill.

———. 1992. *Following the Master.* Grand Rapids: Zondervan.

Willaime, Jean-Paul. 2002. "Le protestantisme", in *Encyclopédie des religions,* edited by Giuseppe Annoscia, 435–439. Paris: Universalis.

Willard, Dallas. 1988. *The Spirit of the Disciplines: Understanding How God Changes Lives.* San Francisco: HarperSanFrancisco.

———. 2009. Conférence donné le 24 mars, cité dans Bill Hull, *The Disciple-making Church: Leading a Body of Belivers on the Journey of Faith.* Grand Rapids: BakerBooks. 2010, 14.

Willis Jr., Avery T. and Mark Snowden. 2010. *Truth that Sticks: How to Communicate Velcro Truth in a Teflon World.* Colorado Springs: NavPress.

Wilson, William. 1987. *New Wilson's Old Testament Word Studies.* Grand Rapids: Kregel Publications.

Wilson-Hartgrove, Jonathan. 2010 (January). "New Monasticism and the Resurrection of American Christianity." *Missiology: An International Review, XXXVIII* (1), 13–19.

Winter, Ralph. 1995. *The Two Structures of God's Redemptive Mission.* Pasadena: William Carey Library.

Wood, A. S. 1978. "Ephesians." In *The Expositor's Bible Commentary* (Vol. 11), edited by F. E. Gaebelein, 3–92. Grand Rapids: Zondervan Publishing House.

Wood, R. 2010 (December). *Mission Frontiers - the online magazine of the U.S. Center for World Mission.* Found on www.missionfrontiers.org/

Wright, Christopher J. H. 2006. *The Mission of God: Unlocking the Bible's Grand Narrative*. Downers Grove: InterVarsity Press Academic.

Wright, N. T. 1994. *Following Jesus: Biblical Reflections on Discipleship*. Grand Rapids: Wm. B. Eerdmans.

Wuest, Kenneth S. 1966. *Ephesians and Colossians in the Greek New Testament* (Vol. 1). Grand Rapids: Wm. B. Eerdmans.

Scripture Index

Old Testament

Genesis
1:28 50
2:7 43
2:24 147
2:3 156
3:8 . . . . 113, 114
3:23-24 113
12:5 21
13:2 21
22:8, 13 117
23:8 174
31:1 112
31:39 105
45:13 112
48:4 174
49:6 174

Exodus
12:11-13 117
19:4-6 113
20:4-5 165
24:13 62
25:8 115
29:38-42 117
29:46 115
29:32-34 114
33:1-5 114
33:13 74
33:16 114
33:18 114
34:6-7 120
34:29-35 83
40:34 114
40:34-38 116

Leviticus
26:11-12 113

Numbers
21:4-9 120

21:6 120
21:8 120
22:4 174

Judges
8:22-32 104
20:2 174

1 Samuel
4:21-22 112
15:23 163
17:47 174

2 Samuel
11-12 106
13 106
14 106
15 106

1 Kings
2:3 174
8:10-11 115
20:1-4 75

1 Chronicles
21 105
25:8 62

2 Chronicles
26 105

Job
30:28 174

Psalms
11:4 112
25:4 74
26:5 174
27:4 118
27:11 74
51:6 161
67:2-3 74
86:11 74

103:12 162
119:35 74
139:23-24 . . . . 160, 161
143:8 74

Proverbs
3:34 80
5:14 174
10:17 147
11:24 147
12:1 147
16:18 164
18:2 148
18:13 142
20:5 148
20:6 147
21:16 174
25:2 147
26:2 159
26:26 174
27:7 147
27:17 103

Ecclesiastes
2:26 79
4:9 68

Isaiah
8:7 112
8:16 62
8:8,16 62
40:3-5 71
42:8 81
50:4 62
53:7 117
54:13 62
58:6-12 147

Jeremiah
6:13 56
11:19 117

13:23 62
23:16, 26 56
23:30 56

Ezekiel
1:27 113

Micah
3:5, 11 56

New Testament

Matthew
1:1-2 71
2:16 221
3:1-17 45
3:7-10 48
3:13-17 43
3:4 155
4:1-11 87
4:8 115
4:18-22 45
4:19 . . . . 44, 69, 148, 209
4:21 196
5:1 58
5:17-20 58
5:23-24 163
5:24-25 47
5:26 57
5:29-30 47
5:34-37 47
5:38-42 47
5:44 47
5:46 134
5:47 134
6:1-7 87
6:1-18 47
6:9 125
6:14-15 162
6:19-21, 25-34 147
6:27 134
6:28 134
6:29 115
6:33 . . . . 47, 148
7:1 47
7:3 134
7:6 47
7:7-8 47
7:12 47
7:15 47
7:15-23 48

7:16 134
7:17-20 7
7:22-23 . . . . 80, 158
7:29 40
8:26 134
8:31 151
9:4 134
9:5 134
9:15 134
9:28 134
10:1, 7-8 40
10:1, 36 58
10:9-10 172
10:24 . . . . 45, 64
10:26-28 47
10:29 112
10:38 65
10:39 124
10:40 44
10:41 16
10:42 57
11:7 134
11:16 134
11:16-19 59
11:27 40
12:11 135
12:29 135
12:34 135
12:48 135
12:49-50 126
13:23 48
14:31 135
15:3 135
15:4 47
15:24 44
15:34 135
16:6 47
16:9 135
16:13 135

16:15 135
16:16-19 175
16:18 14
16:24 164
16:25 124
16:26 135
17:1-9 119
17:17 135
17:20 57
17:25 135
18:1 58
18:10 47
18:12 135
18:13 57
18:15, 21-22 47
18:20 . . . . . 65, 147, 173, 175
18:34-35 161
18:35 163
19:6 47
19:17 135
19:21 170
20:21 135
20:22 135
20:32 135
21:25 135
21:28 135
21:31 57
21:42 135
21:43 48
22:18 135
22:19-21 47
22:37-40 58
22:42 135
22:43-44 40
23:1 58
23:17-19 136
23:33 136
24:1-3 58
24:4, 23-25 158

24:35 40
25:41 151
26:10 136
26:18 37
26:23 191
26:28 46
26:36-56 125
26:39 125
26:40 136
26:53 136
26:54 136
26:55 136
27:46 136
28:18-20 2
28:16-20 . . . . 39, 51
28:18-19 4
28:18-20 . . . . 68, 185
28:19 . . . . . . 14, 43, 45, 47,
          92, 157, 210
28:19-20 . . . . 71, 148
28:20 . . . . 47, 53, 95

Mark

1:9-10 43
1:15 37
1:16-20 45
1:19 196
1:22 40
1:35 87
2:8 136
2:10 40
3:9 129
3:13-15 16
3:13-19 43
3:20 129
3:28 57
3:34-35 126
4:1 87
4:20 48
4:21 136
4:30 136
4:35-41 . . . . 38, 40
4:40 136
5:9 136
5:21-43 40

5:27-32 40
5:30 136
5:39 136
7:18 136
8:12 136
8:17-18 136
8:19 136
8:20 136
8:21 136
8:23 136
8:31 87
8:35 124
9:2-10 119
9:12 137
9:33 137
9:37 44
9:50 137
10:3 137
10:18 137
10:51 137
12:15 137
12:37 129
13:2 137
14:22-25 147
14:32-50 125
14:36 87
14:37 137
16:15 200

Luke

1:1-4 92
1:5-20 74
1:14-17, 31-35, 46-55,
    68-79 72
1:38 74
1:45 74
1:52-53 71
2:9-14, 30-32, 34-35   72
2:32 71
2:41-52 87
2:49 . . . . 72, 137
3:9 48
3:15-18 45
3:21-23 43
3:23-38 71

4:14-9:50 73
4:16-22 71
4:16-30 . . . . 72, 73
4:18 44
4:18-19 72
4:25-27 71
4:28 221
4:43 72
4; 22:53 155
5:1-11 45
5:22 137
5:23 137
5:27-32 71
5:30-32 72
5:1-11 73
6:12 87
6:13 72
6:36 162
6:38 147
6:40 . . . . 64, 146, 196
6:43-49 48
6:46 137
7:11-17 . . . . 40, 71
7:36 71
7:36-50 71
7:50 74
8:9 72
8:14-15 48
8:25 137
8:30 137
8:40-56 71
8:45 137
8:48 74
9:1-2 157
9:23 . . . . 75, 78, 146
9:24 124
9:28-36 119
9:37-43 71
9:37-45 38
9:46 123
9:48 44
9:49-50 207
9:51 73
9:51-19:44 73
9:51-56 71

9:54 72
9:57 73
9:58 87
10:9 157
10:13-15 73
10:15 137
10:16 44
10:16-20 72
10:23 72
10:26 137
10:29-37 71
10:36 137
10:38-42 . . . . . .73, 131, 141
11:1 72
11:20 157
11:37 71
11:40 137
11:127 126
12:14-15 137
12:15 81
12:25 137
12:57 137
13:6-9 48
13:16 72
13:31-35 72
13:34-35 73
14:1 71
14:12-13 71
14:12-14 47
14:26 72
14:31 137
14:34 138
15:4 138
15:8 138
15:11-32 71
16:11 138
17:11-19 71
17:17 138
17:19 74
17:25 72
17:33 124
18:7 138
18:8 138
18:9-14 71
18:43 130

19:1-10 71
19:10 72
19:37-39 72
21:9 72
22:14 87
22:15 47
22:15-20 147
22:24 123
22:27 138
22:31-34 156
22:39-53 125
22:46 138
23:31 138
23:39-43 71
24:17 138
24:19 138
24:26 138
24:36-49 73
24:38 138
24:41 138
24:44-49 72
24:46-47 73

John
1:1, 18 60
1:14 . . . . . .59, 116, 119, 123
1:18 . . . . 113, 118
1:19-34 45
1:29 117
1:32-34 43
1:38 138
2:1-11 118
2:4 138
2:11 121
2:13 117
2:13-22 117
2:18-22 118
2:24 129
2:25 129
2:3 53
3:3 46
3:10 138
3:12 138
3:14-16 119
3:34 57

4:7 138
4:21-24 87
4:24 113
4:34 122
4:34-38 48
4:37 7
4:54 121
5:6 138
5:8-37 87
5:24 57
5:30 126
5:30, 36, 38 44
5:39 175
5:41 . . . . 118, 122
5:44 139
5:47 139
6:2 121
6:5 139
6:29, 57 44
6:38 126
6:61 139
6:62 139
6:67 139
6:70 139
7:6 37
7:16, 29 44
7:18 . . . . 118, 122
7:19 139
7:23 139
7:28 57
8:10 139
8:16 57
8:16, 42 44
8:18 60
8:31-32 . . . . . . .69, 146, 159
8:32 161
8:36 166
8:43 139
8:46 139
8:50, 54 . . . . 118, 123
8:28, 30-32 57
9:4 127
10:10 158
10:30 . . . . 60, 118
10:36 . . . . 44, 139

11:4, 40 118
11:9 139
11:26 139
11:33 139
11:38-44 40
11:41-42 148
12:12 120
12:24 . . . . 48, 123
12:25 124
12:26 124
12:27-28 125
12:28 . . . . 122, 123
12:37 121
13:12 139
13:31 122
13:31-32 123
13:34-35 . . . . 9, 147
14:6 60
14:9 . . . . 59, 60, 139
14:9-10 118
14:12 157
14:13-14 147
14:15 47
14:16 94
14:16-17 142
14:16, 26 218
14:18 38
14:21 . . . . 48, 146
14:26 . . . . . 38, 94, 142, 219
14:30 . . . . 155, 159
15:1-8 48
15:1-16 7
15:2 49
15:4-7 48
15:5 61
15:7 147
15:8 . . . . 7, 47, 49, 219
15:9-10 48
15:13 219
15:14, 16 48
15:15 103
15:15-16 68
15:16 50
15:26 . . . . 38, 94, 218
15:26-27 218

16:7 . . . . 38, 94, 218
16:12-15 218
16:13 . . . . 91, 161
16:13-14 38
16:13-15 94
16:23-24 147
17:1, 5 123
17:4 126
17:5 118
17:6-26 127
17:10 128
17:17 118
17:20-21 . . . . 118, 147,
                        209, 217
17:20-23 208
18:4,7 139
18:11 139
18:21 139
18:23 139
18:33-38 54
18:34 139
20:15 139
20:19-22 94
20:21 . . . . 128, 157
20:21-22 43
20:21-23 . . . . 43, 218
21:5 139
21:15-16 47
21:17 139
21:22 139

Acts
1:1-2 42
1:1-3 43
1:2-3, 9 73
1:8 68
1:9-10 95
1:11 73
2:1-4 94
2:42 132
2:46 34
3:21 73
5:1-11 104
5:12-14 156
5:26 191

8:4 21
9:2 73
9:6, 16 73
10:19 221
10:34-35 221
10:43 74
11:19-21 21
13:1 21
13:16-41 27
13:46 73
14:21-23 33
14:22 73
15:32-41 24
16:7 95
16:14 22
16:18 22
18:2-4 25
18:3 31
19:9 31
19:9, 23 73
19:12 31
19:21 73
19:32-41 174
20:31-35 23
20:17, 28, 34–35 32
20:28 21
20:31 31
20:33-35 26
20:35 30
21:16 91
22:4 73
23:11 73
24:14, 22 73
24:24-26 27
25:10 73
27:24 73

Romans
2:4 162
4:25 37
5:1-11 79
6:3-4 146
6:4-10 37
6:6-7 103
7:23-25 55

8:1 55
8:4-14 147
8:9 . . . . 95, 175
8:10-11 37
8:29 . . . . 69, 148
9:8 50
10:9 41
12:1-2 146
12:2 69
12:3, 16 147
12:8 . . . . 21, 147
12:19 162
13:1-5 163
13:1-12 147
13:14 165
16:3 . . . . 22, 97
16:3, 5 34
16:17 . . . . 96, 220
16:23 22

1 Corinthians

1:10 196
1:12 122
1:13 9
1:27 193
2:1-16 175
2:2 211
2:16 93
3:1 80
3:6 7
3:11 175
3:16 118
4:1 21
4:2-5 147
4:9 96
4:12 23
4:14-16 65
5:7 117
6:4 21
6:9-10 29
6:13 147
6:19 118
6:19-20 164
8:1 80
8:5-6 41

9:6 23
9:12 26
9:22 27
10:31 . . . . 49, 111
10:31-11:1 29
11:1 . . . . 29, 65, 96
11:17, 18, 20,
  33, 34 . . . . 15, 192
11:23 91
11:23-25 147
12:3 41
12:28 21
12:13 147
14:23, 26 . . . . 15, 192
14:31, 35 96
15:3-5 222
15:14 38
15:15, 17, 18, 19   38
15:25-28 41
15:31 124
15:54-55 55
16:19 . . . . 22, 34

2 Corinthians

2:10-11 161
2:14 166
3:13 83
3:17-18 83
3:18 61
4:6 . . . . 83, 128
4:11-12 124
5:16 92
5:17 79
5:17-21 147
5:18-19 55
6:11 141
6:11, 12 24
6:14-18 220
7:2,3 24
9:10 7
10:5 146
11:2-4 158
11:7-11 24
11:8-9 . . . . 24, 25
11:12 24

11:14 158
12:14-16 24
13:11 196

Galatians

1:4 55
1:8-9 220
1:11-12 92
1:18 92
1:23 92
2:11-16 103
2:20 . . . . 76, 96
3:2 96
4:19 69
5:1 165
5:13 147
5:16, 25 147
5:19 147
5:22 7
5:24 . . . . 55, 164
6:1 196

Ephesians

1:10 37
1:10-12 49
1:17 81
2:5-8 195
2:6 161
2:8-9 79
2:20 175
3:7-8 195
3:19-20 128
4:15 24
4:20 96
4:4-5 208
4:11 21
4:11-12 196
4:11-13 14
4:13 80
4:23 148
4:25 161
4:27 . . . . 155, 165
4:28 30
4:32 162
4:1-15 192
5:11 220

5:21 . . . . .67, 103, 141
6:1-3 163
6:5-9 30
6:10-18 165
6:12 156
9:12, 15, 18 24

Philippians
1:3-11, 27-30 30
1:6 143
1:19 95
1:27-30 29
2:3 164
2:3-4 147
2:3-5 103
2:3-8 147
2:4 144
2:5-8 . . . . 67, 87, 217
2:9 40
2:10 41
2:11 41
2:14-16 30
3:3 164
3:7-21 30
3:10-12 78
3:10-13 81
3:17 . . . . 29, 96
3:20 46
4:6-7 147
4:8-9 146
4:9 30
4:9, 11 96
4:15-19 25
4:19 147
4:4,9 65

Colossians
1:7 96
1:9-10 14
1:10 48
1:13 79
1:25 195
1:27 . . . . 61, 83, 128
2:6-7 146
2:10, 15 41
2:14-15 55

3:17 27
3:22 193
3:23 30
4:14 22
4:15 34

1 Thessalonians
1:10 55
2:9 . . . . 23, 25
2:9-12 30
3:10 196
4:3 147
4:11 30
5:12 21
5:12 102
5:14 204

2 Thessalonians
1:1 25
2:2 158
2:15 222
3:6 222
3:7-8 23
3:7-9 25
3:7-10 . . . . 30, 34
3:8 25
3:8-9 29

1 Timothy
2:1-4 163
2:11 96
3:3 81
5:4, 13 96
6:10 81

2 Timothy
1:10 55
2:1 196
2:2 . . . .33, 63, 147, 148, 210
3:1-5 220
3:6-8 101
3:7, 14 96
3:10 97
3:10-14 65
4:7 107
4:18 55
4:19 22

Titus
1:5 21
3:1 30
3:4 96
3:10 220
3:13 22

Philemon
12 34

Hebrews
2:8 155
2:14-15 55
4:15 155
5:7-8 155
5:13 80
7:5, 27 191
10:17 162
10:24-25 147
13:5 81
13:7, 17, 24 21
13:17 . . . . 101, 147
13:21 196

James
1:5 142
1:19 . . . . 142, 148
2:14-17 147
4:1 165
4:6 80
4:6-10 164
5:16 164
5:5,4 67

1 Peter
1:3 50
1:4 55
2:2 7
2:11 165
2:13-16 163
2:18-21 163
2:23 162
3:1-2 163
5:1-10 164
5:5 80
5:5-6 147
5:8 165

5:10 196

2 Peter

1:2-11 143
1:3 79
1:3-11 81
2:2 132
3:18 . . . . 7, 79, 81

1 John

1:1-3 92
1:5-7 160
1:8 . . . . 159, 161
1:9 . . . . 164, 165
3:9 50
5:4-5 166
5:19 159

Jude

1:12 48

Revelation

2:10, 13 147
12:7, 9 151
12:9 156
14:1 77
17:14 117

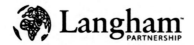

Langham Literature and its imprints are a ministry of Langham Partnership.

Langham Partnership is a global fellowship working in pursuit of the vision God entrusted to its founder John Stott –

to facilitate the growth of the church in maturity and Christ-likeness through raising the standards of biblical preaching and teaching.

Our vision is to see churches in the majority world equipped for mission and growing to maturity in Christ through the ministry of pastors and leaders who believe, teach and live by the Word of God.

Our mission is to strengthen the ministry of the Word of God through:
- nurturing national movements for biblical preaching
- fostering the creation and distribution of evangelical literature
- enhancing evangelical theological education

especially in countries where churches are under-resourced.

Our ministry

Langham Preaching partners with national leaders to nurture indigenous biblical preaching movements for pastors and lay preachers all around the world. With the support of a team of trainers from many countries, a multi-level programme of seminars provides practical training, and is followed by a programme for training local facilitators. Local preachers' groups and national and regional networks ensure continuity and ongoing development, seeking to build vigorous movements committed to Bible exposition.

Langham Literature provides majority world pastors, scholars and seminary libraries with evangelical books and electronic resources through grants, discounts and distribution. The programme also fosters the creation of indigenous evangelical books for pastors in many languages, through training workshops for writers and editors, sponsored writing, translation, strengthening local evangelical publishing houses, and investment in major regional literature projects, such as one volume Bible commentaries like *The Africa Bible Commentary*.

Langham Scholars provides financial support for evangelical doctoral students from the majority world so that, when they return home, they may train pastors and other Christian leaders with sound, biblical and theological teaching. This programme equips those who equip others. Langham Scholars also works in partnership with majority world seminaries in strengthening evangelical theological education. A growing number of Langham Scholars study in high quality doctoral programmes in the majority world itself. As well as teaching the next generation of pastors, graduated Langham Scholars exercise significant influence through their writing and leadership.

To learn more about Langham Partnership and the work we do visit **langham.org**

Lightning Source UK Ltd.
Milton Keynes UK
UKOW02f0750170117
292200UK00001B/99/P